Education, Training and the Future of Work II: Developments in Vocational Education and Training

This volume focuses on the recent changes in education and training policy, mainly in the UK. The considerable developments of the past years and the ways in which they have affected both education and training are examined. The contributors analyse the methods by which we educate our workforce, and look closely at the kind of training now offered to those in work.

Reader II for the Open University module E837.

COMPANION VOLUME
The companion volume in this series is:
Education, Training and the Future of Work I: social, political and economic contexts of policy development
Edited by John Ahier and Geoff Esland.

Both of these Readers are part of a course, Education, Training and the Future of Work, that is itself part of the Open University MA Programme.

Education, Training and the Future of Work II

Developments in vocational education and training

Edited by

Mike Flude and Sandy Sieminski

at The Open University

London and New York in association with The Open University

First published 1999
by Routledge
11 New Fetter Lane, London EC4P 4EE

Simultaneously published in the USA and Canada
by Routledge
29 West 35th Street, New York, NY 10001

© 1999 Compilation, original and editorial matter,
The Open University

Typeset in Garamond by
The Florence Group, Stoodleigh, Devon

Printed and bound in Great Britain by
TJ International Ltd, Padstow, Cornwall

British Library Cataloguing in Publication Data
A catalogue record for this book is available
from the British Library

Library of Congress Cataloguing in Publication Data
Education, training, and the future of work : developments in
vocational education and training / [edited by] Mike Flude
and Sandy Sieminski.
   p.   cm.
Includes bibliographical references and index.
1. Vocational education – Great Britain.   2. Occupational
training – Great Britain.   3. Education and state – Great
Britain.   I. Flude, Michael.   II. Sieminski, Sandy.
LC1047.G7E367 1998
370. 11'3' 0941 – dc21
                                                 98–27622
                                                 CIP

ISBN 0–415–20210–8 (hbk)
ISBN 0–415–20211–6 (pbk)

Contents

Figures and tables

Preface

This is the second of two volumes of readings entitled *Education, Training and the Future of Work*. Volume 1, edited by John Ahier and Geoff Esland, is organized around the theme of the *political, economic and social contexts* of education and training. Volume 2, edited by Mike Flude and Sandy Sieminski, focuses upon *the development of vocational policy*.

Both volumes – which are designed to be complementary – form part of the Open University MA Module, *Education, Training and the Future of Work* (E837). The course itself is based on a Study Guide in which the readings contained in these volumes are integrated within an analysis of a range of themes relating to post-compulsory education and training and the future of work. However, it is our hope that these collections will also appeal to a wider audience with an interest in policy developments in these areas.

Anyone working in this field cannot but be aware that anxieties abound about the future of work. In 1998, after six years of economic growth, and just at the point when it began to stall, the official unemployment level in Britain stood at 1.86 million, having reached well over 3 million during the recession of 1990–92.[1] The significance of these figures is that even when the economic cycle is favourable, unemployment remains at levels which would once have been unthinkable. In his foreword to the report *Unemployment and the Future of Work* published in 1997 by the Council of Churches for Britain and Ireland, the Bishop of Liverpool, the Rt. Revd. David Sheppard asked

> Will there ever be enough jobs to go round?. . . New technology brings prosperity for many people, but for many others it means redundancy and unemployment. As the world economy becomes more and more competitive some people are giving up hope that they will ever work again. Is mass unemployment here to stay?

For those in work, there is a widespread sense of insecurity resulting from the growing use by employers of various forms of 'flexibilization': outsourcing, part-time work, short-term contracts, and unsocial hours. Long working weeks are also common, particularly in Britain, where survey after survey confirms that on average its workforce has the longest working week in Europe. Evidence of the scale of the problem was provided by a survey of managers published by *Management Today* in June 1998 which reported that

A massive 84 per cent of the sample [made up of 5,500 responses] admitted to having made important sacrifices in pursuit of their career. The survey asked managers to consider the biggest personal sacrifice they have made in their career. Missing children growing up and letting work intrude on home life head this listing, although answers reveal a wide range of personal regrets – from missing a school event or the birth of a child, to divorce, the postponement of a parent's funeral and not being with a partner during serious illness or even death.

One of our main aims in preparing these readers has been to extend and deepen the debates about post-compulsory education and training (PCET) by situating them in the broader contexts of economic and employment policy, both in the UK and in the field of international political economy. Many of the agendas that underpin PCET are frequently associated with the dynamic of economic globalization, so that ideological pressure is often directed at individuals – and their schools, colleges and universities – to prepare for participation in a competitive global economy. There is a widespread consensus – at least among 'Anglo-Saxon' style economies – that the new 'post-fordist' forms of production require increasing degrees of 'flexibility' in employment, so that individuals are exhorted to take responsibility for continually updating their skills in a lifetime of learning. 'Portfolio employment' has become the lodestar for the successful, upwardly mobile professional, who is advised to abandon any vestigial craving for the 'job for life' and the 'psychological contract' which characterized employer–employee relationships in an earlier era. Much, too, is made of the economic 'weightlessness' of large parts of international business and trade, due to the fact that a high proportion of transactions now take place via electronic media. Both the financial markets and the Internet have in their different ways become the symbols of a new global information consumerism, giving credence to the view that the traditional boundaries of the nation state are becoming increasingly irrelevant in the new electronic, 'borderless' world. As a consequence, it is claimed, the new technologies will continue to require appropriately skilled people capable of performing effectively in the 'knowledge-based' economies of the future.

Underlying the techno-utopianism which sometimes characterizes the popular discourse surrounding globalization is a rather more sober reality based on the fact that the main economic principles driving it are derived from the international endorsement of free markets, especially in relation to trade, finance and labour. This has been particularly true of the UK, where four successive Conservative administrations were able to establish a de-regulated financial system while scaling down the levels of employment protection previously operating in the labour market. In those sectors of the economy which could not be privatized, highly regulated quasi markets were introduced which had as one of their main objectives the delivery of services on a reducing unit cost basis, so that more was required from fewer employees. The impact of two recessions, a succession of legislative measures designed to weaken the trade unions, and the promotion of enterprise, efficiency and competitiveness in all parts of the economy led to high levels of unemployment and a growing culture of insecurity and long working hours for those in employment. Within less than a generation, the social democratic commitment to state welfare and the promotion of collective responsibility for the alleviation of the grosser forms of inequality and poverty, had been displaced by policies critical of individual and family 'dependency' on the state. The consequence has been that individuals and families have themselves had to bear substantially more of the risks and costs associated with participation in the global labour market. The absence of decently-paid jobs for many young people, coupled with rising personal costs of education and training (especially for those entering higher education) has led to growing numbers becoming trapped in a cycle of debt and insecurity as they struggle to find jobs which will enable them to gain financial and personal independence. Unless the deregulated global economy is able to generate a far higher number of skilled jobs than it has hitherto seemed capable of doing, those young people are likely to find that as they repay their student debts, they will have to find the resources to insure against future insecurity and poverty as well as providing for their own retirement.

For the past two decades, one of the central premises of economic and employment policy in the UK has been that responsibility for generating employment opportunities rests essentially with the individual and those institutions involved in the supply of skills – schools, colleges and universities in particular. According to the 'supply-side' argument, employers are absolved from any moral responsibility for creating the conditions which will generate employment. This has meant, for example, that the role of the City financial institutions, which have been criticized by commentators such as Will Hutton for their negative impact on national investment, have remained largely untouched by the state. Where Conservative governments did become involved in employment generation was in the promotion of inward investment from overseas multinationals, many of which have been prominent in electronics and motor vehicle production. According to a report in *The Observer* (2 August 1998), this policy had by 1998 generated some £160 billion worth of foreign owned business, but it is becoming apparent that certain of the companies involved have become vulnerable to instabilities in the global market – especially those based in Korea, Taiwan and Japan following the Asian financial crisis of 1997. A particularly high profile example of this vulnerability was the decision in July 1998 by the German electronics company Siemens to close down its semi-conductor production facilities on Tyneside, with the loss of at least 1,500 jobs only fifteen months after it was opened by the Queen amid great local fanfares. The cause of the closure was said to be the collapse in the price of semi-conductors due to over supply and seriously reduced demand, arising in part from the collapse of the East Asian economies. In her report on the closure, *The Observer* journalist, Joanna Walters, commenting on Britain's reliance on foreign investment, quoted one of her informants as claiming that

> Britain has become as easy to exit as it is to enter because of flexible, insecure labour conditions and lack of pressure on investors to integrate with the local economy, causing the UK to either stand by and watch as foreign firms pull out when the going gets tough or bail out factories to stop them shifting abroad.
>
> ('Global crisis, local tragedy', *The Observer,* 2 August 1998)

As a number of commentators have pointed out, collapses of this kind will become increasingly typical of the inherent instability of free market global capitalism and are likely to generate even greater insecurity, unless and until the main industrial powers decide to address the need for some form of international market regulation – a debate which has yet to take place.

In spite of their acknowledgement of the importance of the global free market and its relevance to education and training provision, policy makers and their advisers have been reluctant to engage publicly with the critical challenges that are being made to the underlying premises of current policy. In its consultation paper, *The Learning Age,* published in 1998, the Department for Education and Employment, for example, makes no reference to the negative impact of globalization on employment opportunities and chooses not to open up the issue as to whether the vocational courses and systems of qualifications adequately prepare individuals for labour markets which, it appears, will largely continue to operate according to the neo-liberal principles put in place by the New Right. To a large extent, the globalization project and its significance for education and training are deemed to be non-negotiable. As disquieting is the fact that with the growing emphasis on highly prescriptive training courses for educational professionals, in which there is little scope for critical reflection on the *contexts* of practice, there is a diminishing space for engagement with issues of the kind we are raising. It is our hope that the collections of readings we have put together will stimulate what we regard as a necessary debate on the terms of current policy.

Geoff Esland
Chair of *Education, Training and the Future of Work*
Course Team.
August, 1998

Note

1   These figures need to be interpreted within the context of the many changes that have been introduced in the methodology for calculating levels of unemployment. Under the four Conservative administrations after 1979, the formula for calculating unemployment was changed many times. Most of these changes had the effect of reducing the total figure. The basis of calculation used by the fourth Conservative administration after 1992 was a decision to include only those who were claiming benefit. This had the effect of excluding those who were out of work and unable to claim benefit (for example, because their partner was still in work), and some of those who had left the labour market altogether. In May 1998, the Labour Government changed the formula again in order to bring it into line with that used by the ILO. The new methodology employed is based on sampling of the population. The immediate effect of the change was to add an additional 400,000 unemployed to the register, bringing the total to 1.8 million, but even this figure understates the true position of those who would choose to work if employment were available.

Acknowledgements

The editors would particularly like to thank those who have contributed to the compilation and development of these collections. We are especially grateful to Brenda Jarvis who took responsibility for compiling the manuscripts, and we would also like to thank Margaret Bird and Aileen Cousins for the numerous ways in which they helped in bringing the project to fruition. The Course Team is also grateful to Denis Gleeson and Andrew Pollard who were helpful sources of advice in the preparation of the course materials.

Source acknowledgements

The Open University would like to thank all those who have granted permission to reproduce copyright material in this volume. The publishers have made every effort to contact copyright holders with regard to permission to reproduce articles and will be happy to handle any enquiries relating to these.

Chapter 1
Green, A. (1997) 'The roles of the state and the social partners in vocational education and training systems' from *Education, Globalization and the Nation State*, Basingstoke: MacMillan.

Chapter 2
Finegold, D. (1991) 'Education training and economic performance in comparative perspective', from Phillips, D. (ed.) *Oxford Studies in Comparative Education*, Wallingford: Triangle Books.

Chapter 3
Moore, R. And Hickox, M. (1994) 'Vocationalism and educational change', *The Curriculum Journal* 5(3).

Chapter 4
Ball, S. (1990) 'Industrial training or new vocationalism? Structures and discourses' from Ball, S. (ed.) *Politics and policy making in education*, London: Routledge.

Chapter 5
Williams, S. And Raggatt, P. (1998) 'Contextualising public policy in vocational education and training: the origins of competence-based vocational qualifications', *Journal of Education and Work*, 11(3).

Chapter 6
Bates, I. 'The competence and outcomes movement: the landscape of research', updated version of earlier paper in *Studies in Science Education*, Vol. 25 pp. 39–68.

Chapter 7
Field, J. (1995) 'Reality testing in the workplace: are NVQs "employment-led"?', from Hodkinson, P. and Issitt, M. (eds) *The Challenge of Competence:*

Professionalism through Vocational Education and Training, London: Cassell.

Chapter 8

Smithers, A. (1997) 'A critique of NVQs and GNVQs', *Education 14–19: Critical Perspectives,* London: Athlone Press, pp. 55–70.

Chapter 9

Gleeson, D. And Hodkinson, P. 'Ideology and curriculum policy: GVNQ and mass post-compulsory education in England and Wales', from *British Journal of Education and Work* (8)3.

Chapter 10

Bird, M., Esland G., Greenberg, J., Sieminski S. and Yarrow, K. (1998) 'The implementation of GVNQs in further education: a case study'.

Chapter 11

Peck, J. (1991) 'The politics of training in Britain: contradictions in the TEC initiative', from *Capital and Class,* pp. 23–34.

Chapter 12

Hodkinson, P. And Hodkinson, H. (1995) 'Markets, outcomes and the quality of vocational education and training: some lessons from a Youth Credits pilot scheme', from The Vocational Aspects of Education, (47)3.

Chapter 13

Harvey, L. And Knight, P. *Policy and accountability,* Milton Keynes: Open University Press.

Acronyms

CBI	Confederation of British Industry
CTC	City Technology College
DES	Department of Education and Science (forerunner of DfE)
DfE	Department for Education
ED	Education Department
FE	Further Education
FEFC	Further Education Funding Council
GCSE	General Certificate of Secondary Education
GNVQ	General National Vocational Qualification
HE	Higher Education
LEA	Local Education Authority
NACETT	National Advisory Council for Education and Training Targets
NCVQ	National Council for Vocational Qualifications
NTET	National Targets for Education and Training
NVQ	National Vocational Qualification
OFSTED	Office for Standards in Education
TVEI	Technical and Vocational Education Initiative
VET	Vocational Education and Training

Introduction

Geoff Esland, Mike Flude and Sandy Sieminski

Despite the changes that have taken place in the British political context during the 1990s, a number of the issues which continue to dominate debates about education, training and the future of work have changed little over the past two decades. More than twenty years after the event, the criticisms of education and training expressed by James Callaghan in his Ruskin College speech in October 1976 still continue to resonate within official policy discourse. This is especially true of his strictures on school standards and the use of 'progressive' teaching methods, but it also applies to the basic premise of his argument that it is the system of education and training which holds the key to national economic improvement and prosperity. Despite a number of challenges to its validity (see Esland, 1996), this view still remains the cornerstone of current policy.

Although the Conservative government which came into office in 1979 built upon and intensified the ideological stance towards education and training which the previous Labour government had taken, it did so from within a very different set of economic and political objectives. Not only were economic and employment issues accorded a higher priority in educational policy, but in terms of its organization, governance and management, the system itself underwent a major transformation, first through the reforms introduced by the 1988 Education Reform Act and later by the Further and Higher Education Act of 1992. One of the objectives of the legislation was to bring about a reduction in the discretionary areas of professional practice within education and training institutions whilst strengthening market and managerial controls over the ways in which teachers performed their jobs.

As some commentators suspected might happen (see Avis *et al.*, 1996), the political settlement established by the New Right during its eighteen years in power continued to provide the main parameters of policy for the Labour government after it took office in May 1997. Although there have been changes of emphasis and priority, and some alleviation of the more extreme right-wing elements of employment policy, the neo-liberal promotion of free market economic globalization has continued to provide the overarching framework for Britain's political economy as it enters the new millennium.

From this observation, it might be inferred that the political principles established by the New Right during its years in office now form the basis of a 'new consensus'. If the main political parties are divided only over the detail rather than the principle of economic deregulation, and if they share the view that 'supply side' reforms of the education and training system are the primary means of promoting a more 'competitive' economy, then the question arises, is any basis for an alternative perspective capable of challenging the assumptions that prevail in this new consensus.

The significance of this question becomes greater if we extend it to the international context and include other nation states such as the US, Australia and New Zealand, which have forged a similar political consensus around the neo-liberal principles of economic deregulation, privatization and reduced welfare expenditure. Indeed, according to Gray (1998), the consensus also extends to the main international economic NGOs such as the OECD, the World Bank, the IMF and the WTO. These agencies form part of what Gray calls the 'Washington consensus' which collectively provide the main ideological and managerial thrust behind the US pursuit of free market, economic globalization – a goal which he claims to be the ultimate Enlightenment project.

In spite of its dominance, the neo-liberal consensus – particularly as it affects economic, employment and welfare policy – is facing a variety of challenges. Some of these emanate from research and intellectual debate, but there are others which take the form of concerted popular pressure and occasional outbreaks of mass protest at what are perceived as threats to individual survival, social cohesion and environmental integrity. High levels of unemployment across the main industrial economies (not least in the EU) and the economic and social instability affecting many of the Pacific Rim countries after the financial collapse of 1997 are just two examples of the fault lines which lie beneath the international commitment to economic globalization. These and similar manifestations of instability have led Gray and other critics of the global free market – notably the international financier, George Soros (1996) – to predict that as with nineteenth-century attempts to establish a *laissez-faire* international economy, the current policy will become increasingly difficult to sustain.

At the level of rhetoric, at least, education and training policy continues to play an important role in sustaining the ideological commitment to the neo-liberal concept of globalisation, largely because it has now become the default institution for nuturing the psychological conditions necessary for 'competitiveness'. The notion that in order to compete in the global economy, the modern nation state requires a highly trained and 'flexible' workforce, in which 'knowledge- and people-based skills' form the basis of a 'self-perpetuating learning society' (FEFC, 1997: Kennedy Report) has become the *sine qua non* of the age. Under advanced capitalism, symbolic analysis, creation and manipulation are seen as the major new source of commodification, exchange and profit. As technology advances, allowing investment and production to seek out the most profitable locations, the chief source of competitiveness lies in the utilization of symbolic skills – a phenomenon described by one commentator as a characteristic of the 'weightless economy' (Coyle, 1998).

There are, however, a number of problems with this formulation. As Ashton and Green (1996: 70) point out 'the remarkable thing about these claims is that they are typically presented with relatively little theoretical grounding and even less of a basis in solid empirical evidence.' We will note here a number of reservations which we have with the globalization argument.

The first problem relates to the structural impact of economic globalization on employment. At the heart of the international neo-liberal project is the priority attached to 'sound finance' in relation to the securing of 'full employment'. Any nation unable or unwilling to give priority to maintaining low inflation levels is liable to find itself punished by the financial markets (Eatwell, 1995), and possibly subjected to the intervention of the IMF in the running of its economy. The inherently deflationary nature of this policy places limits on national growth rates, but also acts as a deterrent on nation states from using public borrowing to stimulate a flagging economy, and therefore to generate jobs. The consequence has been a massive rise in international levels of unemployment, as nation states have struggled to find their 'natural' or 'non-accelerating inflation rate of unemployment' (NAIRU) – the level to which unemployment can be allowed to fall without causing inflation to rise (see vol. 1, Chapters 5 and 7).

Alongside the priority attached to low inflation lies the other key principle of the neo-liberal global free market: the promotion of economic deregulation – particularly as far as employment policy is concerned. In Britain and the US especially, the effects of two decades of neo-liberal employment legislation have been to strengthen the power of employers *vis-à-vis* the interests of the workforce. The consequence has been that in the cause of 'efficiency' and 'greater productivity', employers have demanded increasing 'flexibility' from their employees whether in the form of part-time working, the use of short-term contracts or the demand for individuals to work unsocial hours. In some cases, companies have gone further through the introduction of out-sourcing and the sub-contracting of services which they formerly undertook themselves. The result has been a massive rise in job insecurity, a culture of long working hours, often based on fear, and a growing polarization in pay levels between the high salaries of boardroom members and those of the great majority of workers.

The third problem with the argument that global competitiveness requires increasingly high level skills is that new technology is as capable of eliminating jobs as it is of creating them. Recent analyses (e.g. Rifkin, 1995) have argued that even relatively high levels of skill are being subsumed within the capability of computerized technology. Aronowitz and DiFazio (1994; see vol. 1 Chapter 4), for example, claim that their research leads them to the conclusion that

> All of the contradictory tendencies involved in the restructuring of global capital and computer-mediated work seem to lead to the same conclusion for workers of all collars – that is, unemployment, under-employment, decreasingly skilled work, and relatively lower wages. . . . High technology will destroy more jobs than it creates. The new technology has fewer parts and fewer workers and produces more product.
>
> (Aronowitz and DiFazio, *The Jobless Future*, p. 3)

If in the interests of promoting 'efficiency' private sector companies seek to use technology to substitute for human labour, even more likely is it that the same process will operate within public sector organisations, restricted as they are by the limits imposed on national public expenditure. Despite the high volumes of work that are in need of being carried out in the labour-intensive sectors such as health, education and the social services, the requirement on public sector managers to deploy their human resources within the expenditure limits imposed on them is what gives rise to the work intensification – and sometimes de-skilling – that we referred to earlier. Here more than anywhere in the economy is the clearest example of work organization being driven by cash limited budgets rather than social 'need' (see vol. 1, Chapter 8).

The fourth point we would make is that the emphasis on the importance of 'supply side' reform as the means of generating competiveness, rests on the assumption that employers are both able and willing to utilize higher levels of skill where they are available. There is evidence to suggest that this may well be true of some sectors but not all, and that many employers are content to compete on price at the lower end of the market. As Keep and Mayhew have argued on a number of occasions (see vol. 1, Chapter 6), many companies choose to tailor their products to a specific market in which the high-skill, high-tech route is not the only option available to them. The

> alternatives include increasing use of crude work-intensification practices, low pay, insecure and casualised employment, and the sub-contracting of more complex parts of production. . . . Producing high-tech, high quality goods and services that require high levels of skill is not, in itself, intrinsically important to a company. The issue of over-riding concern is whether or not its product market strategy allows it to survive and to make adequate . . . levels of profit. If companies can achieve these ends through the production of low-cost, low quality,

high-volume goods and services that require minimal skill levels, then there is little reason for them to alter their strategies.

(Vol. 1, Chapter 6)

Finally, there is the problem of taking at face value the view promulgated by educational policy-makers that the new systems of vocational qualifications are the appropriate ones for meeting the 'requirements for a highly skilled workforce in a global economy.' As with the other assumptions contained within this formula, this one, too, requires examination. Although the 1990s saw an increase in participation rates in post-16 education and training, vocational curricula have continued to experience the low status that has traditionally characterized their position in the British education system. In part this is due to the long history of tripartism, but it also has to do with the accumulation of negative perceptions which young people and their families formed about the succession of post-16 schemes from the late 1970s onwards. These training programmes were widely seen to be devoid of content and as having little relevance to the difficult employment situations in which young people found themselves, and they did little to disarm the cynical perception that they were essentially a means of keeping young people out of the labour market (Field, 1995). The 1990s have seen a different approach to vocational qualifications in the form of NVQs and GNVQs, but this too has attracted a good deal of critical comment. Although the new qualifications have been perceived as offering wider opportunities for access to training than anything that had previously existed, they have also been criticised for concentrating on the accreditation of low-level skills and for their reliance on a competence-based form of assessment which in the view of some commentators has lacked a sufficiently robust knowledge base to meet even current, let alone future, occupational requirements (see vol. 2, Chapters 6 and 7). One of the consequences of this policy has been the creation of a system in which there is polarization between the high-level skills produced by the HE institutions and lower-level skills accredited through the competence based route.

Despite the vigorous repetition by policy makers and others of the globalization formula, there is little evidence in our view on which to base a challenge to the diagnosis put forward by Finegold and Soskice (1988) that a fundamental problem with the British economy is that it is founded on a 'low-skills equilibrium', and that the education and training system reproduces and reinforces that problem (see also vol. 2, Chapter 2). Because of the mono-causal nature of explanations of Britain's economic weakness in which education and training are represented as the main source of economic renewal, other more significant factors have been ignored, not least the low levels of investment – both public and private – which could have generated new economic activity (Hutton, 1995). Furthermore, as Ashton and Green (1996) have argued, the 'high-skills route' to capital accumulation requires a concerted commitment by both state and employers to providing a generously funded system of education and training, in which employers are committed to the effective utilization of high-level skills. In Britain, that approach has not been forthcoming, for the reason that too small a proportion of its businesses appears to require genuinely high-level skills – a situation reflected in the fact that state and employers have resisted the notion of systemic, long-term investment in post-16 education and training. Furthermore, by leaving the provision of PCET to market forces, the state has produced additional barriers to the creation of a high skills route. As Esland *et al.* suggest (vol. 1, Chapter 8), when a competitive market is tied to a vigorously applied centralized funding formula based on falling unit costs, there is every inducement for further and higher education institutions to boost student numbers while scaling down curricular content and choice and making reductions in staffing resources – a process which is perceived by some as a serious threat to the quality of learning.

In our view, these collections of readings offer important exploration and analysis of the issues we are raising. A number of them are critical of the moral and intellectual premises of the current globalization orthodoxy and suggest some alternative approaches. It may be thought that they take an unduly pessimistic view of current policies. For this we are unapologetic. Public discussion of education and training policy has in our view been too narrowly focused for too long, and has been concerned with confirming rather than questioning the principles on which it is based. One of the reasons why there has been so little change to the parameters which govern the development of policy in post-compulsory education and training is that governments themselves have been reluctant to allow broad-based debate to take place in which practitioners themselves could have a role. In its concern to neutralise the influence of 'producer interests' and its desire to persist with a low-trust relationship with those who are employed in the system, the state has closed off an important area of response and feed back from those most closely involved in the implementation of policy. Our hope is that these collections are able to make a small contribution to the opening up of that process.

Volume 2 begins with the chapter by Green in which he considers the role of the state and other social partners (notably employers and trade unions) in vocational and technical education and training in England and Wales and Germany. In the case of England and Wales the dominant tradition has been a voluntaristic or liberal one in which historically there has been a minimum of state intervention. Green traces the impact of shifts in government policy since 1964, and the different forms of state control and social partnership which have underpinned contrasting political interventions across this period. The development of market-led policies in education since 1987 is seen as a return to the voluntaristic principles of the pre-1964 period.

Green argues that the problems which continue to beset education and training in England and Wales mainly derive from two sources.

Firstly, there is still no concerted national approach to training underpinned by the necessary statutory framework governing the roles, rights and responsibilities of different parties. Secondly, there is a marked and growing absence of effective collaboration between social partners and the institutional arrangements to promote this.

This is contrasted with vocational education and training systems in continental Europe, where there has been a much stronger tradition of centralized state regulation and co-ordination than that found in England and Wales. Green considers in detail the distinctive features of the German system and critical roles played by employers and trade unions in the formulation and implementation of vocational education and training policy. The relative success of the German system is attributed to a tradition of social partnership allied to strong state control and co-ordination. On the basis of his comparative analysis, Green then identifies certain properties for any effective mass system of vocational education and training.

The comparative perspective is continued in Chapter 2. Here Finegold examines the relationship between economic performance and education and training and in particular the 'relative failure of Britain to provide sufficient education and training for its workforce'. Initially he identifies various shortcomings in conventional approaches to the relationship between education and training and economic organization deriving from human capital theory and cultural historical explanations. An alternative model is developed by Finegold which examines the incentives that shape the actions of the main investors in education and training: 'namely the individual and his or her family, the company manager and the government policy-maker'. This approach is considered initially in relation to the British situation, where the economy 'has been caught in a low-skills equilibrium, where a majority of firms staffed by poorly trained managers and workers produce relatively low quality goods and services'. Finegold has identified a range of interconnected factors that have shaped the historically low demand for skills within the British economy, and its education and training system. The chapter concludes by arguing that a general improvement in the levels of education and training, and the attainments of those leaving compulsory schooling, might provide the starting point for the breaking out of the low-skills equilibrium.

Moore and Hickox in Chapter 3 broadly agree with Finegold's conclusion but importantly stress the value of a broad-based liberal education rather than the narrowly conceived vocationalist project that has shaped many policy developments in England and Wales. In this chapter they examine how expansionary periods of education give rise to different ideological forms of vocationalism. Although there are some elements of continuity with respect to vocationalism, their analysis highlights the distinctive features of contemporary developments in contrast with policy developments in the 1960s. Whereas in the earlier period debates about the vocationalization of education were underpinned by liberal-humanist values, recent developments express an economic instrumentalism.

In Chapter 4 Stephen Ball considers the origins of the new vocationalism in the 1970s, and the part played by a number of key texts in articulating the 'vocational inadequacy of schools and school leavers'. In contrast to the prevailing cultural explanation which stresses the role of education and various cultural factors in industrial and economic decline, Ball locates these discourses and attendant policy developments in relation to wider structural changes within the national and global capitalist economy.

The next set of chapters looks at developments in national education and training policy in detail. In Chapter 5 Williams and Raggatt consider the origins of the competence-based system of National/Scottish Vocational Qualifications (N/SVQs) drawing on both contemporary source materials and semi-structured interviews with policy makers. Their analysis points to the influence of an interrelated set of economic, institutional and political factors. First they argue, like Ball, that the new vocationalism of the 1970s and early 1980s 'was an expression of a distrust of the established education system, especially further education, not only on the "right", but also amongst "progressive" educationalists employed by government agencies, the MSC in particular.' Second, they point to the influence of a post-industrial analysis of economic change, and the role attributed to education and training in promoting the flexibility and transferability of skills required by new patterns of work organization. Third, they suggest that competence-based qualifications were regarded by policy makers as a means of promoting economic modernization. However, while the reform of vocational qualifications was influenced by such longer term imperatives, Williams and Raggatt suggest that it was the issue of youth unemployment which provided the 'major catalyst for action'.

Following a critical discussion of the development of the competence movement and its impact on education and training, Bates reviews and evaluates the body of research in this field. Four different categories of research are identified: technical literature associated with the developing NVQ/GNVQ system; evaluative studies designed to inform policy and practice; 'spirit of education' studies which critique the fundamental principles of competence-based education and training and sociological studies.

Thus the discussion progresses through drawing on a widening circle of work on competence, moving from the technical and evaluative 'interior' of the movement, where its basic precepts are largely taken for granted, to broader psychological and sociological studies which begin to explore the validity and social significance of the underlying assumptions involved.

In Chapter 7, John Field focuses on the implementation of NVQs, their role and impact in labour market recruitment and effectiveness in meeting skill shortages. Drawing on documentary sources and original research, Field argues that NVQs have failed to address the skill shortage problem: 'there is strong evidence to suggest that the market for NVQs is confined mainly to rudimentary entry qualifications to low-skill-level occupations'. This conclusion is supported by the findings presented in the chapter by Gleeson and Hodkinson. Field also critically evaluates the claim that NVQs are employment-led. He concludes that this qualification substantially derives from 'the professional training lobby working through the MSC and its successor bodies', and that demand for the qualification has been largely created and sustained by government departments.

Whilst sympathetic to a system of vocational training which is employer-led, Alan Smithers in Chapter 8 offers a thoroughgoing critique of the major design features of NVQs and GNVQs, particularly the NCVQ's approach to the content and assessment of qualifications. In contrast to commentators who have called for an integrated system of qualifications, Smithers calls for a coherent and distinct set of qualification pathways for 14–19-year-olds within a national system of national vocational awards. Following a review of the findings and recommendations of the Beaumont (1996), Capey (1996) and Dearing (1996) reports, Smithers considers the significance of the Qualifications and Curriculum Authority in establishing a national system of awards.

The following chapter (Chapter 9) by Gleeson and Hodkinson examines the impact and positioning of GNVQs in relation to a complex set of factors. First, GNVQ, as a vocational middle track, is evaluated in terms of how likely it is to succeed in breaking down post-16 tripartism. Second, they focus on the impact of the 'new managerialism', with its stress on outcomes and performance indicators, in shaping students' learning experiences and undermining the professionalism of teachers. Third, Gleeson and Hodkinson scrutinize the post-Fordist assumptions that have shaped the development of this qualification and opportunities for progression for GNVQ students into employment. Finally, they address the preconditions for GNVQ to be reshaped to meet a broader and more thoroughly educational agenda.

In Chapter 10 Bird *et al.* explore the impact of changes that have taken place in vocational educational programmes as a result of the introduction of GNVQs. Adopting a case study approach, their research focuses on the effects of change in two areas of the vocational curriculum: business studies and health and social care. Consideration is given to the context in which GNVQs have been introduced. The 'incorporation' of colleges in 1992 created a marketplace for funding of provision and has had a profound impact on the organization, management and delivery of GNVQs. The authors raise questions about the impact of change on the roles of professionals and the quality of VET. Their findings suggest features of the new qualification that may benefit some learners and provide a recognized alternative entry qualification to HE. However, they also raise doubts about the ability of an unreformed GNVQ programme to provide the wide range of skills to produce the adaptability in the workforce required for economic prosperity. They argue that any review or revision of GNVQs needs to incorporate the views of professionals who have experience of delivering more structured, knowledge-based vocational educational programmes.

In March 1989 a nationwide network of 82 Training and Enterprise Councils (TECs), 75 in England and 7 in Wales, and 22 Local Enterprise Companies (LECs) in Scotland was established. Soon after its establishment Peck provided a critical analysis of these new institutions that had been created to provide high-level skills training and to foster enterprise within specified geographical areas. He drew attention to a number of inherent contradictions within their design which he predicted would hamper their performance and affect their ability to achieve the objectives set for them. Although Peck's analysis took place in 1991, the issues and concerns he raised have not lost their potency. Despite being promised a substantial amount of autonomy, TECs have been constrained by a tightly defined government agenda of meeting National Education and Training Targets and providing programmes for the unemployed. This has restricted the opportunity they have had for offering high-level education and training and fostering enterprise. A related difficulty that these institutions have also had to confront has been an inability to attract private funds for their work on the scale hoped for. Ultimately, we are forced to question whether this ambitious privatization initiative is an appropriate strategy for bringing about the 'skills revolution' that was promised.

In Chapter 12 Hodkinson and Hodkinson identify the key characteristics of the new paradigm for the management of British VET which is based on the assumption that the quality of VET can be enhanced by the measurement of outcomes and payment of results within a market context. Their research focused on one of the first Youth Credit pilot schemes, which they suggest provides one of the clearest illustrations of the new paradigm in action. Their findings suggest that despite the existence of quality controls within the paradigm there can be no guarantee that a trainee will experience a quality learning process. This leads them to challenge the assumptions on which that the new management paradigm is based. They suggest that urgent consideration needs to be given to what quality training might consist of. For Hodkinson and Hodkinson a quality learning process needs to be coherent and well co-ordinated, with the relationship between on- and off-the-job training carefully integrated. Such factors, they contend, are at present largely ignored within the new paradigm.

Concern about the quality of learners' experience is also pursued by Harvey and Knight in their discussion of policy developments in higher education.

In Chapter 13 they note how higher education policy since the mid-1980s has increasingly come to focus on issues of quality. They maintain that five interrelated themes of accountability, value for money, maintaining standards, measuring outputs, and external quality monitoring have come to dominate the mass higher education system. They argue that the drive for increasing the quality of higher education has not been sufficiently connected to moves to improve and reform teaching and learning processes. According to Harvey and Knight, if higher education is to play a part in producing people who can accommodate to and initiate change in the world economy of the twenty-first century it must focus its attention on the transformative process of learning.

References

Aronowitz, S. and DiFazio, W. (1994) *The Jobless Future*. Minneapolis: University of Minnesota Press.

Ashton, D. and Green, F. (1996) *Education, Training and the Global Economy*. Cheltenham: Edward Elgar.

Avis, J., Bloomer, M., Esland, G., Gleeson, D. and Hodkinson, P. (1996) *Knowledge and Nationhood: Education, Politics and Work*. London: Cassell.

Beaumont, G. (1996) *Review of 100 NVQs and SVQs*. London: NCVQ.

Capey, J. (1996) *GNVQ Assessment Review*. London: NCVQ.

Coyle, D. (1998) 'Jobs in a Weightless World', *Economic Report,* vol. 12, no. 5, May 1998. Employment Policy Institute.

Dearing, R. (1996) *Review of Qualifications for 16–19 Year Olds*. London: SCAA.

Eatwell, J. (1995) 'The International Origins of Unemployment'. In Michie, J. and Grieve Smith, J. (eds), *Managing the Global Economy*. Oxford: Oxford University Press.

Esland, G.M. (1996) 'Education, Training and Nation-State Capitalism: Britain's Failing Strategy'. In Avis, J. *et al.* op. cit.

Field, J. (1995) 'Reality Testing in the Workplace: Are NVQs Employment Led?' In Hodkinson, P. and Issit, M. (eds), *The Challenge of Competence: Profesionalism Through Vocational Education and Training*. London: Cassell.

Finegold, D. and Soskice, F. (1988) 'The Failure of Training in Britain: Analysis and Prescription, *Oxford Review of Economic Policy*, 4(3).

Further Education Funding Council (FEFC) (1997) *Learning Works: Widening Participation in Further Education*, Kennedy Report. Coventry: FEFC.

Gray, J. (1998) *False Dawn: The Delusions of Global Capitalism*. London: Granta Books.

Hutton, W. (1995) *The State We're In*. London: Cape.

Rifkin, J. (1995) *The End of Work: The Decline of the Global Labor Force and the Dawn of the Post-market Era*. New York: Putnam.

Soros, G. (1996) 'The Capitalist Threat', *The Atlantic Monthly*, September.

Chapter 1

The roles of the state and the social partners in vocational education and training systems

Andy Green

The historic demise of the centralized command economies of the communist world has prompted ideologists in the West to proclaim the 'end of history' and the secular evolutionary ascendancy of the liberal, market system as a means of organizing societies and economies (Fukuyama, 1992). However, more sustained examination of the different trajectories of the western capitalist states suggests more discriminating judgements, for while the recent Anglo-American experiments in free-market economics have proved unsustainable, and have merely consolidated the relative decline of Britain and the USA as world powers (Kennedy, 1989), the neo-corporatist, social-market policies of the continental European Union states have, in many cases, proved to be comparatively successful, providing the basis for continued economic innovation and growth through a combination of market dynamism and state regulation. Moreover, whereas advocates of the free market have often explicitly abandoned equity and fair distribution as political goals and have been prepared to see the decline of public services as a necessary cost of rejuvenating private enterprise, elsewhere social justice has remained at least on the political agenda and the effective provision of public services has been seen as a precondition of economic prosperity. The fundamental political debate in industrialized countries still appears now to revolve around the relative merits of free-market economies versus socialized mixed economies and, while this is by no means yet resolved, the case for variations on the 'third way' remains powerful.

Education and training policy, in all advanced economies, occupies a central position in this debate. Not only does it bear critically on questions of both social justice and economic efficiency but it is also subject to very contrary 'solutions' which well illustrate the still marked ideological cleavages within western politics. While all governments appear to recognize the importance of a wide distribution of education and training throughout their populations, especially in the current context of rapid technological advance and intensified global economic competition, the policies they have adopted to achieve this have varied widely.

Typically, Britain and the USA, and some other English-speaking countries like New Zealand, have attempted to raise participation and achievement in education and training systems through institutional reforms that attempt to install market mechanisms, fostering greater competition and efficiency. In Britain this has been accompanied by measures that greatly increase central state control in education as regards curricula and qualifications, while reducing the powers of local education authorities and minimizing the decision-making roles of educationalists and trade unions.

In continental EU states the trends have been somewhat different. Centralized control has generally been reduced by attempts to devolve decision-making to the lowest effective level (the subsidiarity principle). This has generally meant giving more powers to the regions and encouraging the social partners to play increasingly prominent roles at national, regional, local and enterprise levels. The Social Chapter of the Maastricht Treaty, endorsed by all member states except Britain, makes social partnership and subsidiarity the cornerstones of its vocational training policy (CEDEFOP, 1992). However, this devolution, which diffuses control in both vertical and horizontal directions, occurs within the overall context of regulation by the central state, which determines both the roles and responsibilities of the different actors. Neo-liberal policies, involving unfettered control by the markets, have found little favour in systems where the principle remains that public authorities bear ultimate responsibility for collective services.

The different roles played by the state and other social partners in the determination and implementation of policies constitutes one of the most significant variables between different national systems of education and training. This chapter focuses on one particular area of the policy debate – vocational education and training (VET). Its main objective is to offer a preliminary analysis of the roles played by the state and other social partners in different areas of VET within a number of different national systems and to point to some of the effects of such differences. Reference will be made mainly to the systems of VET in England and Germany.

Vocational education and training in England and Wales

VET in England and Wales is frequently seen as one of the weakest areas of the education system, traditionally suffering from a lack of prestige and of coherent planning and organization (Ball, 1991; Green, 1990; Royal Society, 1991; Sanderson, 1994). Currently, despite widespread recent reforms, rates of participation in post-compulsory education and training are still much lower in Britain than most other EU countries, with levels of qualification, particularly in vocational areas, likewise (Green and

Steedman, 1993, 1996; OECD, 1995). The reasons for this are various and complex but much of the explanation arguably hinges on historical traditions of *laissez-faire* which go back deep into history.

The liberal legacy

Britain was one of the last major European countries in the nineteenth century to create a national education system and, contrary to the pattern in continental Europe, the state was particularly slow to intervene in promoting technical education. This was partly due to a general complacency about the importance of technical education that was one of the legacies of an early, successful industrial revolution that appeared to owe little to formal education. It was also partly due to the fact that manufacturers were reluctant to lose child labour to the education system, particularly if they had to pay for it through their taxes, and particularly if it involved training in trade schools that might endanger their trade secrets. Most importantly, however, it was the inevitable consequence of a dominant liberal, *laissez-faire* philosophy that discouraged state intervention in anything except where it was absolutely unavoidable.

The result of this voluntarist policy was that, with the exception of the evening classes provided by the Mechanics Institutes and the Department of Science and Art, there was no technical education to speak of before 1880 except that provided on the job. France by the mid-century had a wide range of vocational schools at different levels. These included 85 elementary trade and agricultural schools; various intermediate vocational schools like the *écoles des arts et métiers* and the *École Centrale* and a number of higher vocational schools *(grandes écoles)* including the celebrated *École Polytechnique.* England had few comparable full-time vocational schools which could impart both the theory and practice of different vocations. Nor, until the higher grade schools were developed, did it have much to compare with the vocationally oriented post-elementary schools on the continent like the German *Realschulen* and the French *écoles primaires supérieures* which numbered 700 by 1887 (Grew and Harrigan, 1991; Day, 1987; Weiss, 1982). In the absence of these institutions England relied largely on the apprenticeship. This was stoutly defended as the most effective way of imparting practical skills but few apprentices received the grounding in scientific principles or indeed basic education which was necessary for the skilled worker promoted to higher supervisory levels at the time when new technology and more complex processes began to make more demands on the scientific and technical knowledge of engineers and managers.

During the last two decades of the nineteenth century the situation did begin to change as the political climate became more conducive to state intervention and as the threat of foreign competition pressed home the importance of improving education and training. However, despite the achievements of the technical education movement in promoting the development of technical colleges and the civic universities, English technical education and training by the end of the century were still significantly underdeveloped by comparison with what had been achieved in many continental states (Barnett, 1986). It was still not widespread and what there was of it was generally still anti-theoretical, low in status and marginalized from mainstream education.

Throughout the first half of the twentieth century vocational education and training continued to lag behind and until the late 1950s remained largely on a voluntary footing. Part-time enrolments at technical colleges grew steadily if unspectacularly, but post-compulsory technical schooling remained a minority experience. Though twice enacted, in 1918 and 1944, compulsory continuation schooling was never implemented and most young people left school without receiving any further education or training. Sporadic attempts were made to develop technical secondary schooling with the pre-Second World War junior technical schools and the post-1944 secondary technical schools, but neither initiative gained much momentum or broke the status monopoly of academic secondary schooling, as recent studies by Gary McCullough (1989) and Michael Sanderson (1994) have shown. By 1937 only around 30,000 pupils attended junior technical schools and attendance at secondary technical schools never grew beyond 4 per cent of the age cohort (Bailey, 1990).

The apprenticeship remained the main vehicle of vocational training throughout the period and was usually completed without any parallel off-the-job general or technical education. For all its strengths as a means for imparting job-specific vocational skills, the apprenticeship system was never an adequate vehicle for meeting the skills needs of the economy. The craft unions tended to see the apprentice system as a means by which they could protect their skill status and differentials through restricting entry into tightly demarcated trades, while employers often valued the system as a way of gaining cheap labour without statutory obligations to provide expensive investment in training to given standards (Rainbird, 1990). Both sides of industry agreed on limiting the numbers of apprentices so that there were repeated skills shortage crises not only before and during the world wars but also increasingly during the expansionary post-1945 period. Not only did the apprentice system provide an inadequate supply of skilled workers but it was deficient in many other ways, as the 1958 Carr Report made plain (Perry, 1976). It involved unduly lengthy periods of time-serving, failed to train to any specified standards, and was overly narrow in the skills it imparted and impoverished in terms of general education and theory; most damagingly, it ignored the training needs of semi-skilled workers and severely limited access to many groups, most notably women (Sheldrake and Vickerstaff, 1987).

Numerous reports (including the government's own 1956 White Paper on Technical Instruction) pointed to the relative deficiencies of British training and the 1945 Ince Report called for the creation of a national training scheme (see Ainley and Corney, 1990). However, no government action was forthcoming. In 1952 the Ministry of Labour and National Service was still upholding the traditional government line that 'employers bear the major responsibility for the training of their own employees' (Sheldrake and Vickerstaff, 1987, p. 27). The *'laissez-faire'* era in British training policy thus continued until the beginning of the 1960s when renewed skills shortages, the challenge of Soviet technology and the bulging youth cohort finally convinced government that policies on vocational training had to change.

Since 1964 and the Industrial Training Act, which marked the first major departure from the traditional *laissez-faire* approach, government policy on training has undergone repeated shifts but only to arrive in the 1990s very much where it started. The period can be divided into three main parts characterized by different forms of state control and social partnership.

The 1964–73 period, defined by the terms of the Industrial Training Act, saw training organized through a devolved form of social partnership between employers and industry with relatively light central state intervention. The period from 1974 to 1979 was the era of the Manpower Services Commission (MSC) under a Labour government, characterized by a more centralized form of social partnership under a highly interventionist government agency. The period from 1979 to 1988 was a transitional period during which central government intervened ever more directly through the MSC to shape training policy while simultaneously dismantling the apparatuses of social partnership in both the education and training fields. Since 1988 there has been a return to the voluntarist model and this time with one of the social partners, the trade unions, largely removed from influence and control. Although numerous initiatives have been tried and despite the fact that vocational education and training has been higher on the political agenda than ever before, the policies of these periods have had limited success in reversing the historic backwardness of British vocational education and training. It is important to see why.

The era of the Industrial Training Boards, 1964–73

The 1964 Act inaugurated the tripartite Industrial Training Boards (ITBs) to promote and co-ordinate training in the different sectors and empowered them to redistribute the costs of training between employers by means of the levy-grant system. Being organized by industrial sectors but without achieving full coverage, this was never quite a national apprenticeship system, still less a national training system for all grades of employees.

However, it was as near as the country had come to such a thing in its history. During the brief ten years while the system was in operation the volume of training did marginally increase (up by 15 per cent in those areas of manufacturing covered by the ITBs between 1964 and 1969) and notable advances were made in improving the quality of training (Sheldrake and Vickerstaff, 1987). Day-release became common in many apprentice schemes; group training schemes proliferated, helping smaller firms to participate in formal training programmes; and the engineering ITB's modular training systems paved the way for greater flexibility and breadth in apprentice training (Perry, 1976). However, the system was far from achieving its objectives.

The quantitative gains in training provision were limited to skilled areas and were, in any case, soon wiped out by the secular decline in apprentice places which followed the onset of the recession in 1973. The ITBs failed to open up access to apprenticeships for previously excluded groups and did little to change the old practices of time-serving and age entry restrictions. Most seriously, little headway was made in the setting and monitoring of standards in training.

These shortcomings were not attributable to the principle of social partnership in training, nor do they undermine the argument for government intervention. What they did show was that a national training system could not be created on the basis of devolved sectoral organization and that the social partners in the different sectors could not be induced to act in a co-ordinated way to create a national system of training to standards without a strong central body to co-ordinate them. Unlike in Germany, Britain's national federations and 'peak bodies' for employers and unions (including the Confederation of British Industry and the Trades Union Congress) lacked binding powers over their members and the local chambers of commerce never attained great influence. The Central Training Council, as the TUC frequently complained, never had adequate powers to compensate for this and to ensure that the system fulfilled its objectives in meeting those long-term skills needs of the national economy which individual employers were always prone to ignore (Perry, 1976; Corney, 1990).

The era of MSC tripartism, 1973–79

The next phase of training policy was inaugurated by the 1973 Employment and Training Act which created the Manpower Services Commission, and can be said to have lasted until the Conservative government was elected in 1979 with a new economic agenda. The tripartite composition of the MSC suggested that the principle of social partnership was still to govern training but this time it was to be co-ordinated through a much more powerful central government agency with considerable public funds at its disposal. The TUC had, it appeared, finally got the Swedish-style central manpower planning body which it had long sought and in its early years the MSC indeed seemed determined to provide the strategic manpower planning and to facilitate the comprehensive national training system which had so long been lacking. In some areas it was remarkably successful. The Training Opportunities Programmes provided a new and viable form of publicly funded accelerated skills training for adults on 6–12-month courses. Numerous other initiatives, although not markedly successful in themselves, did also raise the profile of vocational training to a level not seen before.

However, two factors decisively undermined the MSC's efforts to revolutionize Britain's VET. The first concerned the limited nature of the social partnership which it represented. The MSC, which never gave equal representation to educational interests, soon managed to antagonize the powers in the education sector who viewed it, not without reason as it turned out, as a body that would be used by governments hostile to the education system as a Trojan horse to force changes on that system from without. The MSC, in its relations with education, thus soon came to exacerbate that long-standing historical division between education and training which it was part of its proclaimed mission to eradicate. The split deepened and the possibility of creating an integrated system of post-compulsory education and training receded. The second factor, which lay outside the MSC's control, was the state of the economy. With the deep recession which followed the oil price rises, and the massive increases in youth and adult unemployment which resulted, government training priorities swiftly changed. The MSC was pressed into service to provide emergency unemployment schemes and soon lost sight of its original goal of creating comprehensive and high-quality skills training for the long-term needs of the national economy. The MSC was, in effect, blown off course by economic events. As Ainley and Corney have argued, by 1976 it had all but abandoned its original mission of comprehensive manpower planning and now played a kind of firefighting role, dealing with the social consequences of youth unemployment (Ainley and Corney, 1990).

Training in transition, 1979–87

The third phase in recent training policy covered the years of the first two Thatcher governments and represented something of a transitional phase. Despite early signs that the new government would wind up the Commission in line with its general policy of 'rolling back the frontiers of the state', the MSC remained and even expanded, partly no doubt because the new recession of 1980–81 caused rocketing unemployment and a summer of urban riots which made the MSC's firefighting role ever more important. However, the MSC was to become a different kind of body with a different mission, a shift that was decisively signalled by the government's decision to dispense with its Director, Geoffrey Holland, and replace him by their own man,

David Young (Ainley and Vickerstaff, 1993). Government took increasingly direct control of the MSC, using it now in a more interventionist and authoritarian fashion to impose new forms of vocationalism on the education system and to transform the apprenticeship system, ridding it of time-serving and restrictive trade union controls. The notion of partnership was quickly abandoned. The 1981 Employment Training Act abolished 17 out of the 24 ITBs and replaced them with non-statutory Industry Training Organizations. These rarely included union representatives and the unions were thus deprived of an important forum for representing their views on training. Educational bodies also saw their influence diminished as government initiatives in education increasingly bypassed the DES (as with TVEI, the technical and vocational education initiative) and the local authorities. Relations between the latter and the MSC reached an all-time low in 1985 when government announced its intention to hand over control of a large slice of LEA funding for non-advanced further education to the MSC.

Central government intervention in VET during this phase was probably more intensive than in any other period this century and yet at the end of it British training seems to have been lagging as far behind other countries as ever. What went wrong? The simple answer is that government directed its interventions to the wrong ends. The policies were misconceived. The Youth Training Scheme was set up in a blaze of publicity which proclaimed that this was the first ever comprehensive national training scheme aimed at high-quality training for both the employed and the unemployed. In fact it was cobbled together at breakneck speed without many of the preconditions for high-quality training. The schemes were designed in such a way that they inevitably involved much routine work experience but little supervised training or education. The pressure to provide places to meet government targets was such that schemes were accepted even where there was little likelihood that training would be of a high standard and this was rarely monitored with any rigour. The removal of the statutory grant levy system meant that employers were actually investing less in training than before. Between 1979 and 1987 apprenticeships in manufacturing declined from 155,000 to 58,000 only to be replaced by often lower quality Youth Training Schemes largely paid for by the state (Vickerstaff, 1992). The qualification system was not reformed to provide suitable certification for trainees and consequently less than a third came out with any recognized qualification (Green and Steedman, 1993). Without the prospect of a useful qualification or any guaranteed employment afterwards, trainees inevitably tended to have little motivation on the schemes. In short the Youth Training Scheme never managed to throw off the reputation for low-quality training which had dogged all previous MSC training schemes (Ainley and Corney, 1990).

The return to voluntarism, 1987–

Since 1988 training policy has undergone another radical shift, which has involved the final abandonment of social partnership and a return to the voluntarist principles of the pre-1964 period. A third election victory in 1987, followed by the short-lived 'Lawson' economic boom, encouraged the government to apply in the training field the market-led policies it had been pursuing so vigorously in education. The long dispute with the unions over the Employment Training initiative proved the decisive catalyst for the decision to return to a demand-led, employer-controlled training system. The Youth Training Scheme was substantially deregulated and relaunched as Youth Training, the MSC was abolished and the control of training was handed over to the new, employer-dominated, local Training and Enterprise Councils (TECs). This, according to the Employment Department 1988 White Paper, *Employment for the 1990s*, would 'give leadership of the training system to employers, where it belongs'. Since then further measures have been adopted to place increased responsibility for training on individuals and employers and to replace the corporatist control over training with a new training market.

TECs have been promoted by government as 'one of the most radical and important initiatives ever undertaken in this country' (Shephard, 1992). Originally modelled on the US Private Industry Councils (PICs), the TECs were designed as an entrepreneurial and strategic local mechanism for reversing Britain's skills deficit. They would make training responsive to local economic needs, inject a bottom-line, business-like approach to programme management and use their influence in commerce and industry to persuade employers to take the initiative in solving their own training problems. Unlike the PICs in the USA, they would be responsible not just for training programmes for the disadvantaged but for a range of measures to stimulate all kinds of training and to promote local economic development. Their ability to provide strategic local leadership was seen as a key catalyst for solving Britain's skills problems and for restoring economic competitiveness.

Since 1990 TECs have been formed in 82 areas in England and Wales and there are a further 22 Local Enterprise Councils in Scotland. Their boards, of whom two-thirds must be local business leaders, and the civil servants who service them manage budgets which average around £18 million each and which accounted for a total national budget of £2.3 billion in 1993/4. Originally responsible for training programmes for unemployed youths and adults (the Youth Training Programme and the Employment Training Programme) and for a range of schemes to help local business (Business Growth Training, the Enterprise Allowance Scheme and the Small Firm Service), their responsibilities have been systematically increased during the past five years. They now have a significant role in the finance and governance of further education colleges, play the major part in a range of Education–Business Partnerships and Compacts, and are increasingly involved in the running of local careers services (Bennett *et al.*, 1994). As the role of the local education authorities has declined in relation to secondary schools, colleges and training, so the TECs' importance has increased. They are now *de facto* among the most important agencies of planning in local education and training.

TECs are also centrally involved in several further initiatives which are designed to shift responsibility for training to employers and individuals. First, employers have been exhorted to take more responsibility for training through the promotion of targets for National Vocational Qualifications in firms and through the award of Investors in People kitemarks to companies with demonstrated standards of human resource development. Second, individuals have been encouraged to take more responsibility through schemes like Gateway to Learning and Skills Choice, which have sought to improve the range of careers guidance opportunities available to young people and adults, and also through the introduction of Training Credits (Felstead, 1993).

Training Credits are vouchers which can be used to purchase education and training from a range of accredited providers including colleges, training agencies and employers. Young people are counselled on how to 'spend' the vouchers through a process of Individual Action Planning which identifies suitable career/training progression paths and providers of suitable education or training. When the providers have received the Training Credits from the individual, payments are made through the TECs to providers by instalments and on the attainment of the target outcome (Outcome-Related Funding). The idea of the initiative is to encourage young people to see themselves as consumers making discriminating choices in the training market. According to the Employment Department 'this will put buying power into the hands of young people so that they can choose the training and training provider which best meets their needs' (1992). The . . . White Paper, *Competitiveness: Helping Business to Win* (HM Government, 1994), proposed extending the system to the funding of all post-compulsory education and training.

The limits of voluntarism

There is some evidence that these and other measures have helped to stimulate a more robust training culture in some British firms. By 1994 some half million people had attained National Vocational Qualifications, many within employment; over 800 firms have won the Investors in People awards, with 6,000 more working towards them; and the general level of in-company training activity appears to have improved over the past decade (HM Government, 1994, p. 81).

However, the TECs are still far from fulfilling their mission of creating world-class levels of training and skills (Coffield, 1992; Bennett *et al.*, 1994). The vast majority of firms are still not training their employees to NVQ levels; two-thirds of graduates from Youth Training schemes do not attain NVQs; and only 41 per cent of young people gain qualifications at the 'A' level or NVQ/GNVQ level 3 standard, compared with over 65 per cent in France and Germany (Green and Steedman, 1996). The demand-led or voluntarist approach has still not delivered Britain's long-awaited skills revolution.

The current British government policy on training has been described as the triumph of ideology over experience (Coffield, 1992). Two overarching sets of problems still bedevil Britain's approach to training and these both relate to the historical preference for *laissez-faire* or voluntarist policies. First, there is still no concerted national approach to training underpinned by the necessary statutory framework governing the roles, rights and responsibilities of different parties. Second, there is a marked and growing absence of effective collaboration between social partners and of institutional arrangements to promote this.

There are still no legal obligations on employers to train, to provide paid leave for training, or to contribute funds towards external training. While in other countries employers are bound to pay training taxes or to belong to employer organizations which exert pressure on them to invest in training, this option is still rejected in the UK. In the absence of these requirements and without the restraints of sectoral agreements on wages, it is still relatively easy for employers to avoid training by paying a wage premium to poach trained employees from other firms (Marsden and Ryan, 1985).

TECs have limited means for dealing with these problems. They only have at their disposal the power of persuasion backed up by their control over the allocation of public funds for training. However, these funds represent only a small proportion of the total costs of training in companies and thus do not necessarily provide great leverage (Meager, 1990).

As far as young people themselves are concerned, there are no statutory rights to receive training and, given the prevalence of unregulated occupations, fewer requirements to qualify to find employment than in other countries where the majority of jobs require specified qualifications for entry. Training credits will do little to improve the supply of training since providers are already funded on a per capita basis and the possession of a credit will do little to 'empower' young people. At the age of 16, they are not necessarily in a position to use it to negotiate effectively with future employers about training options, especially in a recessionary labour market (Felstead, 1993).

There is also a concern that the uptake of the new opportunities may be very uneven and that those who are least qualified and less able to make informed choices will fare worst in this kind of training market. Outcome-related funding of training schemes under the Job Training Partnership Act in the USA has often discriminated against the most disadvantaged as training providers have naturally tended to select trainees who are likely to meet the targets and thus ensure payment (Green and Mace, 1994). Unless great care is taken with the specification of performance measures in the UK, the same distortions are likely to arise with Training Credits.

Lack of collaboration between the social partners has also become an increasing problem in British training. TECs were specifically designed as business-led bodies not as partnerships. They not only under-represent unions and education; they also under-represent small business, the public sector employers and sectors without regional headquarters like retailing and finance and insurance (Meager, 1990). They are unelected, unrepresentative bodies which do not have to account to a local electorate or, even, to local business. Recent research suggests that the lack of a sense of ownership in TECs by small and medium-sized firms limits the influence exercised by the TECs and their capacity to provide strategic leadership in local economic development (Bennett et al., 1994).

Trade unions, meanwhile, have been largely removed from any effective role in determining and implementing training policy. They are only minimally represented on the TECs and the Industry Lead Bodies (ILBs) which set standards in training, and have only a minor impact on the examining and awarding bodies like BTEC and City and Guilds. Educational representation has been similarly curtailed, with the TECs generally having few educational representatives and with the removal of LEA representation on college governing bodies.

This breakdown in social partnership may have serious consequences for VET provision. Effective training policy cannot be devised without the active collaboration of the unions, since training cannot be divorced from other issues where unions have legitimate bargaining rights, like the implementation of new technology and labour processes, the definition and grading of jobs and the determination of pay (Rainbird, 1990). Unions can play an essential part in persuading employers to provide more training opportunities and in monitoring the quality of training provided. Where their influence is restricted to the individual firm and to local bargaining, this can only encourage the continuation of the historical pattern of uncoordinated and uneven provision (Winterton and Winterton, 1994).

Union representation is also important at the level of national standard-setting for training. Without significant educational and employee representation the ILBs have frequently defined occupational competencies in the narrowest fashion to meet the immediate needs of employers rather than the longer-term needs of individuals and the economy.

The state and the social partners in continental systems

Historically, the central state has played a much greater part in VET systems in continental Europe, both in terms of setting up and financing provider institutions and via the regulation of curricula and examinations. This continues to be the case today despite the trend towards devolution of power to regional levels and to bodies representing the social partners. Continental European and Scandinavian VET systems clearly vary considerably, from the relatively centralized school-based systems of France and Sweden to the more pluralist, employment-based systems of the German-speaking countries. In each case, however, the social partners play important roles in the system, represented at national, regional and local levels and participating in policy-formation and implementation with respect to various functions, including finance, training delivery, standard-setting, quality monitoring and assessment.

In Germany, France, Denmark and The Netherlands there are tripartite national standard-setting bodies in which unions are fully represented, and a number of countries, including Denmark, France and Italy, impose statutory training taxes on firms. It is also common to see national sectoral agreements between employer and employee organizations which regulate pay levels, link grade levels to qualifications and which seek to distribute the costs of training between different firms. Typically, in all these countries, the state is ultimately responsible for regulating the system and for determining the precise roles and responsibilities of the different social actors in the system.

Germany

Unlike the French system, the system of initial VET in western Germany is relatively decentralized and predominantly work-based. However, as in France, the overall framework is tightly governed by federal legislation and the concept of social partnership underpins the entire system. Wolfgang Streeck (1987) characterizes its organization as 'neo-corporatist' to denote its typical admixture of market and public regulation and the intricate and subtle network of partnership bodies which determine policy and administer the system.

Initially based on the traditional apprenticeship model, the German Dual System has evolved into a highly organized national system of mass VET. The basic structure of the system is easily described. The majority of young people (over 60 per cent) enter an apprenticeship when they leave school, which they do at ages varying between 15 and 19, depending on whether they have been studying at the *Hauptschule*, the *Realschule* or the *Gymnasium*. They sign an apprentice contract with a firm licensed to provide training and thereafter, for between two and four years, spend part of their week (usually three days) in work-based training under the guidance of trained instructors (*Meisters*) and part of their week in the *Berufsschule* studying general subjects and learning the theoretical aspects of their vocation. The vast majority of these (over 90 per cent) obtain their certificates of vocational competence at the end of the training period and are then qualified to enter full employment either with their initial employer or elsewhere.

The system is administered through a variety of corporate bodies operating at national, regional and local levels. At the national level, the Federal Institute of Vocational Training (BIBB) advises the Federal Minister of Education and Science (BMBW), who has ultimate control over training. The BIBB is a public body authorized by the state, whose central board gives equal representation to unions, employers and the *Länder* (11 members each) and includes five federal representatives with 11 votes. The DGB, the German equivalent of the TUC, nominates the employee representatives and the KWB, which brings together the peak organizations of the main chambers of commerce and the main confederations of employers, nominates the employer representatives. At the regional level the main power lies with the chambers of commerce (*Kammern*) and the *Länder* governments. Under the 1969 Act all the chambers have established vocational training committees made up of six representatives for each of the social partners (employers, employees, instructors, colleges). All *Länder* have tripartite training committees representing employers, employees and instructors. At the local level, power lies with the works councils, which must exist in all firms with over 200 employees and whose roles in VET are enshrined in the 1976 Works Constitution Act and the Coordinate-Determination Act (CEDEFOP, 1987). The social partners are involved in all the main functions of the VET system. These include: the setting of objectives, standards and regulations; finance; administration, monitoring and assessment. They each involve the national, regional and local levels.

Objectives, standards and regulations are determined largely at the national level. The main responsibility lies with the Federal Ministry, which is advised by the BIBB. Most decisions require a consensus to be reached among the social partners represented on the BIBB's central board, although this is often only by a bare majority. Federal law frames the entire system, defining the roles and responsibilities of the different social partners; the obligation of firms to join chambers; the obligation of firms to train all their young employees according to the standard terms of the apprentice contract; the obligation of firms providing training to be licensed by the chambers and to employ qualified instructors (*Meisters*); the qualification requirements for entry into classified jobs; training regulations on the duration, content and minimum standards for different classified occupations. At the regional level the *Länder* committees are responsible for co-ordinating these training regulations with the regulations for vocational college provision which they control.

The responsibility for financing the system is also spread between the social partners. The state (federal and *Länder*) finances the vocational colleges and the employers finance the on-the-job training. Trainees make a contribution through their reduced apprentice earnings. Federal government also provides large sums in incentives for employers to train and for special training programmes. National agreements are also reached by the employers and unions in some sectors for training levies on firms. At the regional level the *Land* governments also provide financial incentives for employers to train. The chambers charge their members dues and they often levy firms for funds for external training centres.

Administration, monitoring and assessment occur largely at the regional level. The chambers (under BIBB guidelines) are responsible for training instructors; operating external training sites; approving training firms and monitoring their performance; arbitrating in disputes between employers and trainees; and examination setting and assessment. Monitoring and assessment are conducted by specialist training counsellors employed by the chambers and expert juries comprising vocational instructors and others. At the local level the works councils play an important role in ensuring that training regulations are followed and that the company meets or exceeds the standards laid down. At the national level the performance of the training system is evaluated in the annual BMBW vocational training reports over which the social partners have been consulted through the BIBB. National employee and employer Organizations also have training research departments which monitor training for their sectors (CEDEFOP, 1987).

The Dual System has a number of drawbacks, most of which are endemic to all work-based training systems. The training is relatively narrow and job-specific, particularly in the smaller firms which provide most of it, and this is arguably a disadvantage at a time when new technology and reorganized work processes in leading-edge enterprises increasingly require multiskilled and flexible employees (Casey, 1990). It is also a system which divides the academic and vocational students into different tracks, reproducing within the vocational system the usual hierarchies of labour within which women and migrant workers are confined to disadvantageous positions. However, it is undeniably successful in ensuring that a very high proportion of young people receive training to reasonable standards and attain recognized national qualifications at the end. Despite the additional problems caused by reunification, as the new *Länder* struggle to bring their training into line with the western states, the system still appears to operate effectively, although there has been a drift in recent years away from apprenticeships to full-time academic courses.

A number of factors can be adduced as responsible for the relative success of the system, including the historical and cultural traditions in Germany which place great stress on the importance of education and training and which maintain the high social status of the skilled worker (Hayes, 1984; McLean, 1995). However, roles played by the social partners are also key. Although unions and employers are frequently at odds about aspects of policy, there is a level of basic agreement over objectives which in part accounts for the relative prestige, stability and longevity of the system. The close involvement of employee and employer organizations in policy-formulation and implementation undoubtedly increases the commitment of all parties to making the system work, while at the same time helping to ensure that no pool of expertise is lost to the system and that no interest group can manipulate it to its own exclusive advantage. Regulation through the collective actions of the social partners is also vital for ensuring the effective articulation of training and labour market policy which is critical to the working of the system. It is the national agreements reached between the partners which ensure that apprentice pay levels are set at a level which encourages employers to train, which discourages firms from using additional pay incentives to poach trained employees, and which ensures that the costs of training are fairly spread across a wide range of employers. Equally critical to the success of the operation is the strong regulative role played by the federal state in setting the overall framework and defining the roles of the different parties. The Dual System is a work-based model of training but it is definitively not a free-market one.

The importance of the social partnership model

The historical and comparative analyses pursued in this chapter suggest the fundamental importance of collaboration between the social partners in the effective provision of VET. Such collaboration can only be effective where the state, at national and regional levels, intervenes to co-ordinate the roles and responsibilities of the different partners. Voluntarist policies, which minimize such interventions, have not generally been successful. This is due to the underlying limits of the market as a means of regulating the supply and demand for training (Finegold and Soskice, 1988; Streeck, 1987).

Training is a collective public good from which all social actors benefit. Individual actors, however, may frequently make rational choices not to train. Employers often prefer to poach rather than to invest in training, especially, as in the UK, where there is no strong training culture and where employer associations lack the power to enforce a common code of practice. Furthermore, it is in the employers' interests to provide narrow, job-specific training to minimize the risk of losing their trainees and forfeiting their investment, even though this may not be in the best long-term interests of the firm, let alone the individual or the national economy. Employers tend to think short-term about their training needs and consider training as a cost rather than an investment for the future and this tendency is exacerbated, as in the UK, where the structure of company ownership and the threat of mergers and takeovers puts a premium on showing short-term profit (Hutton, 1995). The supply of training in a market system consequently tends to be insufficient both in quantity and in quality and the costs are not fairly distributed between employers.

There are reciprocal problems on the demand side. Employers may well not seek to employ well-qualified people or pay the rates to attract them because they have grown used to a shortage in the supply of skills and have organized their labour processes accordingly. This is the vicious circle of the 'low-skills equilibrium' for which the market has no answer (Finegold and Soskice, 1988). Likewise, young people may decide not to train because they have insufficient information and life experience to see the long-term advantages (Streeck, 1987) or because they calculate that the pay rewards resulting from the acquisition of qualifications do not warrant the opportunity costs incurred during the process of training. Relatively high wage rates for unqualified young people and poor differentials for those with skills and qualifications have, historically, provided a disincentive that has perpetuated low levels of training in the UK. These and other manifestations of market failure will virtually guarantee the limited effectiveness of a voluntarist training policy.

The foregoing analysis does not provide arguments for the superiority of any particular system or for the advisability of any one country trying to adopt the system of another. What it does attempt to show is that any mass system of VET must have certain properties in order to be effective. These might be defined as coherence, transparency, multi-determination and multi-agency.

Coherence and transparency in institutional structures, curricula and qualification systems are essential in order to promote access and progression for users of training provision and to ensure a close articulation with the labour market. Multi-determination and multi-agency are essential because VET systems are complex organisms, charged with carrying out multiple functions which touch on the vital interests of many different parties and require the investment and expertise of various different groups to operate with maximum efficiency.

Employers, unions and educationalists must all be intimately involved at all levels for VET to be successful. VET without employer input is bound to lose relevance to the world of work, which defeats one of its objects. VET without educational inputs will be narrow and inflexible and dangerously divorced from other areas of education. Without the active involvement of the trade unions VET is unlikely to achieve high quality and will not achieve any functional fit with other aspects of labour market and employment policy relating to job entry requirements, job definition wage determination, labour mobility and so on.

The pluralist representation of interest groups in the design and implementation of VET systems does not, however, obviate the need for strong central co-ordination and control. Systems based on the principle of social partnership only work when one of the partners, the state, defines the roles of the others and determines the shape of the system as a whole.

References

Ainley, P. and Corney, M. (1990) *Training for the Future: The Rise and Fall of the Manpower Services Commission*, London: Cassell.

Ainley, P. and Vickerstaff, S. (1993) 'Transitions from Corporatism: The Privatization of Policy Failure', *Contempory Record*, Vol. 7, No. 3.

Bailey, B. (1990) 'Technical Education and Secondary Schooling, 1905–1945', in P. Summerfield and E. Evans (eds) *Technical Education and the State since 1950*, Manchester: Manchester University Press.

Ball, C. (1991) *Learning Pays*, London: Royal Society of Arts.

Barnett, C. (1986) *The Audit of War: The Illusion and Reality of Britain as a Great Nation*, London: Macmillan.

Bennett, R. J., Wicks, P. and McCoshan, A. (1994) *Local Empowerment and Business Services: Britain's Experiment with Training and Enterprise Councils*, London: UCL Press.

Brennan, J. and McGeevor, P. (1988) *Graduates at Work, Degree Courses and the Labour Market*, London: Jessica Kingsley.

Burrows, A., Harvey, L. and Green, D. (1992b) *The Policy Background to the Quality Debate in Higher Education 1985–1992: A Summary of Key Documents*, Birmingham: QHE.

Casey, B. (1990) *Recent Developments in Germany's Apprenticeship System*, London: Policy Studies Institute.

CEDEFOP (1987) *The Role of the Social Partners in Vocational Training and Further Training in the Federal Republic of Germany*, Berlin: CEDEFOP.

CEDEFOP (1992) 'The Role of the State and the Social Partners; Mechanisms and Spheres of Influence', *Vocational Training*, No. 1, Berlin.

Coffield, F. (1992) 'Training and Enterprise Councils: The Last Throw of Voluntarism', *Policy Studies*, Vol. 13, No. 4.

Day, C. R. (1987) *Education and the Industrial World: The Ecole d'Arts et Métiers and the Rise of French Industrial Engineering*, Cambridge, Mass.: MIT Press.

Employment Department (1992), *People, Jobs and Opportunity*, London: HMSO.

Felstead, A. (1993) 'Putting Individuals in Charge, Leaving Skills Behind', Discussion Paper in Sociology S93 (7), University of Leicester.

Finegold, D. and Soskice, S. (1988) 'The Failure of Training in Britain: Analysis and Prescription', *Oxford Review of Economic Policy*, Vol. 4, No. 3.

Fukuyama, F. (1992) *The End of History and the Last Man*, London: H. Hamilton.

Green, A. (1990) *Education and State Formation: The Rise of Education Systems in England, France and the USA*, London: Macmillan.

Green, A. and Mace, J. (1994) *Funding Training Outcomes, Post-16 Education*, Centre Working Paper, London Institute of Education.

Green, A. and Steedman, H. (1993) *Educational Provision, Educational Attainment and the Needs of Industry: A Review of the Research for Germany, France, Japan, the*

USA, and Britain, Report Series 5, London: National Institute of Economic and Social Research.

Green, A. and Steedman, H. (1996) *International Comparisons of the Skills Supply and Demand*, Report to DFEE, London School of Economics.

Grew, R. and Harrigan, P. (1991) *Schools, State and Society: The Growth of Elementary Schooling in the Nineteenth Century*, Ann Arbor, MI: University of Michigan Press; London: Fontana Press.

Hayes, C. (1984) *Competence and Competition*, London: IMS/NEDO.

HM Government (1994), *Competitiveness: Helping Business to Win*, Cm 2563, London: HMSO.

Hutton, W. (1995) *The State We're In*, London: Jonathan Cape.

Kennedy, P. (1989) *The Rise and Fall of the Great Powers: Economic Change and Military Conflict from 1500 to 2000*, London: Fontana Press.

McCullough, G. (1989) *The Secondary Technical Secondary School: A Useable Past?* London: Falmer.

McLean, M. (1995) 'Education and Training in the New Europe: Economic and Political Contexts', in L. Bash and A. Green (eds) *Youth Education and Work: World Yearbook of Education*, London: Kogan Page.

Marsden, D. and Ryan, P. (1985) 'Work, Labour Markets and Vocational Preparation: Anglo-German Comparisons of Training in Intermediate Skills' in L. Bash and A. Green (eds) *Work Yearbook of Education: Youth, Education and Work*, London: Kogan Page.

Meager, N. (1990) 'TECs: A Revolution in Training and Enterprise, or Old Wine in New Bottles?' *Local Economy*, Vol. 6, May.

OECD (1995) *Education at a Glance*, Paris: OECD.

Perry, P. J. C. (1976) *The Evolution of British Manpower Policy*, London: BACIE.

Rainbird, H. (1990) *Training Matters: Union Perspectives on Industrial Restructuring and Training*, Oxford: Blackwell.

Royal Society (1991) *Beyond GCSE*, London: Royal Society.

Sanderson, M. (1994) *The Missing Stratum: Technical School Education in England, 1900–1990s*, London: Athlone Press.

Sheldrake, J. and Vickerstaff, S. (1987) *The History of Industrial Training in Britain*, Aldershot: Avebury.

Shephard, J. (1992) Speech to the TEC Conference, Birmingham, 2 July.

Streeck, W. (1987) 'Skills and the Limits of Neo-Liberalism: The Enterprise of the Future as a Place of Learning', *Work, Employment and Society*, Vol. 3, No. 1.

Vickerstaff, S. (1992) 'Training for Economic Survival' in P. Brown and H. Lauder (eds) *Education for Economic Survival*, London: Routledge.

Weiss, J. H. (1982) *The Making of Technological Man: The Social Origins of French Engineering Education*, Cambridge, Mass.: MIT Press.

Winterton, J. and Winterton, R. (1994) *Collective Bargaining and Consultation over Continuing Vocational Training*, London: Employment Department.

Chapter 2

Education training and economic performance in comparative perspective

David Finegold

In the last decade education and training reform has become a major issue in most of the advanced industrial countries. Economic change has been a driving force behind this reform movement. Faced with increased integration of world markets, rapid introduction of new technologies and the emergence of efficient, low wage competitors from the Far East, the industrialised countries have been forced to move into high-skill, high value-added market segments if they are to remain competitive. This economic imperative has intensified as countries such as South Korea and Singapore have used a large and successful investment in education and training to advance into increasingly sophisticated product and service markets. While there is an undeniable logic to this argument, it has proved difficult to demonstrate theoretically, or empirically, the relationship between education and training (ET) and economic organisation and performance.

This chapter will explore the relationship between ET and economic organisation and performance in comparative perspective, asking the question: 'Have some advanced industrial countries been more successful than others in creating highly skilled individuals and companies, and if so, why?' The particular empirical focus will be on the relative failure of Britain to provide sufficient education and training for its workforce. The chapter is structured as follows: the first part reviews the traditional approaches to the relationship between ET and economic performance; the second part outlines my own model, which attempts to synthesise two major theoretical approaches to ET and examines the nature of the ET investment decision; and the third part applies this model to the case of Britain to explain why its market-based system fails to provide the same levels of ET and economic performance as its main economic competitors.

The first theoretical perspective on the relationship between ET and economic organisation and performance we need to examine is that of neo-classical economics. This typically involves building abstract models, such as human capital theory, which treat ET as an investment in the same way as investments in physical capital (Becker, 1975). The advantage of this approach is that it forces us to look at the clear causal relationship between investments and the benefits they yield, and to simplify variables to the extent that we can test the relationship between them and aggregate levels of ET. This approach has provided some useful insights into the ET investment decision, such as the distinction that is made between general, transferable skills, which human capital theory predicts will be financed by individuals or the state, and job-specific skills, which the company is likely to pay for. Economic models have also focused on critical factors such as skill differentials and the incentives they provide for individuals to build and develop their own skills.

There are several problems with this type of approach for analysing ET and the economy. The first is that the abstract models become so far removed from reality that it is difficult to apply them to particular cases. This is true, for example, in the difficulty of differentiating between general and job-specific skills in the training that occurs within firms. Second, there is a problem of just what it is that is being measured. The actual concept we are trying to understand, namely improvements in overall skill levels or individuals' capacities, can usually only be measured by proxies such as participation rates in full-time education or performance in examinations. These proxies raise definite problems of comparability between countries; what value, for example, should be attached to a US high school diploma, given that those who attain it have reached no recognised outside standards and, in some cases, may have problems with literacy or numeracy? Similarly, there are difficulties in comparing on-the-job training in Great Britain and Japan, where Great Britain may score higher in terms of incidences of formal training, while the level of skills may be much greater in the Japanese case, where skills are created through informal means, such as job rotation, which do not classify as incidences of training.

The problem with economists' traditional approach is well illustrated by one of the most common variables they use to demonstrate the link between ET and economic performance: skills shortages. If skills shortages persist even during times of high unemployment, then the lack of ET is seen to act as a direct brake on economic growth. There are a number of problems, however, with how we interpret skills shortages. The first is that they tend to be very cyclical and therefore may convey different impressions, depending on where in the business cycle the country is at the time of comparison. Second, the fact that firms report large skills shortages may not in fact indicate that there is a shortage of those skills in the workforce. The problem may be that the wage the employer is willing to pay for a particular job fails to attract sufficient people; or factors such as the work conditions, discrimination in hiring practices or lack of labour mobility may prevent people with the available skills from applying for jobs. In the education sector, for example, recruiting difficulties exist alongside a pool of 400,000 qualified teachers who are no longer working in the profession.

The main problem with skills shortages, however, is that they tend to underestimate the effects that low levels of ET can have on economic performance. Employers are aware of the available supply of skills when they are evaluating uses of new technology and how to organise work, and therefore anticipate this variable when making these strategic decisions. Thus, every vacancy may be filled, but a country could still suffer dramatically from the lack of available well-educated and trained workers because work is organised in such a way that there is a low demand for skills in the workplace and, hence, low productivity.

A final problem with the human capital approach for our purposes is that it tends not to be comparative – it cannot explain why some countries are more successful than others in supplying high levels of education and training.

The obverse of the economist's approach is that of institutional analysis, most traditionally associated with the case study methodology. This involves detailed description and historical analysis of the provision of education and training and the organisation of the economy. The problem with this approach when taken to its extreme is that it treats each case as unique, with particular cultural, historical and sociological characteristics, which therefore makes it very difficult to learn from international comparisons. There are, however, some good recent examples of the institutional method that go beyond the descriptive case study. The first body of research to look at briefly is that of Sig Prais and his colleagues (Prais *et al.*, 1990). In a series of industrial sectors they have matched small groups of British firms with their counterparts in countries such as Germany and France. They began by looking at traditional manufacturing sectors, such as engineering, metal working, and less obvious sectors, such as textiles or kitchen furniture manufacture. They have now moved on to comparisons of service sectors, such as retailing and hotels. The focus of these studies has been on how work organisation and productivity are related to ET and skill levels. A recent study of small to medium-sized hotels found startling differences in labour productivity between Germany and Britain: German hotels were 65 per cent more productive when controlling for other factors. They traced the German advantage to differences in both the amount of training – 35 per cent of the German workforce was qualified as opposed to 14 per cent in the UK – and its quality – German workers had gone through rigorous apprenticeships that provided greater breadth and depth of skills than British training programmes. The greater level of training in Germany enabled particular occupations, such as that of chambermaid and receptionist, to be organised in such a way that fewer workers were needed to provide a higher level of service.

The L'Est School of Societal Analysis has taken a broader approach to ET and the economy. Maurice *et al.* (1986) set out initially to explain the disparities in wage and manning levels between blue and white collar workers in France and Germany. Conventional economic models could not explain the consistent pattern they found across industries. They then shifted to an interdisciplinary approach, studying the social context in which wages were determined. This led them to analyse the different ways in which skills were defined and rewarded in the two countries by tracing career paths and the hierarchy of qualifications. They concluded that differences in wage and career patterns could only be explained with reference to three critical organisational factors: first, the way in which business was organised; Second, the structure of industrial relations; third, the structure of the education, training and qualification system. It is conceded, however, by the developers of this approach that societal analysis still has several limitations. It is relatively static, taking a snapshot picture of a country at one point in time and failing to add a dynamic element of critical importance in times of rapid economic and technological change. The second serious problem with this method is that it fails to allow for the significant variations within countries at either a regional or a sectoral level.

What is needed is a new method for comparing education and training systems that combines recent insights from economic thinking – notably the development of game theory – and an institutional analysis of the incentives that particular actors face. What I propose to do is to construct a simple analytical framework consisting of three players, who represent the main investors in education and training, namely the individual and his or her family, the company manager, and the government policy-maker. Incorporating the advantage of game theory over neo-classical economics, the framework treats the decisions of the three actors as interdependent, with the decision of any one actor on whether to invest in education and training affecting the decisions of the other two. The game can be used to analyse the factors that make these three actors more or less likely to invest in higher-level skills, looking at the specific institutional characteristics of different countries or regions and how they might increase or decrease the likelihood of achieving a high-skill equilibrium. The goal is to move beyond the specifics of national cases to look at the functions served by institutions.

There are several advantages to this approach. The first is that, unlike cultural historical explanations of why Britain provides less ET than its main competitors, the model forces us to look beyond nebulous traits such as British attitudes or an 'anti-industrial culture' to the institutions that perpetuate those attitudes. Many of these so-called irrational cultural attributes may in fact be rational responses to the incentives that particular actors face and, therefore, altering those incentives may enable policy-makers to alter the behaviour of particular actors. The second advantage of this approach is that it allows us to combine different levels of analysis of ET decisions. This chapter is primarily concerned with national systems – the macro-level – and why it is that certain countries have more or less training than others; but the same approach, with the same actors and similar institutional factors, can be used at the meso-level, to analyse industrial districts and the particular structures that allow them to maintain high levels of skills; or at the micro-level – the firm or locality – to analyse what it is that leads the actors in a particular company to invest or not invest in ET. By using these different levels of analysis we may be able to explain variations in skill levels within countries or sectors. Firms that may successfully pursue a high-skill strategy in an overall low-skill environment, for instance, may be subject to a different set of institutional incentives (e.g. a different form of ownership) than surrounding companies.

The game framework was developed by combining numerous different disciplines that bear on the analysis of education and training, drawing on politics, economics, management and business literature, as well as sociology and industrial organisation. Its construction as a game puts the emphasis on probability rather than determinism. Institutional incentives set the odds that players will follow particular routes; each actor, however, retains a degree of autonomy. Players will, for example, have different willingness to take risks, with some electing to pursue a particular route despite disincentives they may face.

I shall now apply this method to the British case, arguing that the economy has been caught in low-skill equilibrium, where a majority of firms staffed by poorly trained managers and workers produce relatively low-quality goods and services. The use of the term 'equilibrium' is meant to emphasise the self-reinforcing nature of societal and state institutions which interact to stifle the demand for improvement in skills. Altering one component in this equilibrium without changing the others is unlikely to shift the country from its low-skill position. What I have argued elsewhere (Finegold and Soskice, 1988) is that this institutional equilibrium has deep historical roots, with its origins in Britain's experience as the world's first industrial nation, and that its effects have continued into the current stage of economic competition, making British companies and individuals less likely to invest in higher-level skills than their main competitors.

The evidence of this low supply and demand for skills is voluminous, and I can review it only briefly here. On the education supply side, the problem begins even before compulsory schooling, where Britain provides much less nursery or pre-school education than its main European competitors. Only 44 per cent of British children in the 1980s were in some form of pre-school education as compared to 85–90 per cent in countries such as France, Italy and Belgium. The next stage in the ET shortfall concerns the levels of achievement within schooling. Britain consistently finishes at the bottom of international comparisons in tests of achievement in such basic subjects as mathematics, science and reading. Although there are numerous problems with these standardised tests, what they reveal in general about the British structure is that, while the élite, the 15–20 per cent going on to higher education, do quite well in their chosen subjects, often finishing at the top of international rankings, the majority fares poorly.

Britain also suffers from low staying-on rates in further and higher education. There are both static and dynamic components to this problem. The static component is that for quite some time Britain has convinced fewer people to stay on in school or college than its competitors; in 1988, roughly half of British 16-year-olds and a third of 17-year-olds stayed on compared with more than 85 per cent of 16- to 18-year-olds in Japan, Sweden and the US. The dynamic element, however, is that Britain has been unable to close this gap with its main competitors; indeed, Britain was one of the only countries in the OECD (Organisation for Economic Cooperation and Development) that failed to increase participation rates during the 1970s. As a result, if we compare Britain and France we find that, whereas they had relatively the same participation rates in the 1960s, now France is well on the way to meeting the Mitterand government's target of having 80 per cent attain the baccalaureate, a broader standard than A-level, by the year 2000; in contrast, Britain continues to have less than half that number staying on until 18 and far fewer than that reaching the A-level standard.

Similarly, if we examine higher education we find just how far behind Britain is falling. In England, roughly 20 per cent of the cohort are now continuing directly into higher education, whereas in South Korea, which a generation ago was defined as a developing nation, the level stands at 36 per cent. To put this number in perspective, even if the British government were to reach its target of increasing the numbers in higher education by 50 per cent in the next decade, which seems unlikely given the government's unwillingness to make the money available to build new universities or polytechnics, and South Korea were not to increase at all, Britain would still be behind. But South Korea is unlikely to remain static, as a recent survey revealed that 85 per cent of South Korean parents expect their children to enter higher education in the next generation.

As a result of these low attainment and participation rates Britain has relatively low levels of qualification in its existing workforce. This low level of qualification is evident not only in terms of success in general examinations, with only a minority of workers having attained even one O-level pass, but also in a particular lack of technical and vocational qualifications. The skills gap is present in such traditional sectors as engineering, particularly at the craftsman level, as well as service sectors, such as retailing, where Britain has a seven to nine times lower supply of qualified workers than France or West Germany (Prais et al., 1990).

The problem continues with the training that individuals are offered within employment. A 1990 OECD survey of further training amongst the industrialised countries found that the British state spent less on training those in employment than any of its main competitors. This deficit is not compensated for by firms; an earlier study, *Competence and Competition* (Hayes *et al.,* 1984), estimated that British employers spent less than 1 per cent of turnover on training, as opposed to an average of 2–3 per cent in West Germany, Japan and the USA. A more recent study, *Training in Britain,* however, made the controversial claim that British employers were spending £18 billion on training each year (Training Agency, 1989). When we look at these figures more closely, however, they reveal the nature of training in Britain; while many workers received intensive training, two-thirds of individuals received no formal training in the last three years and, perhaps most disturbing of all, 42 per cent of those surveyed could never envisage participating in further education or training in their working lives.

In an earlier paper I explored the other side of the skills equation – the low levels of demand for skills among British employers (Finegold and Soskice, 1988). Since that time, further studies have confirmed this finding, notably Porter's *The Competitive Advantage of Nations* (1990). He examined ten industrialised countries and their economic performance between 1970 and 1985, and found that the UK had lost the greatest share in high value-added products and service markets, thus reinforcing earlier evidence that British firms are trapped in a low-skill equilibrium, concentrating on low quality, low-skill markets.

How can we understand the reasons for this failure? By using the game framework outlined earlier, it is possible to identify two factors inherent in the ET investment decision and the institutional structures that discourage the key actors in Britain from developing higher level skills. The first factor is the need for the players to have a long-term outlook if they are to invest in advanced levels of ET. The reason for this is quite simple. It relates to the payback period for ET investment, particularly investment in higher level skills. While the costs of ET must be borne up-front, the returns accumulate only gradually as the individual acquires the skills.

Whether the various actors are able to take a long-term perspective when analysing the decision to invest in ET is not, as it might first appear, a matter of attitudes, but rather a result of the particular institutional incentives they face. If we look first at top-level *company managers*, we find that the key institutional factors that will determine their willingness to invest in education and training will first be the nature of the relationship between financial and industrial capital. To whom are they responsible and what type of performance targets are they trying to meet? In Britain there are numerous studies pointing to the pressures for short-term decision-making by managers as a result of their dependence on the stock market for finance. This was highlighted most recently by the Innovation Advisory Board of the Department of Trade and Industry which called for changes in the tax code and takeover regulations so that British firms would be more willing to invest in those areas necessary for encouraging innovation, such as R&D, new technologies and, of course, training.

While the stock market is a critical factor in determining the willing-ness of top executives to make high-skill investments, most training decisions are made further down the corporate hierarchy. Therefore, it is necessary to look at the way in which companies are structured and, within these structures, whether individual managers are rewarded for investing in education and training. For example, are their assessment and future career prospects dependent on building the skills of their subordinates? Do firm accounting techniques measure all the benefits of training or just the costs? Studies such as Coopers & Lybrand's *A Challenge to Complacency* (1985) have shown that, in general, British firms' structures and reward systems discourage ET investment. The research of Campbell *et al.* (1989) on the microelectronics industry, in fact, found that British managers had to hide their investment in training from upper level management for fear that it would be cut in a recession if it was included in their formal budgets.

The timeframe with which *individuals* evaluate skills investments will be determined both by the incentives within the education and training system and those in the labour market context surrounding the ET system. In Britain, the majority of individuals adopt a short-term perspective towards their own skill development because the education system is driven by a historically élitist examination structure which focuses on the small number of individuals who go on to HE, while branding the vast majority of students as failures (IPPR, 1990). Although the introduction of the National Curriculum and the replacement of O-levels and CSEs with the General Certificate of Secondary Education (GCSE) should improve the incentives within the ET system for average students to work hard until 16 – by introducing continuous assessment and clear stages of progression in a unified system – these reform efforts have, thus far, not been extended successfully into the post-compulsory phase; A-levels, the high-status option that promises entry to HE or a good job, are designed so that only roughly 20 per cent of each age cohort will pass. For the rest, the labour market may actually create an incentive to leave school or college, since employers attach little value to education-based vocational qualifications and recruitment to the best apprenticeships is often restricted to 16-year-olds (Raffe, 1987). This stands in sharp contrast with Germany and Japan, where students of all abilities have clear incentives to work hard during compulsory schooling because their performance is clearly related to their future career prospects and there is no active youth labour market offering relatively high wages, thereby minimising the opportunity costs of remaining in ET.

The second calculation individuals make is whether to continue to pursue ET after finding employment, a decision that will be driven by whether the skills they acquire are likely to be rewarded in the labour market. There are two types of structures that may create these rewards. One is the internal labour market, where British companies have traditionally not been able to reward individuals for building general, transferable skills because of the lack of employment security – like the Japanese 'lifetime employment' model – necessary to justify this investment over the longer term. Thus Britain has had to rely primarily on external labour markets to encourage individuals to invest in their own higher level skills. This works well in certain professions such as medicine, law and accounting where individuals are willing to invest their own time and money in getting certificated because they know that, regardless of which firm they end up in, they are likely to be rewarded with interesting and well-paid jobs. However, an analogous, high-status structure of technical and vocational qualifications does not exist in most UK industrial or service sectors. The National Council for Vocational Qualifications is attempting to address this deficiency, but there are significant doubts as to whether it will succeed in its task.

The final player in the game, the *government policy-maker,* has also been discouraged from taking a long-term perspective on education and training in Britain because of the nature of the institutional incentives faced. The problem centres on the mismatch between the electoral time-cycle and the time-cycle required for investment in higher level skills. It is important to remember that ET policy can serve a number of aims apart from building skills, such as reducing the number of unemployed. In the last decade Britain has undergone an almost endless cycle of reforms and borrowing from other countries' policies, a process Keep (1991) has called the 'pick 'n' mix' approach to policy formulation, rather than a concentration on long-term planning and development necessary for creating high-skill training and education policies. This short-term approach has been reinforced by the lack of institutional support necessary for formulating a high-skill policy, such as comprehensive data on skill needs and existing levels of qualification. An attempt was made to establish this institutional capacity through the creation of the Manpower Services Commission in 1974, but this corporatist project was abandoned by the Conservative government. Even before the MSC was abolished, its ability to take a long-term, strategic view towards ET investment was significantly reduced as it became politicised, forced to respond to the whims of ministers in designing new education and training initiatives.

The second factor that is necessary for high-skill investment decisions to be attractive is that of co-operation within a competitive environment. Co-operation is essential because of the public good nature of the investment in higher-level skills; this includes not only the investment in education and training, but also the expenditure on other key areas – R&D, diffusion of the latest technologies, export marketing – that are essential for success in the current competitive climate. Each of these investments may be beyond the means of a single company or individual, but could be to their mutual benefit if institutional means are devised for overcoming the free-rider or collective action problems.

Let us begin by looking at co-operative relationships between managers. These relationships are crucial because of the persistent structural problem that has plagued British firms, discouraging them from training: the poaching of skilled labour. Britain's inability to prevent poaching can be traced directly to the weakness of British employer organisations. Unlike German or French Chambers of Commerce, British employer organisations have had no sanction with which to deter firms from free-riding on the training system. The 1964 Industrial Training Act was an attempt to discourage free-riders, by imposing a levy on those companies that failed to train, but this mechanism was dismantled along with the training boards in the early 1980s.

It is also necessary to look at the institutions that shape relationships between the various types of actors, such as the relationship between *managers and individuals,* or their representatives, the trade unions. These groups interact through the industrial relations system. The history of British industrial relations – with its roots in the craft guilds and legacy of multiple unions in a single plant – has militated against co-operative labour–management relations by creating a situation where it may not be in any one union's interest to work together with management even though all workers might benefit if cooperative agreements were reached. This institutional barrier to co-operation in Britain, however, has been significantly reduced in the last decade as trade union power has declined, owing to both legislation and, more importantly, falling membership and the decline of those sectors, such as mining and traditional manufacturing, with the strongest unions.

The institutions that govern the relationship between *managers and government* again discourage co-operation in Britain. At the macro-level, the organisations representing capital and labour – the CBI and TUC – lack the power necessary to guarantee the co-operation of their membership, an essential ingredient of lasting corporatist bargains. The result has been that no one actor has taken clear responsibility for the development of higher level skills. The British state has failed to fill this gap, instead relying on voluntarism, or leaving it to the market to ensure a sufficient supply of training for individuals beyond compulsory schooling. Raffe and Rumberger (1992) have pointed to the problems involved in this 'mixed model', where no clear lines of responsibility are drawn between the state and firms; government argues that it is companies' responsibility to train, while companies argue that the government or the individual must make the training investment, with the result that no player picks up the bill for developing higher level skills.

Finally, let us look at institutional mechanisms of co-operation between *government and individuals.* This relationship is critical for ensuring that individuals have the information necessary to make informed choices regarding their own education and training. Britain has suffered from the under-funding of the careers service, and the lack of comprehensive labour market information or skills counselling for those in employment.

If they are not set in a competitive environment, however, co-operative institutions are unlikely to produce a high-skill economy. The reason for emphasising this factor is that co-operation, when combined with a long-term perspective, could be a recipe for stagnation or oligopolistic bureaucracies which would stifle rather than encourage innovation. The essence of competition is that it compels the players to maintain a level of ET investment that enables them to meet or surpass their most successful rivals in the world economy. Here again, if we look at the institutional position of Britain, we find that there have been numerous ways in which competition has historically been discouraged and therefore actors have been able to avoid making the higher skill investment decision. Part of this can be traced to the heritage of empire and the fact that of all the industrialised countries Britain continues to have the highest percentage of trade with the developing world, thereby reducing the pressure to move up-market. British companies have also been shielded from competition by concentrating in the non-tradeable service sector, though this is changing as more and more services become open to foreign companies. The greater integration of the world economy, including the creation of a single European market by the end of 1992, will make it more difficult for British firms to sustain their low-skill strategies.

The foregoing analysis gives some idea of the structural reasons why Britain has invested less in education and training than its main competitors. It is important to keep in mind, however, that even if these institutional incentives could be altered, thereby encouraging actors to invest more in ET, this by itself would not necessarily lead to an improvement in skill levels. The additional factor that must be taken into account is the capacity of the existing system to create higher level skills. If we look first within the education system we find that Britain is already suffering from teacher shortages in key subjects such as mathematics, science and foreign languages, and that these shortages are likely to increase as attempts are made to introduce the National Curriculum. The scale of the problem is partly hidden by the fact that many teachers are responsible for subjects for which they were not originally qualified. The absence of a capacity to deliver high-quality training within employment is an even more severe impediment to a high-skill equilibrium. The low levels of management ET and the accountancy bias of much of the training that takes place discourage managers from making higher level skill investment and, in fact, may cause them to view the up-skilling of employees as a threat rather than an opportunity. Furthermore, as Rose and Wignanek (1990) have pointed out in their comparison of Britain and Germany, spending money on training without first creating a pool of well-trained teachers, equivalent to the German *Meister,* is unlikely to be an efficient means of creating higher level skills.

I shall conclude by looking at the interdependence of the actors in the model, showing how an improvement in the levels of education and training of the majority might provide a way of starting to break out of the low-skill equilibrium. If the basic attainment of those coming out of the compulsory education system is raised, all three players have greater incentives to invest in additional skills. For the individual there is clear evidence from empirical studies that those with higher levels of general education and training attainment are more likely to receive further education and training. From the perspective of the company manager, higher levels of general education not only decrease the need for remedial training that their firms might have to provide, but also decrease the risk of poaching; if the education system provides a higher base of transferable skills, then companies can concentrate more of their training activity on building company or job-specific skills. As Streeck (1989) has argued, elevating the general level of education and training may in fact reverse the traditional poaching argument. German companies have been compelled to move into ever more highly skilled market niches and alter the organisation of work, introducing new technologies in ways that will create demanding jobs, for fear of losing their best employees to competitors. Finally, from the perspective of the government policy-maker, an improvement in the level of attainment of the majority is likely to lead to greater demand for state investment in further education and higher education. Clear evidence of this demand–push factor has come with the introduction of GCSE and the unanticipated surge in higher education enrolments that has followed.

While the elevation of individuals' ET levels may serve to alter the incentives of the other actors, changes on the supply side of the skills equation without corresponding changes on the demand side are unlikely to result in long-term shifts from the equilibrium position. The danger, I fear, is that the ET and economic reforms of the last decade, with their emphasis on market mechanisms that encourage short- over long-term decision-making and competition at the expense of co-operation, will push Britain more deeply into a low-skill equilibrium.

References

Becker, G. (1975) *Human Capital.* Chicago, IL: University of Chicago Press.

Campbell, A., Currie, W. and Warner, M. (1989) 'Innovation, skills and training: microelectronics and manpower in the UK and West Germany', in P. Hirst and J. Zeitlin (eds) *Reversing Industrial Decline: industrial structure and policy in Britain and her competitors.* Oxford, New York, Hamburg: Berg Publishers Ltd.

Coopers & Lybrand (1985) *A Challenge to Complacency.* Sheffield: MSC/NEDO.

Finegold, D. (1991) 'Institution incentives and skill creation preconditions for a high-skill equilibrium', in P. Ryan (ed.) *International Comparisons of Vocational Education and Training for Intermediate Skills.* Lewes: Falmer Press.

Finegold, D. and Soskice, D. (1988) 'The failure of British training: analysis and prescription', *Oxford Review of Economic Policy*, 4, pp. 21–53.

Hayes, C. *et al.* (1984) *Competence and Competition.* London: NEDO/MSC.

Institute for Public Policy Research (1990) *A British Baccalaureate Ending the Division between Education and Training.* London: IPPR, July.

Keep, E. (1991) 'The grass looked greener', in P. Ryan (ed.) *International Comparisons of Vocational Education and Training for Intermediate Skills.* Lewes: Falmer Press.

Maurice, M., Sellier, F. and Silvestre, J. J. (1986) *The Social Foundations of Industrial Power.* Cambridge, MA: MIT Press.

Porter, M. (1990) *The Competitive Advantage of Nations.* London: Macmillan.

Prais, S. (1988) 'Qualified manpower in engineering', *National Institute Economic Review*, February, pp. 76–83.

Prais, S. and Wagner, K. (1983) Schooling standards in Britain and Germany, NIESR Discussion Paper No. 60.

Prais, S. *et al.* (1990) *Productivity, Education and Training.* London: National Institute for Economic and Social Research.

Raffe, D. (1987) 'The context of the Youth Training Scheme: an analysis of its strategy and development', *British Journal of Education and Work*, 1, pp. 1–31.

Raffe, D. and Rumberger, R. (1992) 'Education and training for 16–18 year olds in the UK and US', in D. Finegold *et al.* (eds) *Something Borrowed, Something Blue?*. A study of the Thatcher government's appropriation of American education and training policy, Part 1, *Oxford Studies in Comparative Education*, Vol. 2 (2) pp. 135–157.

Rose, R. and Wignanek, G. (1990) *Training without Trainers?* London: Anglo-German Foundation.

Streeck, W. (1989) 'Skills and the limits of neo-liberalism: the enterprise of the future as a place of learning', *Work, Employment and Society*, 3, pp. 89–104.

Training Agency and Department of Employment (1989) *Training in Britain.* Sheffield: Training Agency.

Chapter 3

Vocationalism and educational change

Rob Moore and Mike Hickox

Introduction

Debates on the 16–19 curriculum tend to be associated with broader issues of expansion and access and, inevitably, with curriculum change. In secondary schools at the time of ROSLA (Raising of the School Leaving Age (to 16)) in 1972/3, expansion and change in the fifth form led on to the development of the 'new sixth' with a wider range of provision departing from the narrowly academic Advanced Level model. In the late 1970s and 1980s, the Further Education (FE) sector responded to the introduction of the Youth Opportunities Programme (YOP) and the Youth Training Scheme (YTS) by introducing innovative, non-advanced vocational and pre-vocational courses (e.g. Certificate in Pre-Vocational Education), often with a stress on social and life skills rather than technical training or academic knowledge (Further Education Unit, 1979). Today, the rapid expansion in higher education has also led to changes in curriculum organization – for instance, the spread of modular courses (especially in the 'new' university sector) and in schemes such as accreditation of prior learning and credit transfer. The situations pre-16 and post-19 crucially contextualize 16–19 provision.

The 16–19 context has to be seen as dynamic. The new status of sixth form colleges, continuing changes in further education, expansion in higher education and the abolition of the binary divide create a radically different situation from that which existed only five years ago. At the same time, the activity of the National Council for Vocational Qualifications (NCVQ), especially at levels 4 and 5 (pre-graduate and graduate level entry), is creating a model of an integrated credential system parallel to and, in certain areas, interpenetrating with received academic and professional arrangements. Higher education expansion has intensified concerns with progression and integration and highlighted the need to construct, across 16–19 provision, coherent pathways through an increasingly complex credential system.

Expansionary periods in education come in waves and it is to be expected that current concerns will reproduce at least some of the major preoccupations of earlier episodes. Such developments call into question established assumptions about the organization of knowledge, its representation in syllabuses and courses and its relationship to institutions, the academic and teaching professions and to students (or even 'customers' or 'clients').

A common thread that unites these expansionary periods is the association of expansion and change with a perceived need to raise the general skill level in society in order to improve economic performance and international competitiveness. Hence, waves of expansion and curriculum change in education have tended to be associated with vocationalism and with criticism of the established institutions and forms of educational provision. However, the way in which vocationalism is used to criticize the established system and precisely how it is seen as facilitating economic regeneration have not remained the same. Expansionary phases take place within differing economic and political contexts and the ideological rationales for expansion and the criticisms of the received educational order vary accordingly. Hence there are dimensions of continuity and similarity, but also significant differences between periods.

Our intention in this chapter is to focus upon the changing forms and role of 'vocationalism' within the process of expanding access and changing provision. In part, as suggested above, our argument is that expansion, as a process, generates particular sets of problems and responses in education. Essentially, those sectors most affected attempt to accommodate not just rapidly expanded numbers, but a changing clientele by extending the range and type of provision. This is realized through courses which introduce new content and methods of teaching and assessment. Also, typically, these new courses tend to make a celebratory claim to increased 'relevance'. This is usually understood in two ways: first, in terms of responding to the 'real' needs of pupils, students or 'clients' (e.g. in social or occupational terms) and involving an acknowledgement of their 'experience' and, second, as better meeting the needs of society (e.g. for citizens, consumers or workers).

Vocationalism in perspective

Placed within the longer-term perspective, today's vocationalists can be seen to be reviving a similar set of justifications to those that underpinned the expansion of the education system in the post-war period. In this Golden Age from the viewpoint of investment in education, the educators were able to appeal to both social democratic, meritocratic and human capital, economic types of argument (Floud and Halsey, 1961). The major difference between then and now is that, today, the social democratic and liberal educational elements of the earlier philosophy have been jettisoned in favour of a more instrumental, New Right, market-oriented approach. These liberal values are now depicted as the reason for education's failure to deliver its earlier promise. On the one hand, progressivism is accused, by neo-conservatives, of undermining educational standards and traditional values, while, on the other, traditionalism is accused, by the vocationalist 'modernizers', of undermining economic efficiency with its 'anti-industrial' values (Whitty, 1991; Jones, 1989).

Contemporary vocationalism, especially in the dominant 'competency' form promoted by NCVQ, is strongly associated, in this way, with a wider political project to 'change the culture' of British institutions by extolling 'enterprise' at the expense of 'liberal' values. Vocationalists attack the received form of educational provision for its 'irrelevant' curriculum, which fails to prepare pupils and students adequately for the 'world of work', and for its academic elitism, distance from everyday experience and contempt for the practical application of knowledge (favouring 'knowing that' rather than 'knowing how'). In doing this, it resurrects earlier arguments about the wastage of talent and the failure to develop the potential of large numbers of 'ordinary' children.

Vocationalism's anti-academic, anti-elitist rhetoric also recalls progressivism's earlier criticisms of traditionalism. It derives much of its recent success from its ability to appeal to a range of distinct political constituencies and to a diverse range of arguments – tough-minded, 'right-wing' arguments concerning economic efficiency and modernization and, also, appeals to social justice, consumer choice and expanded opportunities.

The current situation for 16–19 provision can, therefore, be approached in terms of parallels with earlier periods of educational expansion but must also be seen as exhibiting important differences which reflect changes in the contemporary political and economic context. We are proposing that educational expansion (at whatever level) provokes a problem of 'accommodation' with respect to a changing social clientele which is typically met by new curricula forms that distance themselves from the received model by stressing their 'relevance' and experiential basis in terms of both content and teaching method. (It is interesting to note, here, a parallel with feminist and multicultural approaches.) We can see this pattern repeated in Plowden-style, child-centred progressivism; in the post-ROSLA Newsom approach; in the 'new sixth form' and YTS; and in developments such as modularity in the 'new universities' of today. Vocationalism, in its various forms, is ideally suited to play this accommodatory role and, indeed, has proved far more successful than possible alternatives such as 'community education'.

However, we have suggested that these problems of expansion/accommodation will be realized in different ideological forms depending on the specific economic and political context in which they occur. We will now look in more detail at these differences. In locating vocationalism in this particular way, we are developing a *sociological* rather than a *philosophical* framework for analysis. Although not indifferent to basic questions of definition or insensitive to the various forms of vocationalism proposed in the literature or the intricacies of the education/training debate, our concern, here, is with the manner in which vocationalism is *realized* under given *substantive* conditions. We would suggest that an understanding of these is as important for current 16–19 concerns as would be arriving at some ultimate resolution of the philosophical problems.

Vocationalism in a liberal context

The general context for expansion in schools in the ROSLA period was provided by the Newsom Report of 1963 (Ministry of Education, 1963). A vocational aspect to the upper secondary school curriculum was justified in terms of meeting the needs of pupils. It was seen as a means of reconciling the 'reluctant attenders' (as the Schools Council called them) to the extra year in school. It was essentially a pedagogic response to the perceived needs of non-academic pupils and the problems they could pose in the classroom. The Newsom philosophy defined the place of vocationalism in the curriculum as a means for making school more 'relevant' to the interests of these pupils rather than seeing it as a direct response to 'the needs of industry'. Indeed, not only Newsom but the DES (see Circular 7/74 on work experience: DES, 1974) and interests more immediately involved in 'the world of work' such as the TUC and the CBI were firmly against involving schools directly in preparation for work through explicit, occupational skills training (Moore, 1984; Finn, 1987).

The Newsom concern was with 'relevance', and the broad consensus endorsed the view that work experience schemes and 'the world of work' as a topic be firmly located within a 'wider educational programme' (DES, 1974) rather than being directed towards occupational training or recruitment. Within this broad consensus, 'the world of work' was introduced into the curriculum very much on educationalists' terms. The interests and values of teachers constructed the context in which work experience was treated by the schools and 'the world of work' presented to pupils (Bates *et al.,* 1984: Gleeson, 1983).

There were two interrelated reasons for the situation at that time. The first was the influence of 'human capital theory' that correlated economic development with educational levels in society. What was significant about this approach was that it defined the level of education (e.g. percentages of the population completing primary, secondary and higher stages) as the significant factor rather than the content of the education received (Moore, 1988). Education, regardless of content (science and technology or arts and humanities), developed a general quality of 'trainability' that could, then, be developed for specific occupational purposes by industry itself through training. Hence the content of education could be safely left to the academics and professional educators and to student choice.

Second, the social democratic purpose of education was to promote social mobility and expand pupils' horizons. To prepare them for specific jobs was contrary to this ideal. Particularly for the 'Newsom Child', the implicit purpose of introducing 'the world of work' into the curriculum was to encourage them, in effect, not to aspire simply to the type of unskilled, low level work that typically figured in work experience schemes.

The embedding of 'the world of work' within broader educational programmes in the 1970s and the potential for critical scrutiny by progressive teachers led to increasing criticisms of education's relationship with and attitude to industry. For instance, teachers were accused of promoting hostile and negative attitudes in pupils and emphasizing (e.g. in social education programmes) topics such as trade union membership and workers' rights over the more compliant attitudes expected by employers (Finn, 1987).

At the same time, the association of the post-ROSLA, Newsom curriculum with the spread of progressivism into secondary education drew criticisms of declining standards in basic skills and the overloading of the curriculum by 'fringe subjects' – criticisms articulated by James Callaghan in his Ruskin College speech of 1976 and in Shirley Williams's Green Paper the following year. Ironically, the introduction of a vocationalist element into the school curriculum in the ROSLA period came to be perceived as counter-productive to rather than as promoting the 'needs of industry' (Moore, 1987).

As is well known, the economic crises of the 1970s led to social democratic justifications for educational investment and expansion being subject to attack as the post-war consensus came under increasing pressure. Left-wing critics of the system pointed to its failure to increase social mobility and its tendency to reinforce pre-existing social status. The elitism of the university-dominated academic credential system continued to be criticized by the 'progressivist' lobby and for some the problem was that reforms such as comprehensivization had not been radical enough. However, this type of response was received with less popular enthusiasm than that of the increasingly influential Black Papers, with their questioning of progressivism and comprehensive reform – especially in the wake of the William Tyndale affair of 1976 (Dale, 1989). The fact of economic recession itself undermined social democratic and human capital legitimations of education, given that the expansion of the system had not only failed in its meritocratic aims but had not produced a technical base in the economy sufficiently robust to maintain economic competitiveness.

What this episode illustrates is the possibility of tension between vocational education, when located within a progressive educational paradigm, and political and industrial perceptions of a 'responsible' approach by education to the needs of industry. Under conditions where a liberal education profession enjoys a high degree of institutional autonomy in a period of educational expansion, vocationalism can be developed for essentially pedagogic purposes rather than as an aid to economic policy (essentially, the criticism levelled against British education by organizations such as the International Monetary Fund (IMF) and the Organization for Economic Co-operation and Development (OECD) during the mid-1970s fiscal crisis). Educators utilize its potential to attract and make courses appear 'relevant' to non-traditional, non-academic students in the interests of assimilation and control and are indifferent or even hostile to the immediate labour market needs of employers.

Where a liberal teaching profession enjoys a high degree of auton-omy and can construct 'relevance' for its own pedagogic purposes, the expansion/accommodation problem produces what might be termed an 'anti-industrial vocationalism'. Under these conditions, 'the world of work' is part of the content of a wider liberal humanist curriculum (e.g. social education) rather than a vocationalism where industry constructs a curriculum in its own right – as was the (largely unrealized) aim of the Technical and Vocational Education Initiative (TVEI) (Moore, 1987; Dale *et al.,* 1990; Hickox and Moore, 1990).

Vocationalism and the New Right

Two types of response to the situation described in the previous paragraph can be identified in the 1980s. The first, exemplified by the YTS, is to leave the existing educational arrangements essentially intact, but to intro-duce alongside them an alternative agency providing courses of a preferred type. The Manpower Services Commission (later the Training Agency (TA)) schemes marked a radical departure in that they allowed (through funding power and contract bidding) a non-educational agency to intervene directly in the internal arrangements and conduct of institutions within the educa-tion system. Although TVEI never had the same power to intervene in the schools that YTS had in further education, it still registered the principle that educational autonomy should not be taken for granted or seen as sacro-sanct (Dale *et al.,* 1990).

The second, longer-term response has involved a systematic reduction in the autonomy of the education system itself through the effects of state and market controls. Historically, the first can be seen as preparing the ground for the second. The further education sector, since YTS, has been used as a testing ground for approaches and mechanisms later introduced more widely across the education system – a kind of educational Guernica.

The net effect of these developments has been to change fundamentally the context (and, hence, the content) of vocationalism. Essentially, the liberal educationalist paradigm has given way to one which (a) relates content much more directly and explicitly to skill requirements in the labour market, (b) draws to a significant degree upon an industrial skills training model of transmission (competencies etc.) and (c) sets out to promote 'the enterprise culture' and entrepreneurial attitudes in direct opposition to liberal humanist values and culture. Rather than the general qualities of 'trainability' and the diffuse benefits of education *per se,* as identified by human capital theory, it is specific 'skills' and the promotion of the 'enterprise culture' which are now seen as securing economic growth.

The liberal educational philosophy that has dominated British education has increasingly come under attack from this new vocationalist ideology that seeks to challenge and to reverse the values of liberal humanist education within a broader New Right project of 'culture change'. What has been especially interesting in the British context has been the aggression of this ideology and of its proponents. Consequently 16–19 provision today, and especially its vocational aspects, have to be located within a context of expansion coupled with markedly reduced educational autonomy and institutional 'culture change' directed against liberal educational values. However, in locating this 'new vocationalism', it is important to stress the tensions which exist between it and the neo-conservative and neo-liberal elements of the New Right.

In emphasizing the significance of the ideological context of vocationalism, it is important to avoid the trap of presenting 'ideology' as all of a piece. In fact, the New Right in Britain (and in education in particular) is a disjointed alliance of cultural authoritarians, market libertarians and corporatist modernizers more united by their shared opposition to 'the liberal establishment' than by any common, stable project. We shall now explore some of these complexities within the ideological context, and then consider the major justifications currently offered in support of 'the new vocationalism'.

Vocationalism, the market and the state

The intellectual 'guru' of the contemporary vocationalists has been the military historian Corelli Barnett, who, in *The Audit of War* (1986) and elsewhere, has drawn an unfavourable comparison between the British and German education systems, arguing that whereas the former has aimed to produce a small academic elite geared to employment in the civil service, the German 'Dual System' (combining apprenticeship with vocational training) has underpinned the creation of a highly skilled workforce suited to the needs of a dynamic modern economy. In the contemporary world a better educated and trained workforce is an indispensable prerequisite for any economy that wishes to compete at the level of high quality, 'value added' products – an argument given a new twist by the post-Fordist' model of development (Hickox and Moore, 1992). Failing this, so the argument runs, Britain is condemned to what has been termed a 'low skills equilibrium' (Finegold and Soskice, 1988) whereby low quality training and poor quality production become mutually reinforcing.

This particular, highly influential model of vocationalism highlights the role of the state and a broader political corporatism that must be distinguished quite sharply from that of the 'market liberals' who seek to reform education through attempting to increase consumer choice. Strictly speaking, market liberalism should be neutral concerning the content of the curriculum given that it believes the system should be consumer driven. The customer is always right.

However, for the proponents of vocationalism, education is seen as a vital strategic resource which is too important to be left to the free play of the market and which needs to be centrally directed towards pre-determined objectives. From the vocationalist perspective, therefore, full-blooded consumer-driven reforms (Chubb and Moe, 1991) tend to be seen as suspect for two reasons. First, by their very nature, such reforms are likely to take effect in only a slow and piecemeal fashion – far too slowly to have any effect in creating greater international competitiveness in the near term. Second, even more crucially, since demand in the market inevitably responds to past indicators relating to 'useful' courses, the market liberal consumer-driven model would be of little value in creating a skills base which might reflect the future needs of the economy.

This preference for centralist solutions in the field of education has meant that the vocationalists have shared some common ground with the neo-conservative fraction of the New Right (represented, in particular, by Roger Scruton (1984) and the Salisbury Review group). They also tend to believe that the content of the curriculum should not be left to the free play of market forces. The neo-conservatives have tended to favour a traditional, subject-based curriculum, as embodied in the 1988 Education Reform Act and the National Curriculum, assessed by conventional, written examinations. However, the purpose of the curriculum for the neo-conservatives is to transmit 'traditional values' and forms of authority and, in this respect, they part company with the vocational modernizers. Their attack on 'social engineering', typically directed against left-wing educators, could equally well be directed against the vocationalist effort to impose economic 'relevance' upon education.

At the same time, the vocationalist school has been hostile to the elitism and academic bias associated with neo-conservative educational ideology. Ironically, they favour the experiential aspects of progressive pedagogy which have been so much opposed by, the neo-conservatives. Indeed, the vocationalist hostility to what it sees as a university oriented, mandarin curriculum resonates with the radical themes of the progressives and 'deschoolers' of the 1960s and 1970s.

The vocationalists are essentially arguing from a corporatist, 'statist' position, very different from the neo-liberal 'hands-off' view of the state's role. The free market faction of the New Right, in this key respect, reproduces the condition of relative independence from the state that has dominated the evolution of British education – though justified by market economic rather than professional autonomy principles (Green, 1990). This condition allowed liberal educators to maintain a high degree of control over curriculum content during the post-war period (Dale, 1989) – with the consequences described above. In particular, this situation explains the relatively scant provision of vocational education. By contrast, in a number of continental countries, notably Germany and Sweden, there developed a 'tripartite' system in which the state acted in collaboration with employers and the unions to create a 'social market', one aspect of which was the direction of education to the needs of the economy.

In the late 1980s, advocates of a German-style 'social market' and a more vocational form of education came to be increasingly vocal, given what they perceived to be the apparent failure of the *laissez-faire* Thatcherite reforms to halt the decline of the British economy (Hirst, 1989; Marquand, 1988). This demand for a more interventionist attitude towards the economy has also been echoed by the development of 'Clintonomics' in the United States. In both the US and the UK this is reflected in a demand that the state should provide the 'infrastructure' for private business, one of the most crucial aspects of which is the provision of skills training.

On examination, the current ideological context of education is complex and contradictory. The expansion in numbers at the 16–19 and higher levels has taken place under a general reduction in educational autonomy, but reflecting very different principles and purposes – cultural traditionalism, vocationalist modernism and free market consumerism. Hence the problem of accommodating expansion is being faced by educators within an ideologically unstable and incoherent political and policy framework – indeed, this very complexity can lead to lacunae within the system which educators can effectively exploit in compensation for their formal loss of autonomy to state, managerialist and market controls.

The vocationalist illusion

We have argued that vocationalism represents an attempt to 'repackage' traditional legitimations of education in a new form, at the same time aggressively distancing itself from what seem to be the 'softer' aspects of liberal education. It has been able to exploit the cynicism bred with respect to existing forms of education by the experience of recession. Nevertheless, for all its apparent hard-headed 'realism', the vocationalist claims can be seen as hollow in most essential respects.

Most crucially, vocationalism tends to rest on the assumption that it is possible to predict with accuracy the future needs of the economy. The problems of manpower forecasting, however, are legendary. Even for categories such as engineers, projections for future demand over such short periods as three to five years tend to be wildly inaccurate. Who, at the beginning of the 1980s, would have predicted the major challenges faced within the next decade by the computer mainframe manufacturer IBM, a firm with a considerable reputation for investment in training, and the rise of software manufacturers within the computer industry? State investment in vocational education and training in this area, at the start of the decade, would have inevitably been in skills that were to prove rapidly obsolete.

The vocationalist stress on experiential or real life learning echoes, as we have suggested, many of the themes of the progressivism of the 1960s. But it is open to some of the same objections. By combining a crude experiential philosophy of learning with an equally crude behaviourist definition of 'competency' and 'outcomes' (Jones and Moore, 1993) vocationalism risks ignoring the deeper intellectual competencies that, it can be argued, are necessary to create the truly 'flexible' workers which the occupational structures of post-industrial societies will demand (Hickox and Moore, 1992).

Arguably, given the rapidly changing nature of present-day societies, the last thing that education should attempt to do is to 'freeze' a particular kind of occupational structure at a given point in time. Applied to the occupational sphere this implies that 'experiential' learning on its own is unlikely to provide a secure base for the future skills needed by a rapidly changing economy. Indeed, NVQs have recently come under severe criticism (Smithers, 1993) precisely for their lack of intellectual rigour in matching the academic content of continental forms of vocational education.

Indeed, this objection also applies at a more macro national level, since the recession of the early 1990s has tarnished much of the apparent success of the German and Japanese models that the proponents of vocationalism have used to advance their arguments. Some argue, for example, that the famous German 'Dual System', combining apprenticeship and vocational training, reflects an economy that is excessively biased towards manufacturing industry and which may not be well suited to the needs of a post-industrial economy geared towards service industries and information technology. It is ironic that, just at the time when the German example is being advanced for the British to emulate, for the first time the number of German school leavers opting for academic studies has exceeded those wishing to take up apprenticeships (*Economist,* 1 March 1994).

Equally, it is questionable how far the German system of vocational education can be transferred to the British context, given the very different social context in which the German post-war system evolved. As we have noted, the German 'Dual System' was one aspect of a full-blooded (Clarke *et al.,* 1994) corporatism whereby the state, the major employers and the unions came together to plan the economy. Even in Germany this social consensus has come under heavy pressure in the post-unification period. In Britain, by contrast, corporatism was only weakly developed in the 1960s and 1970s and these developments were themselves dismantled during the Thatcher period (King, 1993).

Vocationalism and the peculiarities of the British

An interesting historical and sociological question is why the academic and the vocational credential systems have become so polarized in Britain in recent years, given that the same situation does not seem to apply to our major competitors. This can be seen to reflect what Corelli Barnett (1986) has seen as a very deep division in British society between the 'theoretical' and the 'practical', a division that has now (ironically, given that vocationalism was partly intended to bridge this divide) been replicated and reinforced by the developing split between vocational and academic forms of education and by opposing systems of credentialism (NVQs v. the A level 'gold standard'). It is interesting to note that in both Germany and Japan vocational education tends to exist as a separate track, superimposed upon a traditional, subject-based form of academic education (Cantor, 1989).

This, in turn (and here we are speculating since little work has been done in this area), reflects a still deeper split in Britain between fractions of the middle class than exists in other European countries. Whereas in France, for example, industrial managers have tended to come from the same kind of academic background as civil servants or members of the liberal professions, in the UK they have tended to be promoted in-house on the basis of experience rather than formal academic qualifications (Green, 1994; Savage et al., 1992).

If, as we have argued, vocationalism will not create a genuine 'skills revolution', which can perhaps only be achieved by a greater emphasis on the teaching of 'hard' science, what might it do? Arguably, one central effect of the vocationalist movement will be simply to increase the overall supply of credentials in the system (NVQs etc.), thus exacerbating the problem of 'credential inflation' (Collins, 1981) which has plagued many industrial societies in recent decades. Psychologically, the net effect of credential inflation is to undermine people's confidence in the value of credentials and of extended educational careers and training. The ironic implication of this is that liberal education (which does not claim this kind of 'relevance' in the first place) is both less susceptible to such problems and more likely, through its more rigorous and general academic content, to provide the 'deep' competence that modern economies really require.

References

Barnett, C. (1986) *The Audit of War: The Illusion and Reality of Britain as a Great Nation.* London: Macmillan.

Bates, I. *et al.* (1984) *Schooling for the Dole?* Basingstoke: Macmillan.

Cantor, L. (1989) *Vocational Education and Training in the Developed World: A Comparative Study*. London: Routledge.

Chubb, J. E. and Moe, T. M. (1991) *Politics, Markets and America's Schools*. New York: Brookings Institution.

Clarke, L., Lange, T., Shackleton, J. R. and Walsh, S. (1994) 'The political economy of training: should Britain try to emulate Germany?' *Political Quarterly* 65(1): 74–92.

Collins, R. (1981) *The Credential Society*. New York: Academic Press.

Dale, R. (1989) *The State and Education Policy*. Milton Keynes: Open University, Press.

Dale, R. (1990) 'The Thatcherite project in education: the case of the City Technology Colleges'. *Critical Social Policy* 27: 4–19.

Dale, R., Bowe, R., Harris, R., Loveys, M., Moore, R., Shilling, C., Sikes, P., Trevitt, J. and Valsecchi, V. (1990) *The TVEI Story – Policy, Practice and Preparation for the Workforce*. Milton Keynes: Open University Press.

DES (1974) *Work Experience* (Circular 7/74). London: HMSO.

Finegold, D. and Soskice, D. (1988) 'The failure of training in Britain: analysis and prescription'. *Oxford Review of Economic Policy* 4(3): 21–53.

Finn, D. (1987) *Training Without Jobs*. Basingstoke: Macmillan.

Floud, J. and Halsey, A. H. (1961) 'English secondary schools and the supply of labour'. In Halsey, A., Floud, J. and Anderson, C. A. (eds) *Education, Economy and Society*. New York: Free Press.

Further Education Unit (1979) *A Basis for Choice*. London: Further Education Unit.

Gamble, A. (1988) *The Free Economy and the Strong State*. London: Macmillan.

Gleeson, D. (ed.) (1983) *Youth Training and the Search for Work*. London: Routledge and Kegan Paul.

Green, A. (1990) *Education and State Formation*. Basingstoke: Macmillan.

Green, A. (1994) 'Postmodernism and state education'. *Journal of Education Policy* 9(1): 67–83.

Hickox, M. and Moore, R. (1990) 'TVEI, vocationalism and the crisis of liberal education', in Flude, M. and Hammer, M. (eds) *The Education Reform Act of 1988*. Lewes: Falmer Press.

Hickox, M. and Moore, R. (1992) 'Education and post-Fordism: a new correspondence?'. In Brown, P. and Lauder, H. (eds) *Education for Economic Survival*. London and New York: Routledge.

Hirst, P. (1989) *After Thatcher*. London: Collins.

Jones, K. (1989) *Right Turn*. London: Hutchinson.

Jones, L. and Moore, R. (1993) 'Education, competence and the control of expertise'. *British Journal of the Sociology of Education* 14(4): 385–97.

King, D. S. (1993) 'The Conservatives and training policy 1979–1992: from a tripartite to a neo-liberal regime.' *Political Studies*, 214–35.

Marquand, D. (1988) *The Unprincipled Society*. London: Jonathan Cape.

Ministry of Education (1963) *Half Our Future*. A Report of the Central Advisory Council for Education (England). London: HMSO.

Moore, R. (1984) 'Schooling and the world of work'. In Bates, I. *et al. Schooling for the Dole?* Basingstoke: Macmillan.

Moore, R. (1987) 'Education and the ideology of production'. *British Journal of the Sociology of Education* 8(2): 227–42.

Moore, R. (1988) 'Education, production and reform'. In Lauder, H. and Brown, P. (eds) *Education in Search of a Future*. Lewes: Falmer Press.

Prais, S. (1989) 'How Europe sees the new British initiative for standardizing vocational qualifications'. *National Economic Review* August.

Savage, M., Barlow, J., Dickens, P. and Fielding, T. (1992) *Property, Bureaucracy and Culture: Middle-Class Formation in Contemporary Britain*. London: Routledge.

Scruton, R. (1984) *The Meaning of Conservatism*. London: Macmillan.

Smithers, A. (1993) *All Our Futures: A Dispatches Report*. London: Channel 4 Publications.

Whitty, G. (1991) 'The New Right and the national curriculum: state control or market forces?'. In Moore, R. and Ozga, J. (eds) *Curriculum Policy*. Oxford: Pergamon Press.

Chapter 4

Industrial training or new vocationalism? Structures and discourses

Stephen Ball

Writing in his autobiography about his speech at Ruskin College in 1976, James Callaghan summarised his concerns and arguments as follows:

> Teachers, I said, must carry parents with them. Industry complained that some school-leavers did not have the basic tools to do the job and many of our best-trained students from university and polytechnics had no desire to join industry. Why was this? Why did so many girls abandon science before leaving school, and why were thirty thousand vacancies in science and engineering at universities and polytechnics not taken up, while the humanities courses were full? Were we sacrificing thoroughness and depth of courses in favour of range and diversity? I favoured a basic curriculum with universal standards. 'The essential tools are basic literacy and numeracy; the understanding of how to live and work together; respect for others; and respect for the individual. This means acquiring basic knowledge, skills and reasoning ability; developing lively inquiring minds and an appetite for further knowledge that will last a lifetime.' The goal of education was to 'equip children to the best of their ability for a lively constructive place in society and also to fit them to do a job of work' and, I emphasised, 'not one or the other, but both'. In today's world there would be fewer jobs for those without skill, and I concluded by asking for a positive response and not a defensive posture in the debate which I hoped would begin.
>
> (Callaghan 1987 p. 411)

. . . The Ruskin speech both drew upon and gave impetus to the New Right's advocacy of parental choice. In this chapter I want to examine in particular the various vocational discourses mobilised by and around the speech and their claims about the relationships between education and the economy. The speech did not initiate these discourses but it gave them legitimacy in the education 'policy community'.

According to James Donald (1979), the Ruskin speech, the Great Debate which followed it and the Government Green Paper, *Education in Schools*

(Cmnd 6869) which was published in July 1977, all played their part, discursively, in 'the creation and imposition of a "new settlement" to replace the old consensus in education' (p. 107). In part this kind of deconstructive/reconstructive process achieved through the logics displayed in the texts: the speech, the debate and the paper. These texts conjured up a commonsense and real account of schools, the purpose of which 'was the validation of existing knowledges through a sort of populist empiricism' (p. 106). . . .

For now I want to pursue chronologically and analytically the 'new vocationalist' impetus provided by the three texts. It is important to begin with the point that these texts, and the many others which quickly followed, do not articulate a single, straightforward vocational message. A number of interrelated criticisms of the vocational inadequacy of schools and school leavers are mounted (see Dale 1985).

1   That schools, particularly those identified with the ideology of progressivism, fail to instil in their students the habits, attitudes and self-discipline which employers require from their workers. They do not encourage and produce good workers (or, perhaps more accurately, good employees). . . .

2   That schools, particularly those identified with the ideology of progressivism, are neglecting basic skills and teaching other inappropriate things, which means that school leavers are unprepared for the technical demands of the workplace.

3   That schools generally maintain and perpetuate a bias towards the academic and against the practical, vocational or industrial, thus encouraging students away from courses like engineering or careers in industry. This position is often identified with the writing of Corelli Barnett (1972) and Martin Wiener (1981) and continues to be put. For example, in 1986, Industry Year:

> We all need industry but we fail to recognize the valuable contribution it makes to society. We are an industrial country with an anti-industrial culture, as recent surveys of attitudes show. This is the *root cause* [my emphasis] of our relative decline, and it is this which Industry Year is attacking.
>
> (*Industry Year* 1986)

The other point to be noted from this illustration is the identification of attitudes located within education and culture as the primary factors in the explanation of industrial and economic decline. Political and economic factors are taken to be of less importance.

4   Related to the above, schools in general are criticised for failing to teach students about the world of work or about the economic import-

ance of industry within society, that is they do not make pupils aware of the source of wealth creation within capitalist societies.

A later addition to these criticisms more directly associated with neo-liberalism and the ideology of Thatcherism was:

5   That schools fail to develop the skills of, or positive orientations towards, entrepreneurship and enterprise.

Clearly there are contradictions embedded in the schools/industry discourse, for example between the encouragement of assertive, independent entrepreneurs, who would found their own businesses, as against fostering attitudes of deference within a body of potential employees. Jamieson (1986 p. 26) notes that:

> It is difficult to describe the schools/industry movement. There are two major difficulties. First, it doesn't stand still. The number of groups, organizations and government agencies constantly grows. Secondly, it has no one focus of attention, save it wants to change the education system in one way or another.

However, the polyvalency of the discourse is one of its great strengths. It has developed as a practical political response to a multifaceted industrial crisis (basically a crisis in the profitability of capitalist industry) and is directed to different levels and aspects of the crisis. It is in part a response to the failures and weaknesses of British industrial management and the need to develop a new cadre of skilled and enthusiastic managers. It also relates to Thatcherism's faith in small business to provide the basis of industrial recovery and thus produce a real and lasting reduction in unemployment. But it is also a response to the high levels of industrial unrest during the 1970s, from the 'three-day week' to the 'winter of discontent'. Further, it is addressed to the low levels of productivity which played their part during the 1970s in rendering British exports uncompetitive. And it is fairly straightforwardly a response to employers' complaints about ill-disciplined and ill-prepared young workers. Finally, the schools/industry movement is part of a large-scale effort directed towards the social management of high levels of youth unemployment.

Many of the specific criticisms carried by these arguments are addressed directly at teachers. In many cases the fault is seen to lie with teachers' attitudes, lack of understanding, political orientations or incompetence. This was most forcefully put, a few months before the launch of the Great Debate, in an influential article written by Arnold Weinstock, Chairman of GEC, with the title 'I Blame the Teachers'.

> Teachers fulfil an essential function in the community but, having themselves chosen not to go into industry they often deliberately, or more

usually unconsciously, instil in their pupils a similar bias. . . . And this is quite apart from the strong though unquantifiable impression an outsider receives that the teaching profession has more than its fair share of people actively politically committed to the overthrow of liberal institutions, democratic will or no democratic will.

(Weinstock 1976)

. . . There are some relationships between new vocationalism and neo-liberal theories, particularly in their common emphasis on the importance of individual endeavour. At the heart of the analytical complex of new vocationalism stands the deficient individual – the school leaver. The explanation of Britain's economic regression and lack of competitiveness is taken to be the lack of individual motivation and skills. Thus, according to the DoE/DES (1986) White Paper *Working Together – Education and Training,* 'motivation is all important so that attitudes change and people acquire the desire to learn, the habit of learning, and the skills learning brings' (1.4). The diagnosis and the solutions appear to be simple, far too simple for many commentators – instil motivation, develop the right attitudes and habits, and economic recovery will be achieved.

. . . Again, though, the new vocationalist discourse is organised around a set of polarities, of problems and solutions. Lack of motivation is set against motivation, lack of skills against skills acquired, wrong attitudes against right ones, bad habits against good, lack of preparation for work against being prepared. As Stronach (1988 p. 60) puts it 'the personalising of economic competitiveness (be motivated, get skilled) offers both an economics of recovery and a metonymics of blame (if *you* were trained and motivated *we* wouldn't be where we are today)'. Indeed, Stronach offers an original and pertinent analysis of new vocationalism. Like many others he rejects the simplicities and audacity of the basic claim, that individual attributes are directly related to national economic well-being, and argues instead that the new vocationalism can be best understood as ritual. 'It is not cynical to argue that these initiatives are essentially responses rather than solutions to "the problem" (p. 66). They 'address' the problem. 'Our vocational initiatives are also contemporary dramas that ritually involve young people in enacting solutions to economic decline' (p. 66). As a ritual, vocationalism serves 'to reassure the powerful as much as it seeks to mystify the powerless' (p. 67). It is, Stronach argues, a form of 'archaic recovery', regeneration, a return to a 'mythicised tradition', a time when workers knew their place, knew their job and capitalism boomed.

Each of the areas of critique listed above, once planted in the political imagination of the major parties, and well fertilised by the discursive outpourings of the Great Debate, was eventually to bear policy fruits. Schools/industry and the new vocationalism quickly became an industry in its own right as innumerable schemes, programmes, initiatives and courses were launched and continue to be launched. Each one of these initiatives offers a response, a solution, to one or more of the areas of concern and deficit.

However, as already indicated, beneath, or beyond, an apparent simplicity and commonality in the vocational impetus there is a degree of dissonance and dislocation. Industry itself is not, of course, of a piece. The needs or concerns of big and small, manufacturing and finance, local, national and multinational, and traditional, service and high-tech businesses are not the same. Industrialists, or those who speak for them, do not necessarily speak with one voice. Those who speak on behalf of industry do not always get things right.

. . . From its beginnings at Ruskin it has been a political discourse. Strategically the various vocational initiatives have played a key role in reworking the governance of education and changing the possibilities of policy making. TVEI has provided a potent exemplar. 'TVEI has emerged as a prototype for implementing educational policy and change' (Gleeson 1987 p. 1). As Dale (1985) argues, TVEI has played a major part in changing the content and orientation of schooling, but in the process the ways and means of changing schooling itself have been changed. . . . In retrospect the TVEI scheme can he seen as the precursor to an increasing variety of forms of categorical funding: directed payments from the centre, from the DES as well as MSC, which are specifically earmarked and which just by-pass Local Authority decision making on educational expenditure. As Dale is suggesting, the MSC has sponsored a new style of policy making and new forms of policy evaluation. The speed of implementation of TVEI and the relative ease with which the compliance of LEAs was achieved served to demonstrate the potential for quick, radical, top-down reform in a system on the defensive, with low morale and reduced funding. The intrusion of the MSC (and the DoE and DTI) in the spheres of influence previously dominated by the DES, the LEAs and teacher unions further reduced and weakened the institutional basis of the old consensus in education. New voices now had a legitimate say in education policy making. The locus of this new discourse in business and commerce articulates the cause of the industrial trainers, and it has a long history stretching back into the nineteenth century (see Reeder 1979 and McCullough 1986).

Beck (1983), looking back at the outcomes of the Great Debate, argues that 'Perhaps the most damaging educational legacy of the Callaghan Government's policy of linking educational practice to industrial regeneration was the legitimacy it gave to forms of educational practice which substitute political socialization for evidential education' (p. 229).

As indicated already, we can identify a key element of style within the social practices of this discourse. Teachers and schools were to find themselves signing contracts with the MSC for the delivery of TVEI courses, and departments or schools, and authorities are in competition for scarce funds, having to make bids and develop effective presentations. The logic of capitalism begins to bite deep into the processes of schooling.

The structuralist scenario

We have looked briefly at some aspects of the new vocationalist discourse; I now want to put that discourse into a non-discursive, economic context. This will enable us to look a little more closely at the economic policies of Thatcherism, and to see how these policies affected education. I will try to link education to capital by looking at changes in the economy and social policy. Thus, we can pursue the aim of setting education within a broader policy perspective. The substantive issue is this: How does education policy over the past ten years look if we attempt to understand it in structural terms, in relation, that is, to the national and international crisis of capitalism of the mid-1970s and the concomitant fiscal crisis of the state? . . .

The notion here is that particular policy ideas and policies-in-practice have certain economic conditions of existence, and when the latter shift, or are perceived to have shifted, then the existing policy repertoire breaks up and a potential is created for a new repertoire.

The structuralist argument proceeds generally as follows. In times of economic growth, high employment and full use of productive capacity, taxation from the profits of capital enables the state to develop welfare services and satisfy demand for increases in the standard of living of workers. Several things are achieved:

1   Policy concessions maintain stability and stifle potential conflicts. Dissatisfaction can, in effect, be bought off. And the development of the social wage – the provision of public health, education, housing, transport services and social welfare – reduces pressure on wage demands aimed at employers.
2   The state takes on responsibility for the disorganising effects of capital (e.g. unemployment, poor health and environmental damage).
3   The state can take over the burden of reproducing the relations of production for capital, thus reducing costs by the provision of public housing, public health and education and training.
4   The state stands in place of industry when social needs do not produce solvent demand (i.e. when they are unprofitable for private enterprise), e.g. recreation, housing and education.

Under these conditions the spheres of production (industry/business) and reproduction (social welfare/education) are strongly separated. Social welfare and public services are firmly within the sphere of reproduction.

In the mid-1970s, in Britain and many other western industrial societies, the economic basis of these social democratic policies began to change dramatically, hastened by the oil price rises of 1973–75. There was:

1 serious decline in the rate of economic growth;
2 massive increases in inflation;
3 rapidly rising rates of unemployment;
4 currency instability.

These changes in economic conditions had severe knock-on effects for the state and for economic policy. Falling profit meant falling revenue from taxes. In order to increase net profitability, capital pressured the state to reduce taxation (e.g. corporation tax, employers' national insurance contributions). The state lost fiscal input in both respects. There were further demands from capital for the state to take over reproduction costs (e.g. apprenticeships and training, pension and health schemes): demand for public funds as a direct assistance to capital in the form of subsidies, regional aid, export credits, the setting up of enterprise zones, etc.; and demand for the relaxation of development controls – enterprise zones, development corporations, suspension of planning controls – setting the needs of capital over and against the needs of the local communities. The pragmatic and reactive response of the state was to cut public expenditure in areas like social welfare, thus reducing the social wage. Reductions in expenditure and investment by both state and capital led to further increases in unemployment. And there was pressure from capital for access to profitable areas of state provision – privatisation – expanding the logic of commodity circulation. . . .

In effect, . . . I want to argue that social welfare has been significantly *restructured* and *repositioned* in response to the crisis in capital accumulation. In education we can see this restructuring and repositioning occurring via three aspects of Thatcherist policy:

1 Controls over and the redirection of spending and expenditure cuts.
2 The attempt to reorient and redefine the meaning of education itself 'what counts as education'.
3 New forms of control over the professional workers of education.

The result or effect of the policy and ideological work done on education in these ways has shifted education out of its firm location within the sphere of reproduction into a closer relation to the sphere of production. Costs which were seen to be a drain upon the profitability of capital can as a result be presented as directly enhancing profit. The strong classification which Bernstein argues has existed, between education and production, which 'creates the condition for the relative autonomy of education, the division of labour between those who are located in production and those who are located in cultural production (education)' (1977 p. 175) is, as a consequence, significantly weakened. . . .

Repositioning and restructuring

Crucially, the repositioning and restructuring of education involves changing the nature of its relative autonomy, with 'the specification "relative", as in relative autonomy, primarily . . . to be understood in the qualitative sense as referring to a particular *kind of relationship*'. (Fritzell 1987 p. 24). In particular, I want to argue that this repositioning involves extensions of aspects of the commodity form, 'the dominant organizational principle of exchange in capitalist societies' (Offe 1984 p. 39), into education, that is, the previously de-commodified manner for the delivery of education is changed. Education is made more subordinate to and less autonomous from the commodity form, and the nature of its relative autonomy is thus changed. . . .

As Fritzell suggests, the nature of relative autonomy in or for education rests upon the tensions which arise between 'the functions of efficient accumulation and legitimation' (p. 27); or, in other words, the kind of relative autonomy enjoyed by education is embodied in the particular ways it fulfils the function of the reproduction of the economic foundation of society. Fritzell outlines two versions of such autonomy.

The first is positive correspondence: here the structuring of schooling is both structurally and functionally tied directly and harmoniously to accumulation and legitimation. (Structural autonomy relates to the correspondence of significant properties and internal relations between systems, here education and the economy. Functional autonomy relates to the adjustment in terms of social consequences between systems. In very simple terms structural autonomy is a matter of similarity of forms and processes; functional autonomy is a matter of outputs. In a broad sense the former relates to social reproduction and the latter to technical.) Seen in terms of positive correspondence, school is a competitive, formal and hierarchical process, knowledge and social roles are fixed, teaching is standardised and is directed towards formal examinations. This provides the framework for what Offe (1976) calls the 'achievement principle'. Examinations serve as personal qualifications providing access to particular occupations. The ideology of merit legitimates this access in terms of individual ability.

The second version of relative autonomy is negative correspondence; this 'concerns functional contributions by means of the *exclusion* of critical tendencies and the *prevention* from destructive developments' (Fritzell 1987 p. 30). Here the process of schooling is distanced from the commodity form; functionally school remains tied to the needs of the economy but structurally *it may appear* to be autonomous. Social education and the personal development and individual capacities of the pupil are given emphasis. Self-realisation and expressive competencies are used as the basis for the evaluation and ranking of students, and access to the labour market is emphasised in terms of social competencies as much as cognitive ones. . . .

Negative correspondence is realised very clearly and directly in the educational projects of new vocationalism. And clearly the new vocationalism has made significant headway in its impact on school-age education in recent years through courses like TVEI and CPVE and the adoption of City and Guilds and BTec courses. However, two important corollaries have to be added to these general comments. First, in some respects the inroads of negative correspondence have been general. For example, the Records of Achievement movement has made considerable headway in many schools and LEAs and has received strong support from Keith Joseph during his period as Secretary of State. Aspects of the new GCSE examination may be seen as take-up of the shift towards more motivational forms of learning and assessment. And the growth in courses of PSHE (personal, social and health education) and ATW (Active Tutorial Work) indicate the spread out of 'pseudo-concrete' activity in schools – courses, that is, which celebrate self-realisation and personal awareness but which display 'lack of interest and awareness as to the deeper structures of individual development in a social context, and in particular the ignorance or bracketing of the individuals' dependency upon the economic structure' (Fritzell 1987 p. 30). Second, however, the sponsorship of negative correspondence has been aimed particularly at the lower two-thirds of the ability range. Courses like CPVE, TVEI (despite the intentions of the MSC), City and Guilds' 365, and BTec's First Award basically service students who have failed at some point in the traditional subject route through school, for whatever reason. In part this can be seen as efficient in correspondence terms – such students are likely to be the earliest entrants into the labour market, and most susceptible to periods of unemployment; they need to be best prepared for interrupted occupational careers – however, this kind of specialisation of the negative correspondence form can also be seen as a deflection. The penetration of new vocationalism has been sponsored by a variety of groups and agencies associated with schools/industry relations and vocational preparation and it receives strong support from many representatives of big business, the industrial trainers. But the inroads of negative correspondence are opposed, particularly in relation to high-ability students, by the supporters of traditional, absolutist forms of curriculum, pedagogy and assessment, the cultural restorationists. The result of such opposition is evident within education policy in terms of limitations imposed on the expansion of the ideology of new vocationalism. Remember, I am suggesting, extending somewhat beyond Fritzell's own argument, that the changes in the internal structure of the schooling process are only one aspect of the penetration of commodity forms into education. The experiences of parents and teachers also need to be taken into account.

I want to discuss the processes of restructuring and the development of negative correspondence in more detail by suggesting five aspects of policy which have been and are acting in and upon the education system as a whole: privatisation, marketisation, differentiation, vocationalisation and proletarianisation.

Privatisation

Privatisation, in the form of selling off assets and nationalised industries, has been a key feature of Thatcherite economic policy. In education the effects of privatisation have been, thus far, more subtle and piecemeal.

1   Perversely, in economic, if not ideological, terms there are various channels for the provision of state aid to the private sector of education – the Assisted Places Scheme is one, and the purchase of LEA and Armed Forces places in private schools is another. Payments are also made to private schools for children with special educational needs. From the point of view of the Conservative government the existence of the private sector provides an example of the possibilities of the market form in education, and the private schools also offer a powerful benchmark of excellence for the state sector to aspire to (Robson and Walford 1989).

2   There has been increased reliance on parental contributions in state schools both in the form of payments for things like music lessons, swimming lessons and school trips (now the subject of charging policies) and extra-curricular activities and in the increase in parental contributions through covenants, PTA fund-raising and cost-savings like redecoration. Pring (1986 p. 72) gives the following examples.

   (a) Department of Industry financed computers to LEA schools on a 50:50 basis, but one authority insisted that the parents find the 50 per cent and running costs.
   (b) Esher Sixth-Form College launched a £20,000 appeal to raise money for computers and library books.
   (c) Parents of Churchill School, Avon, pledged to covenant £60,000 in four years to establish a charitable trust for spending on such 'extras' as library and text books and on scientific and laboratory equipment.

3   The use of private managing agents for YTS courses based on employers' premises is based on government preference for private enterprise. In some cases private managers have been awarded contracts which would

otherwise have gone to Further Education colleges. The private sector is used to encourage competition and to push state provision towards greater efficiency. The increasing use of short-term contracts in Further Education by the MSC for the delivery of courses is intended to have the same galvanising effects.

4   Similar to the above is the putting out to private tender of school cleaning and other support services. Again the private sector has been used to break the direct labour provisions of local authorities. The economic, political and ideological purposes of policy are tightly inter-related here.

5   The increased use of industrial sponsorships and attempts to draw in contributions from business, for example in the funding of City Technology Colleges (CTCs). Schemes like the CTCs, COMPACT, the London Business Partnership, etc. are intended, in part, to draw in direct funding, in money or equipment, from business, for specific programmes in state schools and also to increase the influence of the business community in educational affairs. . . .

Marketisation

That is the introduction of market forces into education.

1   A series of measures since 1980 have strengthened the possibility of parental choice and have increased the importance of competition between schools for enrolments. This began with the requirement for schools to publish examination results and culminated in the Open Enrolment provisions of the 1988 Act. With the creation of an education market, LEAs will no longer be able to protect less popular schools. Schools will be able to admit students up to a standard number, fixed at their 1979 intake. The DES see some closures as inevitable.

> Yes, and the government would recognise that and say, well so be it, if that's the way it is . . . if a school really does produce poor performance, maybe that school should lose its clientele until it has to close.
>
> (Senior civil servant D)

Schools will survive or not on the basis of their reputation and their ability to sell themselves to prospective clients. They will be judged by 'output measures' applied to their 'products'. This also has implications for the nature of teachers' labour in the school. The Hillgate Group, in their pamphlet *The Reform of British Education*, urged that:

HMI's role should be redefined, so as to assign to the inspectorate, as its principal duty, the investigation of schools or Local Authorities which fall below the national attainment standards. They should make much more use of the quantitative indicators, which have been and will become available

(p. 18)

Under the provisions of the 1988 Act Local Authority Inspectors will take on a more direct monitorial role.

2   The Open Enrolment provisions of the ERA are given teeth by being linked to per capita funding arrangements. Schools will be funded primarily in terms of their numbers: more pupils more money, fewer pupils less money. Here again is an indication of the restructuring of educational provision and funding according to the commodity form. A very direct input–output system is being inserted into the process of schooling. In effect pupils are reduced to a form of exchange between parents and schools: 'In exchange a definite quantity of one product changes places with a definite quantity of another' (Bottomore *et al.* 1983 p. 86). Here is a version of the confusion of relations between people with relations to things which Marx called 'commodity fetishism' (Marx 1968 Ch 1. Sect. 4). The relation between teachers and parents and teachers and pupils appears as a relation between intake numbers, capitation payments and examination results. The educational process is obscured. Moreover, the ideology of commodification, the confusion of social relationships with exchange relationships, so basic to the philosophy and culture of Thatcherism, is reconfirmed by its introduction into a fundamental aspect of human development. The social roles constructed out of these exchange relations also act back upon both parent and teacher – the former is confirmed as a consumer, the latter moves closer to classic wage labourer.

3   We can add to the other restructuring aspects of the ERA Local Management of Schools (LMS). By making schools into independent spending units with much greater control of their own budgets we can achieve a number of things. First, the possibility of diversity – an important basis for the New Right conception of an education market – is increased. In the way they make choices about the use of resources, within the constraints of the National Curriculum, differences between schools are likely to increase. Second, and concomitantly, the idea of a common or universal provision of education is broken. Third, the devolution of budgets is likely to lead to the introduction of institutional and regional variations in teachers' pay and variations based upon scarcity (more for shortage-subject teachers) and performance (the use of merit awards). . . . It is likely that in order to maintain market flexibility schools will be tempted to increase the use of temporary contracts for

some staff. Fourth, this brings the model of school organisation closer to that of the industrial organisation with head as Chief Executive and governors as Board of Directors. Good management is thus brought closer to the rigours of profit and loss. The school as an organisation takes on a structural (see Fritzell 1987) correspondence to the organisations of accumulation as the discourses of management and profit take hold (see proletarianisation below).

Taking these points together, ideologically there is a neat and powerful package for reworking the meaning of the educational process, shifting education into a structural relation to the basic commodity form of market exchange.

4   ... The further and logical (for many New Right Conservatives) extension of these procedures is the introduction of vouchers. The argument and push for vouchers emerged first in the *Black Papers* (Boyson 1975) and has been an ever-present possibility in Conservative education policy since. Rhodes Boyson, Arthur Seldon and Stuart Sexton have been the major proponents, and one attempt to introduce vouchers during Keith Joseph's period as Secretary of State proved a close-run thing. The voucher is the embodiment of commodified education and the apotheosis of a Hayekian, neo-liberal free-market state. . . .

5   Finally, here I would draw into this ensemble of policies, developments and possibilities, the work of effectiveness research and the *effective schools movement*. The ideological work done by effectiveness research, linked to notions like accountability, school review and school improvement, should not be underestimated. Again, these concepts draw upon industrial metaphors and practices and link ideologically with the key notions of efficiency and value-for-money. Such terms operate judgementally within the input–output logic of the commodity form and displace and exclude other criteria of judgement. . . . In effect, teachers are entrapped into taking responsibility for their own disciplining through schemes of self-appraisal, school improvement and institutional development. Indeed, teachers are urged to believe that their commitment to such processes will make them more professional. . . . The control of teachers is seen to be the major problem and the major issue – schools need to be made teacher-proof. Also embedded here is the assumption of the possibility of unequivocal consensus about good schooling and good teaching. Professional debates about education are reduced to 'what we all know to be best' or 'what management decides'.

Effectiveness researchers both construct a concept of the ineffective or sick school and draw upon the use of confessional techniques (an admission of transgressions and a ritual of atonement) as a mechanism for the return to health or to a state of grace. The school is to take responsibility for its ailments and its own cure. The confession 'is a ritual of discourse in which the speaking subject is also the subject of statement' (Cousins and Hussain 1984 p. 212). The secular confession is founded on the notion of normal as against abnormal transposed from the religious opposition of sin and piety (Foucault 1978).

As with the notion of consensus, the thrust of effectiveness is the limitation of the range of possibilities for normal education. Once established, such norms can be used to compare and divide and stigmatise. When normalising judgements are turned upon whole schools, each school is immediately set in a field of comparison. This again articulates with the commodity form of education and the educational marketplace. . . .

Differentiation

Briefly, linked to the above, it is possible to identify, by putting separate policies into an ensemble, a further aspect of Conservative Party ideology at work in current policies, that is differentiation, by ability and by specialisation. Differentiation is the basis for *diversity* . . .

1   The private sector is held up as a model for the rest of the education system and, as noted above, has received considerable direct and indirect financial support from the state. The sector has an ideological significance in the discourses about standards and markets which allows for questions of real independence to be glossed over. The Assisted Places Scheme ramifies the ideology of selection and privilege in the private sector by offering an escape route for high-ability students from state schooling. These pupils are creamed off from the comprehensive sector.

> The Scheme has been justified as an extension of parental choice, a restoration of academic opportunities to many children who would not be fully stretched in schools which have to cope with a full range of ability, and as a protection both for those individuals and for the nation's resources of talent against the levelling-down effects attributed to comprehensive reorganisation.
>
> (Fitz *et al.* 1986)

2   Grant Maintained status for opted-out schools has added a further element of diversity. These schools (twenty-nine have been approved as of February 1990) are funded directly by the DES as semi-aautonomous units. They are no longer subject to LEA strategic planning decisions and have reaped significant financial advantage from their new status in the form of building and equipment grants from the DES which are five times higher per pupil than grants available to LEA schools. The majority of schools thus far approved for grant-maintained status have opted out to avoid LEA schemes of school reorganisation.

3   The next layer of schools in the emerging hierarchy of differentiation will be the star schools in the LEA sector, those which are over-subscribed and which turn away pupils and have steady-state or rising budgets. This leaves below them in the pecking order the 'sink' schools – those which are unpopular and under-subscribed. The rhetoric surrounding the parental choice process and its effect on schools is often couched in terms of a standards raising mechanism, but the expectation, . . . is that some schools will lose out.

'Sink' schools will take some pupils deflected from star schools and will also have a captive population of pupils whose parents are unable or unwilling to meet the demands and costs of arranging travel. They may even choose as a survival strategy in the education market to specialise, say, in responding to the needs of pupils with learning difficulties. . . .

4   Into this stratified pattern, although it would seem in small numbers, comes the City Technology College (CTC). Based in part on the rhetoric of the grammar school and inner-city provision for high-ability pupils, in part also modelled on the American magnet school system, and in part a hybrid, business-oriented response to industrialists' complaints about shortages of technologically skilled workers, the CTCs are less significant for their numerical effect than for their symbolic one. They are yet another skim from the comprehensive school pool of ability and from the pool of funds for normal state education. In the period 1989–92 the DES expects to spend £126.6 m on CTCs (and since sponsors enjoy tax relief on covenants the cost to the Treasury is even higher) (*Independent*, 20 June 1989). Their organisation, working conditions and ethos are deliberately fashioned on industrial models. Teacher unions are not recognised and staff have to sign contracts agreeing not to strike. The National Curriculum does not apply in these independent schools. The school day is longer. They were intended, but did not turn out, to be funded directly from industry, weakening again the principle of welfare education.

Taken together, this emerging stratification of schools not only rests upon a competition between schools, it also creates the basis for a large-scale return to competition for places between pupils. The competitive self-interest of families is underlined and the logic of Thatcherist indi-vidualism is ramified in the education system. The education market will tend to weaken social bonds (the social engineering project of comprehensive education is anathema to Conservative thinking) and encourage strategies of exclusion and social closure; that is the gener-ation of boundaries of positional hierarchy.

5   Lastly, it is worth indicating (but I would not over-estimate) the differ-entiation of routes *within* schools. There is, more clearly than for many years, the possibility of early separation of life chances and occupational

entry. Two increasingly distinct routes are emerging. TVEI, CPVE and YTS (Youth Training Schemes) have sketched out a worker-pupil, pre-vocational/vocational route which could be embarked upon from age 14, separate from an academic, subject-based, GCSE, A-level and Higher Education route. Some research evidence already exists which demonstrates a tendency for working-class pupils to follow pre-vocational courses, while children of professional groups tend to take academic courses (Dean and Steeds 1981). Afro-Caribbean pupils may also be over-represented on the pre-vocational courses (Atkins 1982). Atkins (1986) also makes the point that 'Those students who are tracked into the pre-vocational curriculum are led to see this process as a reflection of their personal inadequacy for academic work, as "proved" by their poor showing in school examinations and tests' (p. 48). There is an ironic inversion here in relation to the critique of anti-industrialism which has been so strong in the Conservative educational offensive, an inversion that the MSC has tried to avoid in TVEI courses – that is the identification of pre-vocational routes with failure, as being second-class alternatives for students unable to sustain progress in the academic route. The defence of the academic curriculum (by strident cultural restorationists and the DES) continues to relegate practical, applied knowledge and skills to low status and the pre-vocational credentials continue to be measured against the existing academic benchmarks by parents, teachers and many employers.

Vocationalism

By drawing upon the developments outlined at the begining of this chapter and some points already made in this section, it is possible to identify, as might be expected, a crucial vocational element in the restructuring of education. As suggested already, a primary aspect of the process of making social expenses productive is to establish direct links between expenditure on social needs and the needs of industry. Thus the orientation of education has begun to change from being primarily one of collective consumption to one which ensures that school leavers are better prepared for work roles. This is what Fritzell (1987) calls functional correspondence. As already discussed, this kind of correspondence operates in a number of different ways in different sectors and at different levels of education. Simply put, these might be: technical training or know-how, teaching skills or familiarisation with labour processes: producing particular attitudes and demeanours – deference, punctuality, subservience, etc.; teaching knowledge about wealth creation, and encouraging entrepreneurship and the skills of business.

1   One part of this vocationalism is the general development of the skills of, and a positive attitude towards, production and wealth creation.

A whole range of policies and programmes are relevant here. TVEI and CVPE, with their vocational elements and work experience components, are obviously relevant; so too are more general schemes of work placement. But the Mini-Enterprise in Schools Project (MESP) is a specific example of this sort of development.

> In contrast to the classroom based teaching about industry that remains common among vocational courses, MESP involves students in the actual production and realization of value . . . although student activity is still based at school, they are taken into the market place to sell a good.
>
> (Shilling 1989 p. 115)

The Economic Awareness project, the Schools Curriculum Industry Partnership (SCIP), and the Understanding British Industry project (UBI) are other examples of the dual strategy of attitudinal and cognitive socialisation. Thus, part of the process of establishing schools/ industry links is the fostering of a commitment to the idea of work, and positive attitudes towards industry and enterprise. However, attitudes, knowledge and skills are distributed and targeted very differently within each of these initiatives. Sometimes these different concerns may actually be in conflict. For example, the development of initiative, decision-making and marketing skills appears to have little relevance to many jobs requiring no more than the routine repetitions of general labour. Here work in mini-enterprises may create a disjunction between the capabilities of future employees and the needs of employers. . . .

2   Within school-based pre-vocational courses, considerable emphasis is given to forms of assessment which are intended to motivate pupils while at the same time providing a broad profile of their attributes and abilities – cognitive, affective, social and psycho-motor. Viewed positively, profiles of this kind can give some status to achievements and qualities outside the academic domain, and by discussion and negotiation involve pupils more fully in deciding their own educational needs. While for the pupil these profiles may be justified in instrumental terms – job-getting – they also serve employers' needs of job selection and worker preparation. The whole of the pupil is opened up for assessment and surveillance. . . .

3   Pre-vocational courses like TVEI and CPVE also carry with them a learning message which some employers see as better attuned to the realistic needs of high-tech industry (and self-employment) – flexibility and adaptability. The FEU, on whose work, particularly ABC (A Basis for Choice), the CPVE was based, have been very consistent advocates of the flexibility hypothesis. But while acknowledging the role of these

elements in pre-vocational courses, not all commentators see them as related to the actualities of factory life.

> TVEI aims to disseminate ideas of transferable skills, to accustom pupils to ideas of technological change requiring them to move across job demarcation lines and to change jobs continually throughout their working lives. These may well be desirable objectives, but I would hypothesise that British employers and employees learn attitudes which inhibit effective technological change in Britain *after* they leave school.
>
> (Senker 1986 p. 298)

Doubt is also cast upon the real degree of the matching between national policy imperatives in employment training and the demands of working life and expectations of their workers held by the majority of employers (see Rees *et al.* 1989). If the mismatches are serious then this strengthens the argument that education is being used as a scapegoat for other kinds of failure, and that the disciplining and restructuring of the education/production relation has other purposes. . . .

4   Possibly the most common feature of schools/industry relations is the work experience placement, although different agencies and schemes view its role and intentions differently. Work experience is described by the DES (1984) as 'an insight into the world of work', as 'part of an educational programme', whereas the MSC see it as an 'early' and 'permanent bridge between school and work' (MSC 1984) and thus as providing skills and familiarisation, an initiation into the 'truth' of work (Stronach 1988). But again intentions may not be borne out in practice; some outcomes may actually be counter-productive. Shilling (1987) makes the important point that 'the dominant *view* of work-experience as held by the MSC alongside many schools and industry, often stands in a problematic and contradictory relation to the *practices* experienced by students during their work placement' (p. 419). For a number of pupils work experience is a disappointing, alienating or sometimes combative first engagement with the world of work. The burgeoning COMPACT schemes are a highly developed form of this kind of schools/industry accommodation.

5   Control and policy making in education are now more overtly and directly influenced by the business community. It is now normal for the government to nominate representatives of industry to key committees and decision-making and allocatory bodies concerned with education. A number of industrialists have also been appointed to significant posts in educational bodies.

Proletarianisation

As noted already, the insertion of the commodity form into education is not limited to the experience of pupils; teachers too are becoming subject to new relations of production. The nature of the school as an organisation, as a workplace, is being steadily transformed.

1   The DES clearly see forms of industrial management as the necessary and appropriate method for school organisation. Significant amounts of money are being committed to the management training of heads and deputies, through local INSET schemes and the setting up of a National Training Centre at the University of Bristol. A specialist cadre of school managers is being formed. The attempt is being made to model headship on the Chief Executive role in industry, as noted above.

2   Management techniques, based on a separation of policy from execution, have the effect of further delimiting the professional role of the teacher and have tended to encourage the development of 'them and us' attitudes similar to those in industry. This latter will be enhanced by the devolution of teacher employment from LEAs to schools in the LMS provisions of the ERA. Local Education Authority policies on employment will no longer apply. Schools will not be bound by Equal Opportunities policies or by arrangements for the protection of the jobs of teachers made redundant. There will be no schemes of redeployment to safeguard teachers from the uneven or unexpected effects of falling rolls. . . .

3   The LMS provisions of the ERA also carry with them implications for changes in school ethos. I have already made the point that the key factor in establishing a market in education is linking competition to reward. Schools are to be put in a position of having to make strategic planning decisions about maintaining or expanding their market share – their pupil numbers. Time, effort and money will have to be devoted both to the running of devolved budgets and to policy analysis and planning – most large secondary schools will he dealing with more than £1 million per annum. Schools will either have to spend money on employing bursars or accounts clerks or the like or existing staff will have to take on such responsibilities. Whatever decision is made in a school, the role of senior staff is likely to undergo considerable change. Heads and deputy heads will more than ever be in the business of business. They will have day to day responsibility for the budget and for the management of their staff. The gulf between teachers and the senior management team is again likely to increase. It is also possible that school governors will begin to consider employing executive heads who are not or have never been teachers, but are good managers. In other words, we may see developments like those brought about in recent Health Service reforms. . . .

All in all, these changes amount to a significant change in the labour process, ethos and conditions of work of teaching, a process of *proletarianisation*. What we have is a massive interconnected policy ensemble, a complex of projects, initiatives, schemes, agencies, imperatives and legislation, which is pushing education in new directions and is affecting the way teachers work, the way schools are run and organised, and the nature and delivery of the school curriculum. But this ensemble is not always coherent or co-ordinated. The actual relations between school activities and the world of work are not always clear or logical. Grand intentions are not always realised in practice and may actually be contradicted. The concerns of schools, of industry (and of different schools and different industries), of the state (and of different sectors of the state) rarely come together unproblematically. Thus, the effects of restructuring are general and piecemeal rather than precise and total. Further, the relationship of vocationalism to capital and the economy is complex because capital itself is changing. Nonetheless, the evidence for a general restructuring/repositioning of education in relation to production, and the 'requirements of work', is compelling.

References

Atkins, M. J. (1982) 'Foundation Courses in the Sixth Form: A Case Study', Unpb. Ph.D. Thesis, University of Nottingham.

Atkins, M. J. (1986) 'The Pre-Vocational Curriculum: A Review of the Issues Involved', *Journal of Curriculum Studies*, 19, 1, pp. 45–53.

Barnett, C. (1972) *The Collapse of British Power*, London, Eyre Methuen.

Beck, J. (1983) 'Accountability, Industry and Education', in J. Ahier and M. Flude (eds) *Contempory Education Policy*, Beckenham, Croom Helm.

Bernstein, B. (1977) 'Aspects of the Relations between Education and Production', in *Class Codes and Control* vol. 3, 2nd edn, London, Routledge and Kegan Paul.

Bottomore, T., Harris, L., Kiernan, V. G. and Miliband, R. (1983) *A Dictionary of Marxist Thought*, Oxford, Blackwell.

Boyson, R. (1975) 'The Developing Case for the Educational Voucher', in C. B. Cox and R. Boyson (eds) *Black Papers 1975: The Fight for Education*, London, Dent and Sons.

Callaghan, J. (1987) *Time and Chance*, London, Collins.

Cousins, M. and Hussain, A. (1984) *Michel Foucault*, London, Macmillan.

Dale, R. (1985) 'The Background and Inception of the Technical and Vocational Education Initiative', in R. Dale (ed.) *Education, Training and Employment: Towards a New Vocationalism*, Oxford, Pergamon.

Dean, J. and Steeds, A. (1981) *17 Plus: The New Sixth Form in Schools and FE*, Windsor, Nelson-NFER.

DES (1984) *Work Experience*, Circular 7/84, London, DES.

Donald, J. (1979) 'Green Paper: Noise of Crisis', in R. Dale, G. Esland, R. Fergusson, and M. Macdonald (eds) *Schooling and the National Interest* vol. 1, Lewes, Falmer Press.

Fitz, J., Edwards, T. and Whitty, G. (1986) 'Beneficiaries, Benefits and Costs: An Investigation of the Assisted Places Scheme', *Research Papers in Education*, vol. 1, no. 3.

Foucault, M. (1971) 'Théories et institutions pénales', *Annuaire du Collège de France 1971–72*.

Foucault, M. (1978) *The History of Sexuality* vol. 1, New York, Pantheon.

Fritzell, C. (1987) 'On the Concept of Relative Autonomy in Educational Theory', *British Journal of Sociology of Education*, 8, 1, pp. 23–36.

Gleeson, D. (1987) 'Introduction', in D. Gleeson (ed.) *TVEI and Secondary Education: A Critical Appraisal*, Milton Keynes, Open University Press.

Jamieson, I. (1986) 'Corporate Hegemony or Pedagogic Liberation: The Schools/Industry Movement in England and Wales', in R. Dale (ed.) *Education, Training and Employment: Towards the New Vocationalism*, Oxford, Pergamon.

McCullough, G. (1986) 'Policy, Politics and Education: The Technical and Vocational Initiative', *Journal of Education Policy*, 1, 1, pp. 35–52.

Marx, K. (1986) *Capital*, London, Lawrence and Wishart.

MSC (1984) *TVEI Review*, London, MSC.

Offe, C. (1976) *Industry and Inequality*, London, Edward Arnold.

Offe, C. (1984) *Contradictions of the Welfare State*, London, Hutchinson.

Pring, R. (1986) 'Privatization of Education', in R. Rogers (ed.) *Education and Social Class*, Lewes, Falmer Press.

Reeder, D. (1979) 'A Recurring Debate: Education and Industry', in G. Bernbaum (ed.) *Schooling in Decline*, London, Macmillan.

Rees, G., Williamson, H. and Winckler, V. (1989) 'The "New Vocationalism": Further Education and Local Labour Markets', *Journal of Education Policy*, 4, 3, pp. 227–41.

Robson, M. H. and Walford, G. (1989) 'Independent Schools and Tax Policy under Mrs Thatcher', *Journal of Education Policy*, 4, 2, pp. 149–62.

Senker, P. (1986) 'The Technical and Vocational Educational Initiative: An Interim Assessment', *Journal of Educational Policy*, 1, 4, pp. 293–306.

Shilling, C. (1987) 'Work Experience as a Contradictory Experience', *British Journal of Sociology of Education*, 8, 4, pp. 407–24.

Shilling, C. (1989) 'The Mini-Enterprise in Schools Project: A New Stage in Education–Industry Relations', *Journal of Education Policy*, 4, 2, pp. 115–24.

Stronach, I. (1988) 'Vocationalism and Economic Recovery: The Case against Witchcraft', in S. Brown and R. Wake (eds) *Education in Transition*, Edinburgh, Scottish Council for Research in Education.

Weinstock, A. (1976) 'I Blame the Teachers', *Times Educational Supplement*, 23 January.

Wiener M. (1981) *English Culture and the Decline of Industrial Spirit*, Cambridge, Cambridge University Press.

Chapter 5

Contextualising public policy in vocational education and training

The origins of competence-based vocational qualifications policy in the UK

Steve Williams and Peter Raggatt

Introduction: accounting for the emergence of competence-based vocational qualifications

One of the most contentious aspects of UK vocational education and training policy in recent years has been the rise to prominence of the N/SVQ system of competence-based vocational qualifications (National and Scottish Vocational Qualifications) which are based on the assessment of an individual's performance in the workplace. Although the N/SVQ system has become an increasingly important area of public policy (Keep and Mayhew, 1994), a number of significant concerns and criticisms have arisen regarding the nature and implementation of the qualifications. Among other things, commentators have pointed to the narrowness of the occupational standards on which N/SVQs are based in many cases (Prais, 1989; Hyland, 1994); the reluctance of employers to make use of them (Callender, 1992; Spilsbury *et al.*, 1995); and the failure to bring about a coherent and integrated system of vocational qualifications (Robinson, 1996).

Given the extensive criticism which the N/SVQ policy has attracted, it is surprising how little research into the origins and emergence of competence-based vocational education, training and qualifications has been undertaken (Bates, 1995). Conventional accounts focus on the intellectual roots of the movement, principally the increasing significance of outcomes in American teacher education programmes in the 1960s and 1970s, suggesting that the emphasis on performance objectives within them – which were derived from a tradition of behaviouristic educational psychology – proved attractive to British policy makers in the Manpower Services Commission (MSC) (see Ashworth and Saxon, 1990; Hyland, 1994; Wolf, 1995).

The history of the development of the competence-based qualifications policy within the MSC has also been barely documented, although the broad outlines are well known. The emergence of the need for training based on 'standards of competence' is usually credited to the MSC's New Training Initiative of 1981 (Jessup, 1991). Subsequently, pressure grew within the

MSC, particularly in the context of the Youth Training Scheme (YTS), but also in the adult training programmes, to further this strategic objective. The 1985–6 *Review of Vocational Qualifications in England and Wales* (RVQ) (MSC/DES, 1986) was crucial in moving developments forward in that it proposed that a National Council for Vocational Qualifications should be established to 'design and implement' a coherent framework of National Vocational Qualifications based upon the assessment of an individual's competence. A government White Paper – *Working Together* (DE/DES, 1986) – largely accepted the Review Group's proposals and the new system was formally instituted in October 1986.

While this chronological account is adequate at one level, it still leaves some major questions unresolved. For example, what was it about the American teacher education model that was purportedly so attractive to influential policy makers in the UK's education and training community? What were the political, institutional and structural factors that provided the context within which the policy makers operated? Why was there an imperative for a review of the structure and system of vocational qualifications by 1985 and why was a framework of awards based on competence deemed to be the most appropriate way forward? Where accounts of the development of competence-based qualifications policy do exist, they barely touch on any discussion of the broader factors which might have propelled policy developments in this area (for example, see Jessup, 1991; Hyland, 1994; Wolf, 1995). A multi-dimensional explanation of how policy in this area became established is therefore needed, one in which due weight is given to economic, institutional and political factors (see Ball, 1990; Marsh, 1995).

In this chapter we attempt to provide an account of the origins and emergence of N/SVQ policy which is guided by such an approach. In doing this we have drawn upon both contemporary documentation and secondary sources; and also 29 in-depth and confidential semi-structured interviews with policy makers and other informants who were closely involved in the genesis of competence-based qualifications policy in the UK. Sixteen erstwhile senior officials of the MSC, under whose aegis the policy was developed, were interviewed. Interviews took place with past chairmen and directors of the organisation and also with officials who were formerly responsible for leading policy on youth training, adult training and quality and standards in the YTS. Consultants and project workers, who were employed or contracted by the MSC to develop work-based learning and curricula for the YTS, were also interviewed (5 interviews). Interviews were also carried out with: former officials, at Assistant and Under-Secretary level, from the Department of Education and Science (2 interviews); former government ministers (1 interview); and representatives of further education and some of the major vocational awarding and examining bodies (5 interviews with former chief officers). The interviews were undertaken between January and November 1996 and were tape-recorded.[1]

The aim of the interviews was to allow informants both to discuss their own contribution to the making of vocational qualifications policy and to consider the key imperatives which pushed it in the direction of 'competence' until the establishment of the *Review of Vocational Qualifications in England and Wales* in April 1985. From this research into the policy-making process it became clear that four major interrelated factors were significant, albeit in differing ways, in providing an impetus for reform and each will now be discussed in turn: the 'new vocationalism' in education; economic change and its effect on work and employment; the need to reform work-based restrictive practices in skills formation; and the political pressures caused by high levels of youth unemployment.

Towards greater vocational relevance: the 'new vocationalism'

Historically there is a close association between economic recession and demands for a closer relationship between education and the economy (Reeder, 1979), something which this study of the origins of competence-based vocational qualifications policy in the UK will largely reinforce. The economic recession which developed in the mid-1970s – comprising rising inflation, a falling exchange rate, increasing unemployment and a growing public sector borrowing requirement – was characterised by a decline in the number of jobs available for young people in particular, and this high-lighted the problems experienced by low achievers in education (Fowler, 1979).

While there was no compelling evidence that schools were performing any worse than before (House of Commons, 1977), two major charges were directed at the educational system: that it encouraged anti-industrial attitudes which were inimical to wealth creation and that standards of attainment in basic skills were too low, thus making many school-leavers 'unemployable' (see, for example, CCCS, 1981; MSC, 1975; TES, 1976; Weinstock, 1976; Wiener, 1981).

The notion that education is a key engine of economic regeneration and that there should therefore be strong functional links between education and the world of work was to dominate policy during the 1980s and 1990s. This 'new vocationalism' has influenced policy at all stages of education, and, in so far as it led to an increased emphasis on greater vocational relevance, was an important factor leading to the emergence of competence-based vocational qualifications policy in the UK.

From this perspective it is easy to attribute the emergence of the notion of 'competence' as part of a 'right-wing' trend towards the greater penetration of education by economic imperatives. Yet our research indicates that the development of new kinds of vocational curricula during the late 1970s and early 1980s, the emergent thinking about work-based learning in particular, was influenced by the radical critique of the formal education system in liberal democracies which had been developed by Illich (1971) and Freire (1972) among others. They depicted the educational system as serving Western capitalism through the propagation of practices which reproduced economic and labour market inequalities. Thus, among the 'progressive' educationalists who were working in, or in association with, the MSC there was a concern that in producing significant numbers of 'low achievers' the educational system was failing to mitigate inequality. This resulted in a sense of disillusionment over the performance of schools and colleges.

> There was certainly a feeling around that education had not done a very good job. It was not serving the needs of employment. . . . A lot of the key (MSC) project workers were FE (further education) based, but radicals who recognised the problems FE was having.
>
> (Consultant)

Curriculum innovators attached to the MSC and its associated agencies became increasingly interested in the notions of work-based learning, experiential learning, the accreditation of prior learning and the assessment of learning outcomes rather than teaching and course inputs. It was hoped that the individual learner would come to replace bureaucratic and ineffective educational establishments as the dominant influence in the education system. Such novel and distinctive approaches to learning and the consequent production of qualifications seemed potentially more effective in delivering opportunities for young people. Thus the 'new vocationalism' of the 1970s and early 1980s was the expression of a distrust of the established educational system, especially further education, not only on the 'right' but also among 'progressive' educationalists employed by government agencies, the MSC in particular, to work on the development of programmes for the young unemployed. A former senior DES official noted that:

> [The] new vocationalism was not so simple a concept. You'd often get so-called left-wing and so-called right-wing positions meeting up in the middle. In the early 1980s there was the coming together of a more humane and socially aware approach to the education of the disadvantaged on the one hand, and on the other a greater sense of vocational relevance.

While policy makers and development workers in the MSC were, in the context of rising youth unemployment, experimenting with different ways of designing curricula and assessment methods for vocational education and training, the DES itself had little influence over the direction of policy in this area. From the mid-1970s, the DES had been confronted by the MSC, an organisation which 'challenged the long-cherished notion of "education for life" and attempted to replace it with "education and training for work"' (Ainley and Corney, 1990, p. 3). Indeed, a 1975 report for the Training Services Agency within the MSC, *Vocational Preparation for Young People*, has been credited as starting the 'great debate' over vocational relevance with a critique of schools (Ainley and Corney, 1990).

The capacity of the DES to develop and introduce a more vocational curriculum or to improve provision for low achievers by other means was impeded in three ways. First, it lacked power. The DES typically worked through discussion and negotiation with local education authorities and teacher organisations. It had no control over the curriculum or examinations, nor could it direct how central government funding was used by local education authorities. Second, the election of a Conservative government in 1979 further weakened the influence of the DES. According to a former senior MSC official, when it came to the need to design and implement a more extensive and coherent system of vocational education and training there were political factors which worked in favour of the MSC:

> Mrs Thatcher had a prejudice against the DES as such and a prejudice against educationalists as such. So she was prejudiced in the MSC direction to begin with. . . . Over there at the DES was this outfit she could remember all too familiarly,[2] which she regarded as being in the pockets of the LEAs (Local Education Authorities) on the one hand and the teachers on the other.

Third, Mrs Thatcher may have had her prejudices, but the DES also suffered a more profound difficulty in providing policy leadership when dealing with vocational education. It did not think the issue was an important area of policy: externally and internally there were criticisms of the DES's attitude towards vocational education:

> The majority, I think, of the MSC people were totally behind us, absolutely totally behind it. Almost without exception the Department of Education side were against it. They were against it on two of the worst possible grounds, one turf and that's awful . . . secondly, ideological. They actually were not in favour of technical and vocational education.
>
> (Employment Minister)

> [In the DES] FE was regarded as a bit of a backwater; nobody understood it very much.
>
> (DES official)

The DES thus became a minor 'bit player' in the development of vocational education and training during the 1980s and it was the MSC which increasingly dominated policy innovation in this area. The influence and power of the MSC in both schools and further education increased; the introduction of the Technical and Vocational Education Initiative (TVEI) in 1982 and the MSC's takeover of 25 per cent of the budget for work-related non-advanced further education in 1984 can be cited as key examples of the way in which it acted as the vanguard of the 'new vocationalism' movement. For the purposes of this chapter, then, it is important to note that the MSC not only dominated policy formulation in vocational education and training during the late 1970s and early 1980s but also promoted very heavily the view that it should be more closely aligned to the world of work.

> There was a two-fold concern. One of them, a crude one I thought, was to get them [the young unemployed] off the streets and the unemployment count, but also, and a slightly more high-minded one, to repair the gaps that frankly the education system seemed to have left. So the MSC did give them something to relate to ... by making it more close to the world of work in some way and by making sure that it did have a strong work experience element in it.
>
> (MSC official)

Although the concept of occupational competence was understood in only a vague sense at this time, the idea that it might have an important part to play in preparing young people for the labour market, particularly in the context of the YTS (see below), was responsible for ensuring that it received a considerable amount of attention among MSC policy makers.

The changing nature of work and employment

Clearly, then, a desire to align education with the needs of industry to a greater degree was one of the major policy imperatives in this area during the 1970s and early 1980s, and the emergence of the competence-based qualifications policy can be seen in part as an outcome of this. Yet while policy makers laid a heavy emphasis on this 'new vocationalism' they were also concerned that the very nature of work and employment itself was experiencing some fundamental changes. In putting the case for substantial improvements in skills training, and in looking towards standards of competence as a way of achieving this, policy makers in the MSC were increasingly influenced by some of the central tenets of post-industrialism.

Among other things, advocates of post-industrialism argued that the service sector of the economy was not only growing at the expense of manufacturing, but was increasingly coming to replace it as the principal source of employment in modern societies; and that the increasingly extensive util-isation of information technology was also becoming ever more evident within industry. Such changes were seen to imply that broader knowledge-based skills were more appropriate in working environments no longer typified by manual labour (see Bell, 1973). However, it was the economic recession of 1980–81, particularly the massive decline in manufacturing industry and the concomitant reduction in employment therein, which prompted policy makers to re-think the nature of the provision of skills and qualifications in the UK in a much more radical way. The MSC's New Training Initiative was, in part, inspired by post-industrial thinking:

> The new markets and technologies require a more highly skilled, better educated and more mobile workforce in which a much larger number of professional and technical staff are supported by a range of more or less highly trained workers who perform a range of tasks and who are involved in a process rather than the repetitive assembly or manufac-ture of a part of a specific product.
>
> (MSC, 1981, p. 3)

There was thus a growing concern not only not to be propping up an apprenticeship system which to a large extent was specific to a part of the economy – manufacturing industry – that appeared to be declining in signif-icance, but also a desire to establish practicable methods of providing skills and accrediting qualifications in the increasingly important service sector. The retail, hotel and catering and caring occupations, for example, were typified by low levels of skill attainment and an absence of an appropriate qualifications framework. These were also areas into which a high propor-tion of YTS participants were drawn from 1983 onwards. Clearly, the unsuitability of the traditional apprenticeship model, despite having been subjected to reform in some areas, particularly in engineering, ruled out its revival as a way of engendering a more skilled and qualified workforce, not least because it was associated with restrictive practices (see below). A former senior MSC official recalled that:

> part of it was that there's a whole dimension . . . of skill competence . . . of standards of achievement and educational training needed over a much wider spectrum of occupations and that the country will not be all right if you simply get manufacturing apprenticeship back.

The growing impact of new technology and the associated shift to an economy which was dependent upon 'knowledge' work, both in services and in the remnants of manufacturing industry, was the second key aspect of the post-industrialist thesis which appealed to MSC policy makers. Yet there was an awareness within the MSC that not only would the demise of the Fordist model of economic organisation imply a dampening of demand for low level manual skills, but that it would also inspire a greater degree of flux both within organisations and in the labour market more generally. Officials were increasingly aware, therefore, that a key aspect of any reformed and improved system of vocational education and training should be the extent to which it would both recognise and promote increased flexibility.

Contemporary research being undertaken at the then Institute of Manpower Studies (IMS), which had close links with the MSC, asserted that employers were looking at new ways of organising their employment practices, most notably through a greater use of a 'peripheral' workforce of part-time and temporary employees (Atkinson, 1984). Given the perception held by policy makers that during their working lives individuals would increasingly be required to undertake not only a higher number of different jobs but also a greater variety of jobs, a former senior MSC official argued that they were concerned with promoting:

> Generally, those skills that could be transferable, were transferable. Skills that did build upon mathematical skills and communication skills, building in quite a good understanding of new technology, specifically in relation to whatever the specific area of interest, technician area, was. Particularly seeking to develop adaptability, and also seeking to develop a willingness to face up to the whole concept of change, much of which was technology led or was coming to be technology led.

Moreover, the growing emphasis placed by the MSC upon flexibility and transferability in developing education and training for employment led to an increasing realisation that to talk about and encourage the development of 'skills' was increasingly archaic. The concept of 'skill', it was argued, implied a link with a particular occupation. Yet MSC policy makers were seeking to move away from the notion of discrete occupational skills towards broadly based competences that could be acquired and utilised by individuals in a variety of different contexts. An influential consultant for the MSC recalled that at that time:

> Our starting point was to say, stop looking at skill and start looking at the outcomes that people will need to achieve. [The] issue is not about training people to be an operative, it's about how they are going to interact, resolve problems, plan the work they are going to do.

While the New Training Initiative was inspired in part by the acceptance of key tenets of the post-industrial thesis within the MSC, it is also evident that the 1981 policy statements did in turn prompt investigations into the attributes and qualifications – if not the competences – that an economy increasingly dominated by the service sector and new technology would require; for example, in the IMS work on transferable skills and occupational training families (Hayes *et al.*, 1982).

Yet there are two problems with this emphasis on the MSC's wish to play a vanguard role in the reconfiguration of the economy. First, as we shall see below, the effort to establish and implement the Youth Training Scheme necessarily dominated its agenda in the early to mid-1980s. Thus, in explaining the emergence of competence-based qualifications policy, there is a danger of overstating the significance of the MSC's strategic thinking in the area of employment and labour market change. Second, the extent to which post-industrial change was generating greater demand for more broadly based and transferable skills in the workplace is highly questionable. To take one example from the period, in a study of clerical work in a bank, an insurance company and a local authority Crompton and Jones (1984) discovered that the introduction of new technology, far from leading to an upskilling of work, had largely had a deleterious effect upon it.[3]

Nevertheless, the notion that economic modernisation was contingent upon greater numbers of more highly and broadly skilled workers was prominent within the upper echelons of the MSC, and the need for action was reinforced by influential reports which revealed that in comparative terms the provision of skills and qualifications in the UK was poor (Hayes *et al.*, 1984; Coopers & Lybrand, 1985). One former senior MSC official confessed that 'overall our national training performance was awful and probably deteriorating compared with our competitors', while another noted that by '1984 there was definitely an increasing awareness of our relative underperformance in the skills area'. Therefore, despite being diverted by the necessity of managing record levels of unemployment, by the mid-1980s policy makers within the MSC were nonetheless determined to set about initiating long-lasting reforms to the structure of skills and qualifications provision in the UK.

Removing the barriers to economic modernisation

The last section showed the extent to which by the early 1980s policy makers in the MSC had become aware that the nature of both employment change and wider economic change necessitated an overhaul of the UK's system of vocational education and training. There was also an increasing awareness that the principal existing method of work-based skill formation – the apprenticeship system – was not only unknown in many growing parts of the economy, but was also typified by the sort of artificial barriers and restrictive practices that were seen to hinder economic modernisation. Thus the development of competence-based vocational qualifications – in so far as they represent a way of accrediting training to standards and are independent of time-serving – can be identified, at least in part, as an outcome of the desire by policy makers to attenuate 'restrictive practices' in the hope of modernising the British economy.

It is in this context that the notion of improved training to 'standards' first appears in the public policy arena. *The Royal Commission on Trade Unions and Employers' Associations,* popularly known as the Donovan Commission, sat from 1965 to 1968 with the purpose of examining and making recommendations for the improvement of British industrial relations, particularly the pervasive workplace bargaining and the restrictive practices and strike activity which appeared to characterise it. Training was identified by the Commission as one of the areas where constraints on managers were rife, and it was asserted that 'training is an area in which restrictive traditions have especially deep roots in British industry and where the pressure of technological advance makes the need for a radical change in outlook particularly urgent' (Royal Commission, 1968, p. 85). Furthermore, the Donovan report went on to state that there was 'no doubt that an urgent need exists to secure the rapid and general adoption of systems of training which accord with the social and economic needs of a modern industrial society', and called for 'objective standards to be laid down by which qualifications may be judged' (Royal Commission, 1968, pp. 92–3).

While a number of the Donovan recommendations became implemented in the 1970s, there appear to have been few noticeable moves to restructure training provision along standards-based lines. Moreover, a series of influential reports and studies reinforced the 'pre-supposition that labour practices were a central cause of lower levels of labour productivity' (Cutler, 1992, p. 167), and were thus having an adverse impact on the British economy.[4]

There was, however, increasing pressure within the engineering industry for more emphasis to be placed on training to standards as a way of countering the restrictive practices which were seen to be associated with the time-served apprenticeship (Senker, 1992), and it appears that the election of a Conservative government in 1979, with its antipathy towards organised labour, proved to be a crucial force for reform. Senker notes the increasing groundswell of opposition to the bipartite industrial training boards (ITBs). The Centre for Policy Studies – a right-wing think tank – not only recommended that the ITBs be abolished (as many of them were to be in 1981), but it also suggested that

> because of the rigidity of apprenticeships – especially their length and restrictions on entry – there should be a move away from a 'time-serving' concept of apprenticeship training towards an 'achievement' basis, so that apprentices who have reached the required standard, regardless of the length of their apprenticeship, are deemed to be qualified.
>
> (Senker, 1992, p. 61)

Perhaps the most conspicuous example of the connection between countering restrictive practices and the need for training to standards which was increasingly being made at this time came in the Centre for Policy Review Staff's 1980 analysis of the British VET system (CPRS, 1980). Among other things, *Education, Training and Industrial Performance* condemned what it called the 'rigid' and 'conservative' vocational training system which existed and deemed it central to the continuation of 'restrictive labour practices' (p. 17). It also called for greater objective standards for vocational qualifications and, in passing, referred to the need for a competence-based system of vocational training.

A wish to ease, and hopefully eliminate, restrictive practices in skills training was a key imperative for the MSC's New Training Initiative of 1981 and its call for the introduction of standards of competence (DE, 1981). Indeed, an earlier MSC policy document – *Training For Skills* (MSC, 1977a) – had already called for training to 'agreed standards in appropriate skills' (p. 20). The changing political climate of the 1980s, however, allowed policy makers more scope for reform. A former senior MSC official recalled that:

> The notion of standards was somehow there in the [New] Training Initiative. I think that was mainly as a result of trying to get away from time-serving. [Training] was being used as a form of restrictive practice really, for trade unions to restrict entry and therefore raise skill shortages – raise wages by creating skill shortages.

Furthermore, the extent to which the apprenticeship system, despite having been subjected to some reforms – reductions in the length of time in the engineering sector for example – and the accusation that unions used it to restrict access to jobs impelled policy makers to consider radical alternative methods of skills provision. According to another former MSC official: 'In some industries, printing being the prime and notorious example, the trade unions were using restrictive practices to limit numbers entering. . . . The whole thing from an employer's point of view was getting less and less worth the candle.'

The New Training Initiative of 1981, and the emphasis on training to recognised standards of competence contained within it, was therefore in part an outcome of the concern among policy makers that the anachronistic methods of skills formation associated with the traditional apprenticeship were not only obsolete but, as we have noted above, should also not be exported to other sectors. In the period immediately following the publication of the New Training Initiative, much of the MSC's attention was taken up with the development and initial implementation of the YTS. Nevertheless, in parts of industry, in chemicals and printing for instance, employers began to reform their skills training processes more along standards-based lines (interview data; Stuart, 1996); and in the engineering industry pressure from a group of influential employers resulted in the eventual abandonment of all vestiges of time serving in 1986 (Senker, 1992). While this growth of interest was inspired in part by the MSC's New Training Initiative, it can also be taken as evidence of the wider reassertion of managerial prerogative that occurred in employment relations more generally at the time as the political climate became more hostile to organised labour.

Since, by the early 1980s, the need for establishing standards of training was both a policy imperative and was increasingly recognised by many parts of industry as being desirable, the question of accrediting qualifications based on such training arose. As the next section will show, this was a debate that was largely inspired by the experience of the YTS.

Enhancing quality in youth training

In accounting for the emergence of the competence-based qualifications policy, it would be mistaken to lay too heavy an emphasis on the capacity of officials to translate strategic thinking into concrete policy outcomes. While long-term economic, institutional and political factors provided the context for the reform of vocational education and training on competence-based lines, perhaps the most important imperative for competence-based *qualifications* arose from the politically driven necessity in the early 1980s to mitigate, in the short term, the impact of rising levels of youth unemployment.

While the MSC had been established principally to provide strategic national manpower planning, akin to the Swedish model, rising unemployment, particularly increasing youth unemployment, in the mid-1970s had diverted it into a fire-fighting role at an early stage (Ainley and Corney, 1990).[5] By 1976 over 800,000 young people were registered as unemployed and youth unemployment was rising three times as fast as unemployment among the working population as a whole. The MSC was quickly directed into instituting schemes designed to manage youth unemployment, particularly given the increasing realisation that it was becoming established as a permanent feature of the labour market. Following the *Young People and Work* report (MSC, 1977b), the government approved a major expansion of youth training provision through the newly created Special Programmes Division of the MSC. Perhaps the most significant of the MSC's initiatives was the Youth Opportunities Programme (YOP) which provided 162,000 places in 1978/9 rising to 553,000 in 1981/2 (Finn, 1984).

While the principal short-term imperative was to manage youth unemployment, there was also a growing realisation among policy makers that, as measures to alleviate the problem took on an increasingly permanent character, a new type of vocationally oriented curriculum was needed. Thus the MSC and the newly established Further Education Unit (FEU) of the DES took steps to develop and implement work-related curricula suitable for young people on training schemes. Perhaps the most notable development was the establishment of the Unified Vocational Preparation (UVP) programme in 1976. Its objective was to provide 'a limited programme of experimental schemes of vocational preparation for those young people who left school and entered jobs where hitherto they received little or no systematic education and training' (Farley, 1985, p. 77). For the purposes of this chapter, the most significant aspect of the attempts to design a work-related curriculum for the young unemployed was the recognition that 'traditional' college-based models of further education were unsuited to the needs of these people, to whom the prospect of spending more time attending college would be abhorrent. Thus it is in this context that one can identify an imperative, albeit a somewhat implicit one, to move away from the traditional 'input' paradigm towards a model of vocational education and training in which the outcomes that individuals achieve are given recognition; see, for example, the FEU's (1979) document *A Basis For Choice*.

Notwithstanding the significance of these developments, the sharp economic recession of 1980–81 proved to be a watershed. Not only was there a rapid decline in the number of jobs open to young people, but there was also a decrease in the provision of apprenticeships in British industry (Gospel, 1995). At a time of growing government concern about the potential for social disorder created by such a high level of youth unemployment (Keep, 1986), the MSC, in its 1981 New Training Initiative, was able to put forward proposals for a radical overhaul of the UK's youth training arrangements. The new one-year Youth Training Scheme became operational in April 1983.

While the government's main concern was to manage politically sensitive high levels of unemployment, the main priority of officials was to ensure that individuals received good quality vocational education and training in the new YTS, not least because of an awareness that criticisms of poor quality in the MSC's youth training programmes were well directed. One leading educationalist of the period who was close to the MSC leadership stated that:

> I have already indicated the appalling quality of YOP and the first stages of YTS, because everybody was recognising it as more about solving, trying to solve temporarily anyway, the unemployment problem in the early days, rather than producing a proper training scheme.

The MSC, however, envisaged the new YTS as being first and foremost an appropriate training scheme, in line with its strategic aim of establishing a 'permanent bridge between school and work' (Ainley and Corney, 1990).

According to a former senior MSC official:

A big effort had to go in, first of all, to get YTS off the ground in terms of numbers, over 350,000 at the time, but also to make it a credible scheme; and the qualifications dimension was an important part of developing a credible training scheme.

Initially, it was envisaged that the leaving certificate, which young people received on completing their YTS programme, would be an appropriate way of certifying their achievement and of easing their passage into the labour market. A former MSC official recalled that:

There was an increasing feeling that youth training should be more about forming part of young people's transition into the labour market and not just be about stopgap programmes aimed at keeping people off the streets. The corollary of that was that you had to have a good leaving certificate.

From an early stage it was widely recognised, however, that this certificate had been a failure, not least because of ambiguities about what it actually represented (Finn, 1986). Nevertheless, the MSC generated and oversaw a considerable amount of research and development into the appropriate contents of a work-based YTS curriculum. The Core Skills project, for example, developed out of UVP curriculum development work and, with the benefit of finance from the European Social Fund, investigated appropriate work-based methods of learning and skill formation suitable for use in the YTS (Levy, 1986, p. 7). Likewise, the work on transferable skills and 'occupational training families' undertaken by the IMS, which has already been noted above, was developed in the context of establishing an appropriate work-based curriculum for the YTS. However, Finn (1987) has argued that not only did such concepts help to conceal the low levels of skill that typified most YTS programmes in reality, but that they were also 'resisted by employers and young people alike. Employers preferred to train young people in skills which could be used immediately' (p. 180).

Nevertheless, the need for a recognised qualification became even more apparent as policy makers began to design the principles of a two-year YTS programme (Ainley and Corney, 1990). A former senior MSC official argued that this generated pressure for a review of the qualifications issue: 'I think that by the time we got to devising, in 1985, with the promise of more government money, a two year YTS, that's when this really took off in fact', while another emphasised the priority that was given to finding appropriate methods of certifying achievement in various occupations, but confessed that 'it soon became apparent there weren't many about' (see Finn, 1987). The recently instituted Scottish Action Plan (SED, 1983), and its attempt to rationalise the system of vocational education and qualifications north of the border on modular and outcome-based lines, also induced a considerable amount of interest within the MSC.

Thus the government White Paper of April 1985, *Education and Training for Young People* (DE/DES, 1985), not only announced the setting up of a two-year YTS, to begin in April 1986, which would 'differ from the existing YTS in that its objective will be that all trainees should have the opportunity to seek recognised vocational qualifications' (p. 7), but it also instituted a Review of Vocational Qualifications in England and Wales. While the focus of this review, which, as we have seen, was to lead to the establishment of the NCVQ and the NVQ system of competence-based qualifications, was to be on the entire vocational qualifications system, the White Paper makes it clear that the 'review is expected to concentrate initially on improving the structure of qualifications to meet the needs of the extended Youth Training Scheme' (p. 9). In this context, policy makers in the MSC became increasingly attracted to the concept of 'competence-based' qualifications for two major reasons.

First, given the context of the 'new vocationalism', not only was it deemed inappropriate for the further education sector to have a dominant role, but there was also, as we have already noted, an awareness that for many of the young people being catered for by the YTS the inclusion of a formal 'classroom' approach would be a major disincentive to participation. Thus it was envisaged that any new system of vocational qualifications would need to be founded upon work-based learning. Second, the sheer scale of the YTS operation nationwide also ruled out traditional methods of assessing the vocational capabilities of individuals. The MSC was under a great deal of pressure to maintain and enhance quality within YTS. It did not have the capacity, however, to ensure that all providers of YTS programmes were either providing participants with a proper vocational education and training input or that they had staff with an adequate knowledge of assessment. As a consequence, the MSC shifted the emphasis to looking at the measurable outcomes that YTS participants could display. By 1985 therefore, with the institution of the Review of Vocational Qualifications and the development of the two-year YTS, the concept of 'competence-based' vocational qualifications had become increasingly attractive to policy makers (see DE/DES, 1985, pp. 8–9).

Therefore, while there were more longer-term imperatives, of the kind we have examined in earlier sections of this chapter, for the reform of the UK's vocational education and training structure which attracted policy makers to the competence-based model, the issue of youth unemployment provided the major catalyst for action, and for the development of competence-based *qualifications* in particular, in the mid-1980s as officials were able to develop policy in this area on the back of political worries about high youth unemployment.

The dominant political motivation [behind the Review of Vocational Qualifications] had to do with the fact that there were all these bloody schemes. YTS was just the latest and there were no qualifications which appeared to be appropriate. Ministers were shit scared – you can quote me on that – that there were all these kids going through these schemes with bugger all to show at the end.

(DES official)

Concluding discussion

In this chapter we have argued that the emergence of competence-based qualifications policy in the UK in the 1980s, as manifested by the N/SVQ system, can be ascribed to four factors: the growth of a 'new vocationalism' in education; the perceived change in the nature of the economy and employment; the concern to remove artificial barriers to economic modernisation; and the imperative to manage unprecedented (in the post-war period at least) levels of youth unemployment. While for analytical purposes we have examined these factors discretely, it is evident that they are heavily interrelated. This can be seen in three ways, for example. First, although economic recession and the decline of manufacturing industry in the early 1980s led to a rapid diminution in the provision of apprenticeships, policy makers rejected the option of trying to sustain the apprenticeship system, not least because of the restrictive practices it was perceived as embracing. Second, the growth of youth unemployment in the 1970s, and its continuing high level in the 1980s, caused officials to give the concept and the components of vocationally oriented curricula a much greater degree of attention. Third, a high proportion of YTS programmes were directed towards the tertiary part of the economy where there had hitherto been an absence of appropriate vocational qualifications, in retailing, hotel and catering and care in particular.

Thus the interrelated factors we have identified impelled policy makers towards the propagation of occupational 'competence' as a means of improving the provision of skills in and across the workforce. The concept of 'competence' was never precisely defined but, understood in a general sense, it had a number of positive attributes which appealed to different constituencies. It could be seen as: directly work related and oriented to the needs of employers; part of the revival of managerial prerogative; focused on outcomes and the progress of the individual learner and therefore attractive to educational progressives who were critical of existing forms of vocational education provision; consonant with wider economic change, especially the shift from manufacturing to services and the perceived elaboration of an economy characterised by greater employment flexibility; and, as the basis of a qualifications structure, an effective and efficient way of measuring the success of the YTS and of individual providers.

While the emergence of competence-based vocational education and training was the expression of several long-term policy objectives, it was the presence of a combination of factors – economic recession and the decline of manufacturing industry, a Conservative government which was hostile to organised labour and the economic distortions it was perceived to generate and the growing power of the MSC (at the expense of the DES) – in the early to mid-1980s which allowed policy makers the scope to innovate. Nevertheless, it was the relatively short-term pressure on the MSC to establish 'quality' in the YTS that was to result in the 1985–86 *Review of Vocational Qualifications in England and Wales* and the development of a system of vocational *qualifications* in which competence was operationalised and prescribed.

Above all, this chapter has shown the extent to which the N/SVQ system of competence-based qualifications in the UK was the product of a number of interrelated economic, political and institutional factors. While the short-term political imperative to manage high levels of youth unemployment dominated the agenda of politicians in the early to mid-1980s, senior officials within the MSC were nonetheless able to use this issue to propagate some of their more strategic aims. One of these was the development of a system of vocational education and training which would have the close involvement of employers, would be rational and coherent, and would recognise both economic change and the concomitant upskilling which was seen to accompany it. A national system of competence-based vocational qualifications was seen to be a central aspect of this policy. Given the primacy of these strategic aims, which this analysis of the origins of the system of competence-based vocational qualifications has revealed, the problems that the competence-based vocational qualifications policy has had in attracting the enthusiasm of employers, in promoting and recognising upskilling and in rationalising the structure of vocational qualifications, at least in England and Wales, must be a matter for further investigation.

Notes

1   The MSC had been established in 1973 and was set up as a non-departmental government body, under the aegis of the then Department of Employment (DE), to develop and administer both the national network of job centres and the provision of industrial training. Its tripartite character – employer and trade union representatives sat on the Commission itself – subsequently gave the MSC a significant degree of influence. It was wound up in 1988 and its functions were absorbed into the DE. For further details see Ainley and Corney (1990). The Department of Education and Science (DES) initiated and monitored policy developments in relation to schools, further education and higher education. In July 1995, as the Department for Education, it was combined with the DE to form the Department for Education and Employment.
2   Margaret Thatcher had been Secretary of State for Education between 1970 and 1974.

3   More fundamentally, Kumar (1986) has raised a number of questions about the appropriateness of the concept of 'post-industrialism', especially the novelty of the supposed shift from a manufacturing to a service-based economy.
4   For example, see Caves (1980), Prais (1981) and Pratten (1976). For a wide-ranging critique of this body of work see Nichols (1986).
5   Ainley and Corney comment that after '1976 the MSC became preoccupied with the management of youth unemployment' (1990, p. 36).

References

Ainley, P. and Corney, M. (1990) *Training for the Future: The Rise and Fall of the Manpower Services Commission*. London: Cassell.

Ashworth, P. and Saxton, J. (1990) 'On competence', *Journal of Further and Higher Education*, 14, 2, 3–25.

Atkinson, J. (1984) 'Manpower strategies for flexible organisations', *Personnel Management*, August, 28–31.

Ball, S. (1990) *Politics and Policy-making in Education: Explorations in Policy Sociology*. London: Routledge.

Bates, I. (1995) 'The competence movement: conceptualising recent research', *Studies in Science Education*, 25, 39–68.

Bell, D. (1973) *The Coming of Post-industrial Society*. New York: Basic Books.

Callender, C. (1992) *Will NVQs Work? Evidence from the Construction Industry*, Institute of Manpower Studies Report 228, Brighton: Institute of Manpower Studies.

Caves, R. (1980) 'Productivity differences among industries', in R. Caves and L. Krauso (eds) *Britain's Economic Performance*. Washington, DC: The Brookings Institute, 135–192.

Central Policy Review Staff (CPRS) (1980) *Education, Training and Industrial Performance*. London: CPRS.

Centre for Contemporary Cultural Studies (CCCS) (1981) *Unpopular Education: Schooling and Social Democracy in England since 1944*. London: Croom Helm.

Coopers & Lybrand (1985) *A Challenge to Complacency*. London: Coopers & Lybrand.

Crompton, R. and Jones, G. (1984) *White Collar Proletariat: Deskilling and Gender in Clerical Work*. Basingstoke: Macmillan.

Cutler, T. (1992) 'Vocational training and British economic performance: a further instalment of the "British Labour Problem"?', *Work, Employment and Society*, 6, 2, 161–183.

Department of Employment (DE) (1981) *A New Training Initiative: A Programme for Action*. London: HMSO.

Department of Employment/Department of Education and Science (DE/DES) (1985) *Education and Training for Young People*. London: HMSO.

Department of Employment/Department of Education and Science (DE/DES) (1986) *Working Together – Education and Training*. London: HMSO.

Department of Industry (1977) *Industry, Education and Management: A Discussion Paper*. London: HMSO.

Farley, M. (1985) 'Trends and structural changes in English vocational education', in R. Dale (ed.) *Education, Training and Employment: Towards a New Vocationalism?* Oxford: Pergamon Press.

Finn, D. (1984) 'The Manpower Services Commission and the Youth Training Scheme: a permanent bridge to work', in R. Dale (ed.) *Education, Training and Employment: Towards a New Vocationalism?* Oxford: Pergamon Press.

Finn, D. (1986) 'YTS: the Jewel in the MSC's Crown?', in C. Benn and J. Fairley (eds) *Challenging the MSC*. London: Pluto Press.

Finn, D. (1987) *Training without Jobs*. London: Macmillan.

Fowler, G. (1979) 'The politics of education', in G. Bernbaum, (ed.) *Schooling in Decline*. Basingstoke: Macmillan.

Freire, P. (1972) *Pedagogy of the Oppressed*. London: Sheed and Wood.

Further Education Unit (FEU) (1979) *A Basis for Choice*. London: FEU.

Gospel, H. (1995) 'The decline of apprenticeship training in Britain', *Industrial Relations Journal*, 26, 1, 32–44.

Hayes, C., Fonda, N. and Anderson, A. (1982) *Training for Skill Ownership*. Brighton: IMS.

Hayes, C., Fonda, N. and Anderson, A. (1984) *Competence and Competition: Training and Education in the Federal Republic of Germany, the US and Japan*. London: NEDC/MSC.

House of Commons (1977) *The Attainment of the School Leaver*. London: HMSO.

Hyland, T. (1994) *Competence, Education and NVQs: Dissenting Perspectives*. London: Cassell.

Illich, I. (1971) *Deschooling Society*. London: Calder and Boyars.

Jessup, G. (1991) *Outcomes, NVQs and the Emerging Model of Education and Training*. London: Falmer Press.

Keep, E. (1986) 'Designing the stable door: a study of how YTS was planned', *Warwick Papers in Industrial Relations*, 8, Warwick: University of Warwick.

Keep, E. and Mayhew, K. (1994) 'The changing structure of training provision', in T. Buxton, P. Chapman and P. Temple (eds) *Britain's Economic Performance*. London: Routledge.

Kumar, K. (1986) *Prophecy and Progress: The Sociology of Industrial and Post Industrial Societies*. London: Penguin.

Levy, M. (1986) *Work Based Learning: Core Skills Project Research Report*. Bristol: FESC.

Manpower Services Commission (MSC) (1975) *Vocational Preparation for Young People*. Sheffield: MSC.

Manpower Services Commission (MSC) (1977a) *Training for Skills*. Sheffield: MSC.

Manpower Services Commission (MSC) (1977b) *Young People and Work*. Sheffield: MSC.

Manpower Services Commission (MSC) (1981) *A New Training Initiative: A Consultation Document*. Sheffield: MSC.

Manpower Services Commission/Department of Education and Science (MSC/DES) (1986) *Review of Vocational Qualifications in England and Wales*. London: HMSO.

Marsh, D. (1995) 'Explaining "Thatcherite" policies: beyond uni-dimensional explanation', *Political Studies*, 43, 595–613.

Nichols, T. (1986) *The British Worker Question*. London: Routledge.

Prais, S. (1981) *Productivity and Industrial Structure*. Cambridge: Cambridge University Press.

Prais, S. (1989) 'How Europe would see the new British initiative for standardising vocational qualifications', *National Institute Economic Review*, August, 52–54.

Pratten, C. (1976) *Labour Productivity Differentials within International Companies*. Cambridge: Cambridge University Press.

Reeder, D. (1979) 'A recurring debate: education and industry', in G. Bernbaum (ed.) *Schooling in Decline*. London: Macmillan.

Robinson, P. (1996) Rhetoric and Reality: *Britain's New Vocational Qualifications*. London: Centre for Economic Performance.

Royal Commission (1968) *Report of the Royal Commission on Trade Unions and Employers' Associations 1965–1968*. London: HMSO.

Scottish Education Department (SED) (1983) *16s to 18s in Scotland: An Action Plan*. Edinburgh: SED.

Senker, P. (1992) *Industrial Training in a Cold Climate*. Aldershot: Avebury.

Spilsbury, M., Moralee, J. and Evans, C. (1995) *Employers' Use of the NVQ System*, Institute of Employment Studies Report 293, Brighton: Institute of Employment Studies.

Stuart, M. (1996) 'The industrial relations of training: a reconsideration of training arrangements', *Industrial Relations Journal*, 27, 3, 253–265.

Times Educational Supplement (TES) (1976) 'Extracts from the Yellow Book', 15 October, pp. 2–3.

Weinstock, A. (1976) 'I blame the teachers', *Times Educational Supplement*, 23 January.

Wiener, M. (1981) *English Culture and the Decline of the Industrial Spirit 1850–1980*. Cambridge: Cambridge University Press.

Wolf, A. (1995) *Competence and Assessment*. Buckingham: Open University Press.

Chapter 6

The competence and outcomes movement

The landscape of research

Inge Bates

Introduction

In the last decade we have witnessed the advance of the competence movement across all spheres and levels of post-16 education and training, but
its penetration is deepest in the technical, vocational and, to a lesser extent,
scientific fields. It has gone furthest, in other words, in areas where education tapers into vocational preparation, whether at craft, technical or
professional levels. Hence competence-based approaches are now being developed for occupations ranging from motor mechanic to medicine. In Britain,
the 'Trojan Horse' for the competence movement, has been the development of a system of National Vocational Qualifications and their sister
qualifications, General National Vocational Qualifications, henceforward
referred to as the NVQ/GNVQ framework. As we shall see, this framework, which is intended to span the entire range of qualifications including
those at degree level, requires the development of competence-based pedagogy. Parallel trends are evident in New Zealand, Australia and the United
States (Dawkins, 1989; Watson, 1991; Marks, 1994) and there are signs
of emerging interest in Europe arising from the single market and need for
transparency of information on qualifications (Twining, 1994). It is in
Britain, however, where competence has become wedded to a national system
of qualifications, that the movement has become most sharply defined,
uniform in its manifestations and most deeply entrenched.

This chapter reviews the development of the competence movement
mainly in a British context, and the related literature, concentrating chiefly on the period 1985–95. The overall argument of the chapter is that
the rate of development of the competence movement now outstrips
our understanding of both its effectiveness and its social significance; more
metaphorically, it has become a colossus, skating on rather thin ice.
The relatively slender support from research raises the more interesting
question, however, of what factors have promoted and sustain the movement. Further research on effectiveness and impact is now considerably
overdue – but the larger issues concerning social influences on the emergence

of competence formations and its broader social significance are also pressing.

An examination of the literature on 'competence' in recent years and its implications for education reveals that initially it was peculiarly insulated from critical academic scrutiny. The absence of academic attention was first noted by Burke, one of the more significant British academics working on competence, who noted as early as 1989 that 'one might have surmised that Competency Based Learning would have assumed a prominent and important focus for research and debate in British universities. This is not the case' (Burke, 1989b, p. 3). More recently, work by Jones and Moore (1993) raises the possibility that this silence in the academic literature may in part be seen as socially constructed. They suggest that the competence movement can be usefully understood as an example of a 'pedagogic discourse' (Bernstein, 1990), one of the very functions of which is to protect official forms of educational knowledge or policy from academic exploration through the creation of strong systems of 'classification', or strong boundaries, between the different spheres of knowledge production. . . .

This discussion begins by tracing the growing importance of competence-based education and training (CBET) as an aspect of Government policy and its application to technical and vocational education. Particular attention is given to the breadth of possible meanings of the term 'competence', debates over this issue and the emergence of a dominant definition in the context of the British National Vocational Qualification system. Having established the contours of the movement, I shall distinguish four broad categories of research: a very substantial, *technical* literature arising from the development of CBET, particularly in the context of the NVQ/GNVQ system; *evaluative* studies designed to inform policy and practice for industrial and vocational training purposes; a wide swathe of literature which I shall loosely categorise under the heading '*spirit of education*' *studies;* and finally, a relatively thin strand of *sociological perspectives* which begin to grapple with the broader significance of the competence movement. . . .

This categorisation, like any, has limitations. It is not exhaustive; the categories are not entirely discrete; there are salient sub-categories and themes, some of which will be discussed. The object here in designating large categories, or even 'schools' of thought on competence, rooted in different disciplines and paradigms, is to begin to develop a 'big picture' of research in this field commensurate with both the increasing influence of the movement and the scale of the potential research endeavour. The need for an aerial view is further underlined by the highly fragmentary state of current research and the resulting need to assemble disparate perspectives in order to prepare the ground for more productive study. In the final part of the chapter I shall outline possible avenues for research.

The role of competence in recent developments in vocational education and training

The paucity of academic debate on competence is not immediately apparent from a literature search. For example, examination of the ERIC database and British Education Index over the period 1985–95 generates several hundred references to English language material on competence produced in the last decade. A more intimate knowledge of the subject matter, however, suggests that this level and quality of coverage may pale into insignificance relative to the scale and rapidity of the current spread of competence-based approaches. We need first to examine these developments if we are to assess more accurately the extent to which the current research endeavour has an adequate purchase on the issues involved.

Central to understanding the competence movement in Britain in the last decade is an appreciation of the fact that competence is a central concept in the emerging system of National and General National Vocational Qualifications (NVQs and GNVQs). Consequently, the British literature on this subject is largely inseparable from the related literature on the development and implementation of these qualifications. It is important to recognise, however, that the NVQ/GNVQ framework organises the meaning of the term 'competence' in very specific ways which, while having the advantage of establishing consistency of usage, results in a loss of richness and cultural diversity.

In a general sense the development of competence can be seen in terms of the shaping and development of human capacities in relation to everyday social purposes, or in other words as a very basic and unremarkable human practice. This is perhaps more apparent if we consider pre-modern societies, where explicit connections between educational activities and social purposes are more likely to be in evidence than the more oblique and circuitous links which have characterised these relationships in modern societies. For example, Norberg-Hodge's account of education in the Ladakh community notes that:

> For generation after generation Ladakhis grew up learning *how to* provide themselves with clothing and shelter; *how to* make shoes out of yak skin and robes from the wool of sheep; *how to* build houses of mud and stone. Education was location specific.
>
> (Norberg-Hodge, 1991, p. 111, emphases added)

This presumably was the ultimately desirable and 'natural' approach to the cultivation of competence in everyday settings for which Gilbert Jessup, father of the NVQ philosophy (see Jessup, 1991), was striving. However, in modern societies – with the rise of more academic forms of education – the development of human abilities has become focused on more abstract and generalised forms of knowledge. It is in this context that the turn to competence formations appears strange and has encountered resistance. This resistance, as we shall see, however, is multi-layered, springing in part from the challenge to the domination of the academic curriculum which the competence movement represents but also from critiques of the particular version of competence promoted by official bodies. In the face of this double-edged resistance, considerable resources have been invested in bolstering its legitimacy.

The older broader meanings of the term 'competence' have been noted by a number of writers whose work will be discussed more fully below. The debate is perhaps cast most widely by Jones and Moore (1995), who suggest that all social science is concerned with competence:

> The use of the term 'competence' by the competency movement appears to imply that it is pre-eminently concerned with competence in a way that other approaches are not. However, *Competence* is in fact a general and fundamental concern of all behavioural and social sciences from ethnology, through linguistics and psychology to anthropology and sociology. . . . Hence *the* competency movement and its distinctive approach should not be seen as representing a special interest in competence, but, rather, as just one of the many and varied ways in which the behavioural and social sciences have addressed it.

It is against the backdrop of competence-based education viewed as a universal and fundamental social and pedagogic practice that we need to examine recent developments. As will become apparent, what is emerging is a dominant definition which has narrowed and reified the meaning of the term. . . .

At present there is no published, original, historical research on the recent growth of the competence movement in Britain and this itself represents an important lacuna. This brief outline is based on official reports and Government White Papers which have marked stages in the development of CBET, together with some secondary sources which deal with the development of CBET in Britain, largely for purposes of contextualising discussion of current developments. The latter are scattered across a wide variety of literature, including the promotional literature and broader discussion papers (e.g. Tuxworth, 1989; Ashworth and Saxton, 1990; Hyland, 1991). Most writers trace CBET to models of teacher education which became popular in the United States in the 1960s (Silver, 1988; Tuxworth, 1989; Ashworth and Saxton, 1990) and which originated from earlier versions of Performance Based Teacher Education (Tuxworth, 1989). In the United States – as in Britain – it came to prominence in the context of calls for greater accountability in education, fuelled by the heightened interest in human resources characteristic of the 'Cold War' period. Its genealogy can be traced backwards further, to include the behavioural objectives movement in curriculum design (see e.g. Tyler, 1949; Bloom, *et al.,* 1956) and further still to the rise of Taylorism in management.

Research undertaken into American models suggests that the version now dominant in Britain is broadly similar. For example, Grant *et al.* (1979) used the following definition of competence as a basis for their research into American developments:

> Competence-based education tends to be a form of education that derives a curriculum from an *analysis of prospective or actual role* in modern society and that attempts to certify student progress on the *basis of demonstrated performance* in some or all aspects of that role. Theoretically, such demonstrations of competence are *independent of time-served* in formal educational settings.
>
> (Grant, *et al.*, 1979, emphasis added)

The approach to CBET adopted in Britain by the National Council for Vocational Qualifications (NCVQ) resonates closely with this model, incorporating all three of the key features highlighted in the above quotation: the derivation of the goals of training from the analysis of occupational roles; the translation of these goals into training 'outputs' in the form of performance criteria rather than the more traditional teaching parameters of training 'inputs' such as syllabuses; and the freeing up of possibilities for individuals to progress at their own speed on the basis of readily available opportunities for performance assessment rather than coverage of course content. These practices – prior 'functional analysis' of occupations, the specification of what is to be learned in terms of performance criteria and self-paced learning, have come to be regarded as the defining characteristics of CBET in Britain.

Precisely how CBET came to play such a dominant role in British vocational training policy is a question which historians of the movement will need to unravel. From the published literature various elements of a possible story can be assembled but there remain many missing pieces. CBET appears to have first entered official thinking in the context of the problems posed by the development of the Youth Training Scheme, created in 1981 partly in response to escalating youth unemployment. The publication of *A New Training Initiative* (DOE, 1981) which launched the scheme emphasised the importance of 'standards of a new kind' and throughout the 1980s the Manpower Services Commission's Standards Programme appears to have been grappling with the problem of embedding-national standards in youth training provision (Debling, 1989; Jessup, 1991). In reports and official papers of the 1980s the language of 'outcomes' and 'competence' was increasingly used, initially alongside more familiar educational terms such as 'objectives' (Jonathon, 1987).

By the mid-1980s, however, as the Government moved towards a complete overhaul of vocational education and training strategy, the term 'competence' became decidedly dominant. It was adopted, for example, in the most influential publication of this period, *The Review of Vocational Qualifications* (MSC/DES, 1986) and further endorsed in the White Paper which followed *Working Together, Education and Training* (DOE/DES, 1986). Together these papers laid the foundations for developing a new system of vocational qualifications related 'more directly and clearly to competence required (and acquired) in work' (DOE/DES, 1986). The NCVQ was then formally established in October 1986 to implement the remit set out in the White Paper, which included responsibility to 'identify and bring about the changes necessary to achieve the specification and implementation of standards of occupational *competence* to meet the needs of the full range of employment' (emphasis added). With the setting up of NCVQ, Gilbert Jessup – who had played a key role in the development of the concept of competence within the Manpower Services Commission – now became Head of Research and Development in the new organisation. His prominent role throughout this period points to the need to take account of the role of key actors in this movement, as well as economic, political and social factors.

The NCVQ proceeded to establish a framework for all vocational qualifications based on five levels and set in motion a system of 'kitemarking' qualifications which satisfy NVQ criteria and rank them on one of these levels. An essential criterion for recognition was that qualifications must be based on statements of competence. The derivation of competencies for particular occupations was made the responsibility of industry, operating through Industry Lead Bodies. Lead Bodies normally work with consultants with experience in analysing jobs for this purpose using a process described as 'functional analysis'. As described by Paul Ellis of NCVQ, the process involves 'progressive disaggregation by occupational experts to break down the key purpose [of the industry] into smaller components' and ultimately into performance criteria (Ellis, 1992, p. 202). These performance criteria, grouped in 'elements of competence' which, in turn, are grouped in 'modules', now form the basis of all qualifications recognised as NVQs, in contrast with the more typical content-based syllabuses which traditionally defined the content of vocational education and training.

While NCVQ itself had no legal powers and could not force awarding bodies or organisations involved in the provision of training to adopt competence-based approaches, it was acting in concert with other very significant players. It operated in tandem with the Standards Branch within what was originally the Manpower Services Commission, where an extensive programme of work has supported the development of standards in industry. Youth training was based on NVQs and the highly influential Confederation of British Industry report *Towards a Skills Revolution* formulated 'world class targets' in terms of NVQs to be achieved by specified dates (CBI, 1989). By the end of 1993 NVQs up to level 5 were in place covering about 80 per cent of the workforce (Debling, 1994, p. 10) and the development of competence-based qualifications for professional qualifications was well under way. Throughout the 1990s NVQs, joined in 1991 by their 'sister' qualification GNVQs, have continued to occupy a privileged position in successive Government White Papers (see, for example, DES, 1991). In the newer GNVQs the language of competence has been replaced by alternative terminology and there is a greater emphasis on the development of theoretical knowledge and understanding. Nevertheless, while the concept of competence is less prominent, the basic principle of defining curricular parameters primarily in terms of measures of pupil performance, or learning outcomes, has been retained. The 1994 White Paper *Competitiveness, Helping Business to Win* (HMSO, 1994) endorsed new 'National Targets for Education and Training', again formulated in terms of NVQs or GNVQs. These targets state that 50 per cent of young people should reach NVQ Level 3 (or its equivalent) by the year 2000, which would mean that 50 per cent would have experienced induction into vocational education and training through competence-based approaches.

Moreover, the hand of NCVQ was strengthened not only by sustained official approbation but by Government's legal powers. The Government's intention to enforce all vocational training to be linked with NVQs and GNVQs was made explicit in an announcement in the White Paper of 1991, *Education and Training for the 21st Century* (DES, 1991, vol. 1, para. 3.10). This states that the Secretary of State will use reserve powers under the 1988 Education Reform Act as a means of 'requiring colleges and schools to offer only NVQs (and thus only CBET) to students pursuing vocational options'.

From the perspective of education, the competence movement has materialised in the form of NVQs and GNVQs and as a product of Government policy. In exploring the scale of the movement it is important to recognise, however, that competence is also integral to current cultural changes affecting the world of work. There is now, for example, a growing interest in competence as a means of human resource management (see, for example, Prahalad and Hamel, 1990; Lawler, 1994). A mark of the level of this interest was the launching in 1994 of a journal, *Competency*, by Industrial Relations Services, which reviews competence-related developments in industry. Many of the initiatives reported in this journal involve the analysis of the 'competence' requirements of specific firms. The interest employers have shown in competence frameworks (as distinct from NVQs) is also evidenced in an Institute for Manpower Services survey which reveals that employers 'did not introduce competencies because everybody was doing it' but as part of a clear strategy of business planning and assessment of internal skill requirements (*Competency*, vol. 1, no. 4, p. 5). Moreover, if we define the competence movement more broadly to include the increasing use of performance criteria to manage and measure organisational and individual performance, it is even more starkly evident that we are dealing with a highly pervasive and seemingly relentless social trend. This suggests that we may need to view the arrival of competence-based pedagogy as epiphenomenal, as a surfacing in education of deeper changes in strucrures and processes of social control over work and training and as a means of synchronising these historically separate spheres. Consequently, while we may observe some significant modifications in the paradigm and terminology, it seems likely that the pivotal position of competence formations in technical and vocational education will grow stronger rather than decline.

This skeletal account is intended to adumbrate the proportions of the phenomenon we are dealing with in order to assess better the current state of research. In essence, the entire gamut of post-16 provision for technical and vocational education throughout work-based, further and higher education is in the process of reconstruction on the basis of competence-based approaches. Where the language of competence is not used, we nevertheless find models for defining both curricula and work performance in terms of the measurement of outcomes. The version of competence which is currently dominant derives from Department of Employment thinking and hinges upon tight pre-specification and subsequent measurement of the intended consequences of learning. This model of CBET removes the determination of what is to be learned from the orbit of influence of practising teachers and trainers, who instead become 'deliverers' and 'assessors' of learning outcomes. In theory, it is the ultimate teacher-proof model. Furthermore, in contrast with many previous educational changes, for example the curriculum movement associated with the Schools Council projects of the 1960s and 1970s, the move towards CBET does not depend upon voluntary participation and persuasion but on a high degree of compulsion. As presently constituted, Government policy on National Vocational Qualifications means that education and training linked with all types and levels of occupation will be brought within this framework. . . .

The technical construction of CBET

In a previous paper (Bates, 1989) I have analysed the considerable scope for further development and reinterpretation of educational aims as broad policy is translated into more specific texts for purposes of operationalisation. It is partly because of the importance of this domain for the purposes of understanding the making of educational meanings that this review will include a brief tour of the technical literature on CBET, the volume of which also serves to provide further illustration of the scale and scope of the movement.

The pivotal role of CBET in relation to NVQs has resulted in extensive mapping and description of the processes, principles and issues involved. The seminal work here is Jessup's book *Outcomes: NVQs and the Emerging*

Model of Education and Training (Jessup, 1991), which provides a lucid and fairly comprehensive overview of the rationale and operation of NVQs and the role of 'competence'. The book includes accounts of: the former Manpower Service Commission's Standards Programme which informed the early development of competence-based training; the principles of assessment; and the implications of competence-based approaches for employers, further and higher education and individuals. It concludes with a discussion of outstanding issues to be tackled for the further development of CBET. Central among these is the question of whether the NVQ competence model takes sufficient account of the role of knowledge and understanding in effective work performance. The discussion of these points foreshadows a continuing debate on the role of knowledge and its assessment in competence-based approaches, with some commentators arguing (for example, Callender, 1992; Smithers, 1993) that the NVQ criteria under-represent the role of theoretical understanding in the development of competence. These critiques, together with NCVQ's own 'in-house' evaluation studies, have led to increasing attention to knowledge issues in the technical literature (see, for example, Employment Department 1993 and 1994). After the publication of Jessup's book, the main vehicles for communication of the ongoing programme of development work associated with NVQs and GNVQs were two professional journals: *The NVQ Monitor,* published by NCVQ itself, and *Competence and Assessment,* published by the former Employment Department. These monitored and reviewed current issues and initiatives arising from the development of National Vocational Qualifications and included a regular update on new NVQs and GNVQs as they become accredited. . . .

A tier below the general guidance literature is the documentation detailing the requirements for specific NVQs and GNVQs. This again is a very substantial body of material, since each qualification may be represented by several hundred pages of text, detailing the units and performance criteria and evidence required. The amount of material is further inflated by the fact that each qualification may be marketed by several awarding bodies. While the requirements for any particular qualification must remain constant across awarding bodies, there are differences in style, presentation and guidance provided. There are no obvious precedents in the history of education and training in Britain for the production of such massive quantities of text detailing curricular specifications and consequently no obvious model of analysis. . . .

Moving deeper into the crucible of production of CBET, we find the literature on 'functional analysis', which is the term used to describe the methods through which competencies are derived. This literature deserves more attention than it has so far attracted since the viability of the entire NVQ framework, in addition to competence-based qualifications which fall outside this framework, depends significantly on the suitability of such methods to their task. The development of the process of functional analysis – initially by the Manpower Services Commission (MSC), later by the Training, Enterprise and Education Division (TEED) of the Employment Department – is detailed in a series of reports and articles (e.g. Mansfield and Matthews, 1985; Fennel, 1991; Mansfield, 1989a; Mitchell, 1989; Debling, 1989). These various papers contextualise and describe functional analysis as a process which involves gradually breaking down ('progressive disaggregation') the purpose (or 'mission') of an occupational area until all areas of competence and ultimately performance criteria, are specified. Responsibility for functional analysis for the purposes of NVQs lies with Lead Bodies but in practice the central role normally falls to consultants working in association with the Employment Department. . . . Detailed studies of the processes involved in functional analysis are needed if we are to move towards a position where we can illuminate the socio-political dimensions involved in processes of selection and specification which lead to the construction of sets of competences.

The process of functional analysis has been undergoing constant refinement and further development and, as one of its proponents once acknowledged, it is not, as yet, 'a highly developed method with well-developed rules and procedures' (Mansfield, 1989b, p. 5). Chief among the problems identified by those involved in its development have been: the need for the process to take account of future as well as present occupational requirements (Jessup, 1991); the need for the range of competencies included to cover work roles in their broadest sense and not simply technical activities (Mansfield, 1989a); the problem of identifying and adequately representing the types of knowledge and understanding relevant to competence in the performance criteria (Wolf, 1989; Mitchell and Wolf, 1991); and the need to incorporate ethical statements in competence formations (Steadman et al., 1994). Given these surrounding difficulties, the question arises as to whether such a crude and as yet unrefined methodology should constitute the key instrument for a national curriculum reform.

Standing at greater distance from the competence lobby, Marshall (1991) and Stuart and Hamlyn (1992) have argued that functional analysis reflects functionalist traditions in sociology and is consequently vulnerable to the various sociological critiques of functionalism. For example, it reflects a unitary model of employer and employee interests and thus does not take into account the possibility of conflicting perspectives on work priorities. Barnett makes a similar point: 'What counts as good practice in social work, the law, medicine and so on are contested goods . . . the identification of the occupational standards is not something that can be settled, and competences read off in any absolute fashion' (Barnett, 1994, p. 73). . . .

These critiques and their implications for how jobs might be analysed merit further development. In fairness, however, to the authors of functional analysis, there are brief acknowledgements in the official literature that the process of developing competencies is indeed 'partly political' (Jessup, 1991, p. 43) and of 'the need to involve those in employment as widely as possible in determining or endorsing the competence statements' (Jessup, 1991, p. 45). Nevertheless, the exploration of social and political factors involved in the sifting and shaping of competence statements remains largely unaddressed. We consequently have little access as yet to ways of understanding more precisely the interrelationships between the selections of knowledge involved in competencies and the 'distribution of power and principles of social control' (Bernstein, 1971).

Evaluative studies of CBET

A major perspective in the literature on any curriculum change is always evaluative and CBET is no exception here. The term 'evaluation' is being used here in the narrow sense to refer to work which tends to bracket out any critique of the central ideas and assumptions of CBET and to focus instead on how far CBET programmes achieve their stated aims and objectives and/or on specific problems of implementation. As we shall see later, however, there is also a much wider body of research which might more loosely be called 'evaluative' but where the focus is extended to include critical analyses of underlying theories and assumptions.

It is noticeable, though, that studies of CBET in the traditional curriculum evaluation mould are surprisingly few. In contrast, the curriculum change movement in Britain of the sixties and seventies was accompanied by a long wave of 'illuminative' evaluation (Parlett and Hamilton, 1977) and the Technical and Vocational Education Initiative (TVEI) spawned extensive national and local evaluation studies. Whilst the CBET movement and the impact of NVQs and GNVQs have generated press coverage, independent evaluation studies remain scarce.[1]

Official reviews have only been undertaken in the wake of critical press reports, together with less than satisfactory OFSTED reports (e.g. OFSTED, 1996). The chief reviews, the Beaumont Report on NVQs (NVQ, 1994) and the Capey Report on GNVQs (NCVQ, 1995), have endorsed both qualifications but recommended substantial reductions in the burdens of assessment and administration involved. Further studies, notably by Alison Wolf (FEDA, 1995) and the Further Education Funding Council (FEFC, 1994), support these conclusions.

Despite these critical appraisals, there have been some small-scale evaluation studies which identify a number of positive benefits consistent with the claims concerning the democratic, 'empowering' and egalitarian thrust of CBET (Jessup, 1991, p. 115; Knasel and Meed, 1994, p. 7). Benefits noted include the widened access to vocational training for mature students as a result of flexible attendance patterns and accreditation of prior learning (Bryson, Edgar and McAleavy, 1990; McIlgorm, 1992); opening up intimate aspects of teaching to public scrutiny and debate (Candy and Harris, 1990); and improved student motivation and satisfaction.

The effects on student motivation are particularly salient with a number of researchers – covering examples of programmes in Australia, Canada and Britain – reporting that CBET was associated with high levels of student satisfaction, and improved motivation and self-reliance (Candy and Harris, 1990; Watson, 1991; Toye and Vigor, 1994). Raggatt, (1994) elaborates on this:

> Increased motivation was manifested in a number of ways: students often chose to work through their breaks and lunch periods; to come in for extra sessions . . . went voluntarily to the library or resources centre to work on underpinning knowledge and understanding; tried to 'pass a bit each day'; talked to each other about their work; were keen to track their own development.
>
> (Raggatt, 1994, p. 64)

These effects are seen as associated with the public and accessible criteria for success, together with the opportunities for self-pacing and individualised instruction associated with the competence model.

Findings on student responses to CBET are by no means invariably positive, however. Work by Stark (1992), based on a qualitative study of students experiencing competence-based teacher training for further education, suggests that the students were angry with and resistant to the new approaches, particularly at the outset of the course. There are also signs that trainees varied in their capacity to cope with and take advantage of independent learning. For example, Candy and Harris (1990) quote one lecturer as reporting that: 'this programme allows less motivated students to become less motivated'. These findings suggest that the impact of CBET on student motivation deserves much closer scrutiny, with particular attention to the broader social and cultural factors shaping students' responses. It is possible, for example, that 'independent learning' may depend more heavily on factors associated with social background and family supportiveness than more traditional, didactic forms of teaching and training.[2]

Most of the problems and pitfalls identified in connection with the shift to CBET centre on the changes involved for teachers and trainers. Whereas the findings on student and trainee responses tend to be fairly positive, the findings on teacher perspectives are much more ambiguous. This contrast itself raises interesting questions. A central theme here in the research on teachers is the analysis of the role changes which CBET involves. These changes are typically reported in terms of a change from 'teacher centred' to 'student centred' methods or from 'directing instruction' to 'facilitating learning' (Candy and Harris, 1990, p. 41). However, as Hyland (1994) argues, we need to regard the use of these terms with caution since, as practised in the context of CBET, they have travelled a long way from their roots in liberal and experiential traditions. . . .

A variety of more specific consequences stemming from these changes are reported, including problems associated with the volume of assessment and administration (Raggatt, 1994; McIlgorm, 1992; Bryson, Edgar and McAleavy, 1990); increased work load (Candy and Harris, 1990); the need to develop appropriate resources and learning materials (Haffenden and Brown, 1989a, 1989b; Watson, 1991); and the need for major programmes of staff development to prepare staff for the changes involved (Haffenden and Brown, 1989a, 1989b; Burke, 1989a; Watson, 1991; Haffenden, Blackman and Brown, 1992). Accounts of how staff involved experience these changes vary greatly in emphasis, with some studies suggesting they produced feelings of dissatisfaction such as 'powerlessness' and 'frustration' (Candy and Harris, 1990) and others, such as Stark and McAleavy (1992), suggesting staff found the role changes stimulating and challenging. There is no work as yet which illuminates the contextual factors which might account for such divergent responses.

A final theme in the literature on CBET written from the perspective of evaluation is the question of course content, or what counts as knowledge. The major concern is the narrowing of the curriculum and lack of provision for theoretical knowledge which may result from CBET. In the context of evaluation studies, the 'knowledge' issue rears its head mainly in the form of empirical work on users' perspectives. Two categories of users have been canvassed on the question of the appropriateness of the curricula associated with CBET: teacher/trainers and employers. Studies of teachers indicate very mixed views on the resulting curriculum. While the more realistic preparation for many aspects of employment seems to be appreciated, there are numerous references to staff concerns about the marginalisation of theoretical knowledge involved in CBET and the implications of this for effective and responsible work performance (e.g. Hyland and Weller, 1994; Smithers, 1993; Prais, 1989; Raggatt, 1994). A study by Bryson, Edgar and McAleavy highlights specifically the response of science teachers in further education:

> Debate centred on the nature of quality in knowledge acquisition. The hairdressers tended to focus on the practical applications of knowledge whereas some science teachers felt that some areas of knowledge were holistic and could not be segmented. . . . In addition the nature of the programme meant that the number of hours allocated to science had decreased and some science teachers argued that a reduction in time allocated meant a reduction in quality.
>
> (Bryson, Edgar and McAleavy, 1990, p. 117)

These findings point to the need for researchers on teacher/trainer perspectives to take account of the potential interplay between curriculum values and professional interests.

Perhaps of more interest from the standpoint of policy makers are the results of surveys of employers' perspectives on the value of NVQs for industry. Since CBET, and NVQs particularly, are represented in the official literature as 'employer led', we might expect the most positive response in this quarter. However, here again the evidence available is limited and contradictory. For example, the picture of take-up of competence-based NVQs varies according to the indicators used. A recent Institute of Manpower Studies survey based on a questionnaire to 1,506 employers concludes that 44 per cent of employers with 500 employees or more were using NVQs in their training (Toye and Vigor, 1994) yet when these figures are compared with the numbers of NVQ certificates actually awarded take-up looks much thinner. For example, NCVQ figures show that only 500,000 certificates had been awarded by winter 1993 (*NVQ Monitor*, 1993). The above IMS survey drew the conclusion that 'in general there was considerable support for the principle of competence-based training' (Toye and Vigor, 1994, p. 21). Again this stands in contrast to a slightly different reading of employers' perspectives offered in a recent Confederation of British Industry (CBI, 1994, p. 7) report which proposes that 'the biggest barrier to NVQ take-up reported by employers is the qualifications' lack of perceived relevance to individual and company need' . . . Nevertheless, despite what appear to be deep reservations about competence-based approaches in some industries, the CBI has repeatedly reaffirmed its commitment to the competence movement and its endorsement of the National Vocational Qualification framework: 'NVQs represent a fundamental change for the better in the way that competence in an occupation is defined, measured and recognised' (CBI, 1994, p. 5).

Given the findings considered above, we have to be cautious in drawing any firm conclusions about the relevance of competence-based approaches to the needs of industry. A serious empirical investigation of this issue poses complex problems. For example, 'industry' and 'employers' cannot be treated as a monolithic entity but span very diverse sets of interests. The positions and priorities of the CBI, multinational companies and small businesses are all likely to differ in significant ways, as also will the perspectives of employers, trade unions and labour. A further complicating factor is that employers may have a wide range of reasons for rejecting or embracing concepts of competence and NVQs, which have little to do with assessments of their value for improving work performance. For example, take-up may be related to the professional and career interests of training and personnel managers. Third, one of the major concerns of employers about the value of NVQs is likely to be the impact on profit. However, the impact of training 'inputs' on business performance cannot yet be rigorously demonstrated. Since the *raison d'être* for the competence movement rests so heavily on the claims made concerning its relevance to employment, deeper empirical investigation of these issues is much needed. . . .

More generally, the scope for evaluative research on competence-based education and training is considerable. Indeed, it is somewhat surprising that the comprehensive overhaul of post-16 provision resulting from the introduction of NVQs and GNVQs was not the subject of an independent national evaluation such as accompanied the Technical and Vocational Education Initiative. To summarise, the findings of the evaluative studies up to 1995 suggest that the impact of competence-based approaches has been at its most positive in the area of student and trainee motivation. If this is indeed the case, this achievement of NVQs and GNVQs cannot be lightly dismissed. Given the history of difficulty in motivating the types of students and trainees involved in the lower level NVQs/GNVQs, it is a highly significant finding. There are clearly further issues to be investigated here and lessons to be drawn. Studies of teachers and trainers document the impact of substantial role changes and detail the types of staff development required. Interestingly, though, whereas one might have expected teachers to be encouraged by the enthusiasm reported amongst trainees, the findings suggest their perspectives are actually very mixed and the indications are that they are experiencing the changes involved more in terms of deprofessionalisation, loss of influence and work overload. Student enthusiasm and teacher satisfaction do not necessarily correlate. There are a wide range of contextual factors which merit further investigation here. Finally, the response of 'industry' and relevance of the new approaches to industrial needs deserve much closer scrutiny.

'Spirit of education' studies

At the heart of the work considered here is a critique of CBET on the grounds that it runs counter to what might be termed the 'spirit of education'. While this is an eclectic body of work, which includes different emphases and perspectives, considered collectively it provides a fairly comprehensive critical analysis of many of the fundamental principles of CBET. At the risk of simplifying a number of different approaches, the central line of argument might be summarised as follows.

To be effective, education needs to be grounded in appropriate assumptions about human behaviour and learning. In recent years researchers have tended to eschew models of learning rooted in behavioural psychology which focus on producing requisite changes in behaviour through conditioned responses to stimuli. Prevailing models draw more upon phenomenological and interactionist perspectives, emphasising the importance of individual agency in the construction of meanings and the need for education to treat learning as a creative process in which the outcomes are to some extent unpredictable. CBET, insofar as it relies heavily on shaping learning through the specification and measurement of behavioural outcomes and sidesteps considerations about the process of learning, is viewed as resting on outdated behaviourist approaches and as treating both teachers and learners as passive agents in the process of 'delivering' learning. Thus the model of learning implicit in CBET has come to be regarded by some critics as mechanistic, reductionist and unlikely to foster the fullest possible development of human potential. The application of these sorts of critiques to approaches to education which centre on the specification and measurement of predetermined outcomes is by no means new or unique to current changes in technical and vocational preparation. The rational curriculum planning movement which dominated American curriculum development in the 1950s (e.g. Tyler, 1949; Bloom, *et al.,* 1956) gave rise to similar concerns, with writers such as Stenhouse (1975) arguing that an emphasis on pre-specified objectives is antithetical to learning. . . .

One of the most persistent critics of CBET, and particularly NVQs, is Hyland, whose series of papers have explored many facets of the competence movement both conceptually and empirically, together with its policy implications (see, e.g., Hyland, 1991, 1993, 1994; Hyland and Weller, 1994). Amongst the wealth of angles from which he has comprehensively circled this subject is an article in similar vein to the approaches considered above which explores the incompatibility between CBET, NVQs and 'experiential' learning, defined by Kolb (1993) as 'a process whereby knowledge is created by the transformation of experience' (Hyland, 1994). Hyland argues – and here his case is possibly overstated – that this tradition has been the dominant ideological tradition in further and adult education in recent years. It is a tradition to which he sees CBET as fundamentally opposed:

> Instead of an holistic framework, CBE atomises and fragments learning into measurable chunks; rather than valuing process and experience, CBE is concerned only with performance outcomes and, most importantly, instead of encouraging critical reflection on alternative perspectives, CBE offers a mono-cultural view based on the satisfaction of narrow performance criteria and directed towards fixed and predetermined ends.
>
> (Hyland, 1994, p. 235)

The conflict between the two traditions is then examined empirically through research into the practice of further education, focused on lecturers attempting to remould their approaches to fit the NVQ model of CBET. Hyland concludes that the NCVQ model restricts and frustrates their preferred approach.

While some educationalists have struggled to stand above the rising tide of CBET and have concerned themselves chiefly with critique, others –

possibly concluding that its advance is in any case inexorable – have sought to channel the movement in what are deemed to be more constructive and educationally appropriate directions. This 'reconstructionist' tendency is most visible in work on professional education and training, where debate about the appropriateness and applicability of competence-based approaches is now gathering pace.[3] Particularly notable here is the work of Eraut, brought together recently in *Developing Professional Knowledge and Competence* (Eraut, 1994). Eraut approaches this terrain from a long history of research into appropriate models for professional education and training revolving around the excavation and explication of underlying principles of professional practice with the aim of bringing 'the largely intuitive aspects of practice under some kind of professional control' (Eraut, 1989, p. 184). From this perspective Eraut questions the primacy of the concepts of performance and performance evidence in NCVQ literature, arguing that the emphasis on actual performance does not take sufficient account of the need to develop and assess individual potential or 'capability', particularly in the context of complex professional roles. This leads to a proposal to expand the notion of evidence required for professional qualifications to include 'capability' evidence.

There are now a growing number of explorations of *rapprochement* between experiential and 'reflective practitioner' traditions and the competence movement. Winter (1992), for example, describing the development of competence-based degree qualifications in social work argues for the inclusion of 'core assessment criteria' which would be devised to take account of knowledge and values relevant to professional practice. Focusing on teacher training Whitty and Willmot (1991) offer a critical assessment of the current state of debate from which they conclude that while there is 'insufficient experience to justify the national imposition of any particular approach there is considerable scope for further exploration' (p. 317). Such exploration has been taken further by Tomlinson (1995a; 1995b) who proposes that a competence-based model of teacher training should 'embody the idea of competence as *capacity* in any profile formulation' (emphasis added). Broadening the scope of debate beyond professional training, Hodkinson suggests that the need to be able to respond creatively at work is not exclusive to the professions but common to many jobs.

> The receptionist must be able to deal with the unique situations as well as the familiar. A jobbing builder is often faced with new problems of repair or maintenance. Even routine jobs are changing increasingly frequently, for example in response to new technology.
>
> (Hodkinson, 1992, p. 35)

This leads him to recommend an 'interactive' model of competence, rooted in interactionist social theory, rather than behaviourist traditions. Such a model is seen as dispensing with static, fixed versions of competence and offering a basis for a more dynamic and flexible approach.

Having separated out both critical and 'reconstructionist' strands in the educational literature on competence, it is important to note that what I am highlighting here are differences in emphasis rather than clearly demarcated positions.

Across the board, the various critiques and discussions of competence also have a great deal in common. At root what they share is a resistance to the drive towards bringing educational meanings into the realms of the known and calculable on the grounds that this will lead to the impoverishment of learning. On occasion this is expressed as an impassioned attack on competence models. For example, Smithers (1993) warns that the NCVQ reforms threaten a 'disaster of epic proportions', and Marshall (1991, p. 64) concludes that 'the current model will set back education in Britain in an incalculable way'. At other times the emphasis is on domesticating the competence movement and bringing it within the fold of education theory.

What is to be made of the meaning of these critiques and in particular the volume and intensity which characterise discussion? While the arguments developed clearly have important merits, they can also be seen as reflecting a process of academic contestation of the territory of education and training in the context of rapid erosion of the responsibilities and control of the teaching profession. This explanation should not be seen as necessarily detracting from the intrinsic merits of the critiques developed, which need to be assessed in their own right. The point here is simply to emphasise that debates about competence and related research need to be seen as socially situated in a highly charged political arena.

Sociological perspectives

This takes us to a much thinner but growing strand of research in which competence becomes the subject of a potentially more far-reaching enquiry. There is a limited collection of studies and projects which have begun to consider social and historical factors involved in the competence movement and allied trends, exploring, for example: their social origins and significance; the particular ways in which competency formations construct and reshape processes of education, training and the control of labour; and the resulting social interaction in the course of policy implementation, for example in staffrooms and classrooms.

First, the work on the social origins of the recent competence movement has made it clear that the question of explaining its resurgence in the last decade has begun to exercise a number of writers. It will be apparent from the research reviewed above that we need to look beyond the pedagogic merits of this movement in order to understand its current momentum and to consider broader explanations of its considerable resilience in the face of critique. One promising avenue is to examine ways in which competence keys in with broader social trends. This is an ambitious project but one which several writers have begun to wrestle with, pointing to factors such as: the rise of technocratic approaches to management in the context of a legitimation crisis involving a breakdown of traditional norms and values (Broadfoot, 1985); changes in the organisation of work characterised in terms of post-Fordism (Rassool, 1993); similar trends in work but theorised in terms of a further wave of Fordism (Field, 1991); or the continuation of modernism (Edwards, 1993). A different approach again has been to analyse competence-based training in terms of increasing performance surveillance in education and work (Bates, 1991). This tentative analysis linked the competence movement with Bernstein's concepts of classification and framing (Bernstein, 1971) and Foucault's work on discipline and surveillance (Foucault, 1977), suggesting that competence involves tightening the classification and framing of vocational training in order to increase the scope for surveillance and social control.

The exploration of competence in relation to social change and social control is now benefiting from more focused work on these themes, notably by Jones and Moore (1993) and Barnett (1994). The most developed theoretical attack to date is a paper in which Jones and Moore argue that competence needs to be seen in terms of growing state control of the professions:

> The crucial feature of this movement is the manner in which the State, through agencies such as MSC and NCVQ has, over the past two decades or so, progressively extended its direct control over the sphere of professional expertise.
>
> (Jones and Moore, 1993, p. 390)

They then unpack the means by which this increased control is achieved, linking specific features of the competence movement with Giddens' theories of social regulation (Giddens, 1991) and Bernstein's work on pedagogic discourse (Bernstein, 1990). . . . It is in this general sociological context that our own work on 'The Social Construction of Competence' is situated (Bates, 1993; see also Bates, 1991; Bates and Dutson, 1995; Bates 1998a, 1998b). Drawing on previous work on processes of developing and implementing vocational curricula (Bates, 1989), this project examines competence at two levels – origination and implementation – focusing on NVQs and GNVQs. Our research so far reveals complex adaptations of the competence paradigm as it passes through multi-layered terrains from policy-making to practice. Such findings are testimony to the creative agency of social actors – teachers and young people – in re-interpreting control mechanisms to suit their own professional values and contextualized concerns.

The basic thrust of the sociological research in competence is to argue that, contrary to the learner-emancipatory ethos of the official discourse, the movement needs to be understood in terms of tightening social regulation and control. The intensification of control is seen as a means of achieving a major transformation in orientations towards work and part of a wider project of cultural change related to changing economic circumstances. More concretely, competence has been explained as a movement reflecting the late twentieth-century *Weltanschauung,* with its characteristic emphasis on markets, performance measurement and the merging of education and work for purposes of improving economic performance. So far, however, much of the work is quite speculative and theoretical rather than empirically grounded.

Research implications

There are many ways of determining what a curriculum should comprise and many ways of teaching and learning. The reconstruction of education and training around concepts of competence replaces this rich cultural diversity with a more narrow band of practice. The competence model in its dominant form in Britain treats the production of learning as a process susceptible to central governance through a systems approach based on the specification, monitoring and assessment of outcomes. It is a model which has aroused much debate amongst practitioners and researchers, particularly as those centrally involved in technical, vocational and professional education and training question current notions of competence and resist the changes involved in their traditional professional responsibilities.

Despite its scale and significance, however, the competence movement in Britain remains poorly reflected in high quality research as opposed to critique, defence and thin evaluation. This disproportionality needs explaining. Researchers have begun to tackle the competence colossus from a number of angles – as reviewed here – but so far their efforts have not been concerted, there has been little cross-fertilisation of ideas and little impact on policy. The advance of the competence movement calls for a wider, more insightful research agenda, fanning out from the narrowly developmental and evaluative to socio-psychological explorations of the nature of teaching and learning, to macro socio-historical questions of origins, influences and impact. In the summary below I shall translate these into some more specific research possibilities.

1 Discourse analysis and the technical construction of CBET

CBET is *par excellence* a textually mediated discourse, that is, it is substantially embodied in and mediated through text. In Britain these texts will consist of detailed specifications of competencies and performance criteria for countless vocational qualifications. This contrasts with previous examples of curriculum change where materials have often been exemplars, intended to encourage teachers to develop new approaches. This suggests the need to expand the focus of educational enquiry to include more emphasis on content analysis of competence texts. Models of discourse analysis are likely to prove useful here but more work needs to be done on appropriate models. Areas these need to cover include: the nature and characteristics of selections of knowledge included; occupational values embodied; comparison with previous curricular parameters for similar qualifications; and underlying assumptions about organisation and resourcing of learning.

2 Evaluation studies

Large-scale evaluation studies, using quantitative and qualitative methodologies, are needed to examine the impact of competence-based approaches on the processes and quality of learning. Given the substantial material and political interests now invested in NVQs and GNVQs, fully independent studies are particularly needed. Current research points to at least three important foci for further evaluative work: the impact of CBET on student/trainee responses; the impact on the roles of teachers and trainers; and the relevance of qualification specifications to 'industry'.

3 'Spirit of education' studies

CBET reverses much of traditional educational practice with its emphasis on outputs rather than inputs and has been viewed as reducing the scope for teachers and students to act as creative participants in learning. It will be important to examine more closely and empirically the implications of competence models for the development of the creative 'lifelong' learner and to identify contextual variables. This may be particularly important as these models begin to penetrate higher education and professional training, where forms of knowledge and abilities required may be less compatible with the competence paradigm.

4 Sociological approaches

There are two kinds of analysis which are appropriate here. First, socio-historical studies are needed, for example of the emergence of the competence movement – in different countries, or of critical stages in the development of any particular movement. In our present state of understanding we cannot assign weight to the different theoretical explanations of competence without more historically based research. Second, studies are needed of the social reconstruction of specific domains of education and training and of the social and political processes involved at all levels of operationalisation and implementation. Such work might initially be most fruitfully focused on training for occupations which most clearly involve socially sensitive issues in order to explore the difficulties and processes involved in arriving at consensus over common standards in the context of professional dissensus.

Progress in any or all of the above directions will be important since our present state of understanding of CBET and its embodiment in the British NVQ/GNVQ framework is an insufficient basis to form considered judgements. Moreover, with such major political, ideological and material interests invested in both sides of the debate on competence, and such different traditions involved, clarification of issues, together with reflexive and informed understanding, are called for all the more.

Acknowledgement

I am grateful to Professor Edgar Jenkins, editor of Studies in Science Education, who prompted the writing of the original version of this paper, published in *Studies in Science Education* vol. 25 (1995), pp. 39–68.

Notes

1 Since 1995 two ERSC funded research projects at the University of Leeds covering NVQs and GNVQs have gradually been reporting their findings (Bates, ESRC R000 23 3908 and Higham, Sharp and Yeomans, ESRC R000 235 911).
2 The relationship between family background and the experience of independent learning is the focus of a forthcoming project within the ESRC programme Youth, Citizenship and Social Change (Bates and Allatt, *Youth, Family and Education* 1998–2001).
3 For examples of discussion of CBET in relation to training for the professions see Winter (1992) on social work; Whitty and Wilmott (1991) on teaching; Haffenden and Brown (1989a and 1989b) and Chown and Last (1993) on further education teaching; Challis, Usherwood and Joesbury (1994) on medicine; McNair (1992) on vocational guidance.

References

Ashworth, P.D. and Saxton, J. (1990) 'On Competence', *Journal of Further and Higher Education*, 14 (2), 3–25.
Barnett, R. (1994) *The Limits of Competence: Knowledge, Higher Education and Society.* Buckingham, Society for Research into Higher Education and Open University Press.
Bates, I. (1989) 'Versions of Vocationalism: An Analysis of Social and Political Influences on Curriculum Policy and Practice', *British Journal of Sociology of Education,* 10 (2), 215–31.

Bates, I. (1991) 'Closely Observed Training: An Exploration of Links between Social Structures, Training and Identity', *International Studies in Sociology of Education*, 1, 225–43.

Bates, I. (1993) 'The Social Construction of Competence: Qualitative Studies of Vocational Training', Proposal to the Economic and Social Research Council.

Bates, I. (1998a) 'The "Empowerment" Dimension in the GNVQ: A Critical Exploration of Discourse, Pedagogic Apparatus and School Implementation', *Evaluation and Research in Education*, 12 (1), 7–22.

Bates, I. (1998b) 'Resisting "Empowerment" and Realizing Power: an exploration of aspects of the GNVQ', *Journal of Education and Work*, 11 (2), 187–204.

Bates, I. and Dutson, J. (1995) 'A Bermuda Triangle? A Case Study of Competence-based Vocational Training', *British Journal of Education and Work*, 8 (2), 41–59.

Bernstein, B. (1971) 'On the Classification and Framing of Educational Knowledge', in M.F.D. Young (ed.) *Knowledge and Control*. London, Collier Macmillan.

Bernstein, B. (1990) *The Structuring of Pedagogic Discourse, Class Codes and Control*, volume 4. London, Routledge.

Bloom, B.S. *et al.* (1956) *Taxonomy of Educational Objectives, I: Cognitive Domain*. London, Longman.

Broadfoot, P. (1985) 'Changing Patterns of Educational Accountability in England and France', *Comparative Education*, 21 (3), 273–86.

Bryson, J., Edgar, C. and McAleavy, G. (1990) 'From Concept to Practice: Implementing a Competence-based Programme in a College Hairdressing Curriculum', *The Vocational Aspect of Education*, 42 (113), 113–18.

Burke, J.W. (1989a) 'The Implementation of NVQs', in Burke (1989b).

Burke, J.W. (ed.) (1989b) *Competency Based Education and Training*. Lewes, Falmer Press.

Callender, C. (1992) *Will NVQs Work? Evidence from the Construction Industry*. Sussex, University of Sussex/Institute of Manpower Studies.

Candy, P. and Harris, R. (1990) 'Implementing Competency Based Vocational Education: A View from Within', *Journal of Further and Higher Education*, 14 (2), 38–57.

CBI (1989) *Towards a Skills Revolution*. London, Confederation of British Industry.

CBI (1994) *The CBI Review of NVQs and SVQs*. London, Confederation of British Industry.

Challis, M., Usherwood, T. and Joesbury, H. (1994) 'Assessment of Specified Competences in Undergraduate General Medical Training', *Competence and Assessment*, 25, 19–21.

Chown, A. and Last, J. (1993) 'Can the NCVQ Model be Used for Teacher Training?', *Journal of Further and Higher Education*, 17 (2), 15–25.

Dawkins, J.S. (1989) *Improving Australia's Training System*. Canberra, Australian Government Publishing Service.

Debling, G. (1989) 'The Employment Department/Training Agency Standards Programme and NVQs: Implications for Education', in Burke (1989b).

Debling, G. (1994) 'Competence and Assessment: Five Years On and What Next?' in *Competence and Assessment Compendium*, no 3. Employment Department Learning Methods Branch.

DES (1991) *Education and Training for the 21st Century*. London, HMSO. Two volumes.

DOE (1981) *A New Training Initiative: A Programme for Action.* London, HMSO. Cmnd. 8455.

DOE, DES (1986) *Working Together: Education and Training.* London, HMSO. Cmnd. 9823.

Edwards, R. (1993) 'A Spanner in the Works: Luddism and Competence', *Adults Learning* 4 (5), 124–6.

Ellis, P. (1992) 'Saying it All in Standards', *Education and Training Technology International,* 29 (3), 198–205.

Employment Department (1989, onwards) *Competence and Assessment.*

Employment Department (1993) 'Knowledge and Understanding: Its Place in Relation to NVQs and SVQs', *Competence and Assessment,* Briefing Note no. 9.

Employment Department (1994) 'The Place of Knowledge and Understanding in the Development of National Vocational Qualifications and Scottish Vocational Qualifications', *Competence and Assessment,* Briefing Note no. 10.

Eraut, M. (1989) 'Initial Teacher Training and the NCVQ Model', in Burke (1989b).

Eraut, M. (1994) *Developing Professional Knowledge and Competence.* London, Falmer Press.

FEDA (1995) *GNVQs 1994–95: A National Survey Report.* London, FEDA.

FEFC (1994) *GNVQs in Further Education.* London, FEFC.

Fennel, E. (ed.) (1991) *Development of Assessable Standards for National Certification.* Sheffield, Employment Department.

FEU (1984) *Towards a Competency-based System.* London, Further Education Unit.

Field, J. (1991) 'Competency and the Pedagogy of Labour', *Studies in the Education of Adults,* 23 (1), 41–52.

Foucault, M. (1977) *Discipline and Punish: The Birth of the Prison.* Harmondsworth, Penguin.

Giddens, A. (1991) *Modernity and Self-Identity.* Cambridge, Polity Press.

Grant, G. *et al.* (1979) *On Competence: A Critical Analysis of Competence-based Reforms in Higher Education.* San Francisco, Jossey-Bass.

Haffenden, I. and Brown, A. (1989a) 'Towards the Implementation of NVQs in Colleges of FE', in Burke (1989b).

Haffenden, I. and Brown, A. (1989b) 'A Study of the New Vocational Qualifications: Interim Findings and Implications for Teacher Education', *Journal of Further and Higher Education,* 13 (3), 46–57.

Haffenden, I., Blackman, S. and Brown, A.R. (1992) 'Research Partnership and an Issues Framework: A Review of the Methodology of an Overarching Project on Competence Funded by the Further Education Unit and the Training Agency', *British Educational Research Journal,* 18 (1), 25–36.

HMSO (1994) *Competitiveness, Helping Business to Win.* London, HMSO. Cmnd 2563.

Hodkinson, P. (1992) 'Alternative Models of Competence in Vocational Education and Training', *Journal of Further and Higher Education,* 16 (2), 30–9.

Hyland, T. (1991) 'Taking Care of Business: Vocationalism, Competence and the Enterprise Culture', *Educational Studies,* 17 (1), 77–87.

Hyland, T. (1993) 'Professional Development and Competence-based Education', *Educational Studies,* 19 (1), 123–32.

Hyland, T. (1994) 'Silk Purses and Sows' Ears: NVQs, GNVQs and Experiential Learning', *Cambridge Journal of Education,* 24 (2), 233–43.

Hyland, T. and Weller, P. (1994) *Implementing GNVQs in Post-16 Education.* University of Warwick, Continuing Education Research Centre.

Industrial Relations Services (1994) *Competency,* 1.

Jessup, G. (1991) *Outcomes: NVQs and the Emerging Model of Education and Training.* London, Falmer Press.

Jonathon, R. (1987) 'The Youth Training Scheme and Core Skills: An Educational Analysis', in M. Holt (ed.) *Skills and Vocationalism: The Easy Answer.* Milton Keynes, Open University Press.

Jones, L. and Moore, R. (1993) 'Education, Competence and the Control of Expertise', *British Journal of Sociology of Education,* 14 (4), 385–97.

Jones, L. and Moore, R. (1995) 'Appropriating Competence: The Competency Movement, the New Right and the "Culture Change" Project', *British Journal of Education and Work* 8 (2), 78–92.

Knasel, E. and Meed, J. (1994) *Becoming Competent: Effective Learning for Occupational Competence.* Sheffield, Employment Department and Learning Methods Branch, Report no. 27.

Kolb, D. (1993) 'The Process of Experiential Learning', in M. Thorpe, R. Edwards and A. Hanson (eds), *Culture and Processes of Adult Learning.* London, Routledge/ Open University.

Lawler, E. (1994) 'From Job-based to Competence-based Organizations', *Journal of Organizational Behaviour,* 15 (1), 3–15.

McIlgorm, E. (1992) 'Implementing a CBVE Programme within the Constraints of the FE Framework', *Journal of Further and Higher Education,* 16 (2), 71–9.

McNair, S. (1992) 'New Maps for Old: Guidance and the Reform of Vocational Qualifications', *British Journal of Guidance and Counselling,* 20 (2), 129–49.

Mansfield, B. (1989a) 'Competence and Standards', in Burke (1989b).

Mansfield, B. (1989b) 'Functional Analysis – A Personal Approach', *Competence and Assessment,* Special Issue 1. Sheffield, Employment Department.

Mansfield, B. and Matthews, D. (1985) *Job Competence – a Description for Use in Vocational Education and Training.* Bristol, Further Education Staff College.

Marks, R. (1994) 'Standards in the States', *Competence and Assessment,* 26. Sheffield, Employment Department.

Marshall, K. (1991) 'NVQs: An Assessment of the "Outcomes" Approach in Education and Training', *Journal of Further and Higher Education,* 15 (3), 56–64.

Mitchell, L. (1989) 'The Definition of Standards and Their Assessment', in Burke (1989b).

Mitchell, L. and Wolf, A. (1991) 'Understanding the Place of Knowledge and Understanding in a Competence Based Approach', in Fennel (1991).

MSC and DES (1986) *Review of Vocational Qualifications in England and Wales.* London, HMSO.

NCVQ (1993) *The NVQ Monitor.* London, National Council for Vocational Qualifications, published bi-annually.

NCVQ (1994) *The Beaumont Report.* London, NCVQ.

NCVQ (1995) GNVQ Assessment Review, *The Capey Report.* London, NCVQ.

Norberg-Hodge, H. (1991) *Ancient Futures: Learning from Ladakh.* London, Rider.

OFSTED (1996) *Assessment of General and National Vocational Qualifications in Schools, 1995–96.* London, HMSO.

Parlett, M. and Hamilton, D. (1977) 'Evaluation as Illumination: A New Approach to the Study of Innovatory Programmes', in D. Hamilton *et al.*, *Beyond the Numbers Game*. London, Macmillan.

Prahalad, C.K. and Hamel, G. (1990) 'The Core Competence of the Corporation', *Harvard Business Review*, 68 (3), 79–93.

Prais, S. (1989) 'How Europe Would See the New British Initiative for Standardizing Vocational Qualifications', *National Institute Economic Review*, August, 225–7.

Raggatt, P. (1994) 'Implementing NVQs in Colleges: Progress, Perceptions and Issues', *Journal of Further and Higher Education*, 18 (1), 59–74.

Rassool, N. (1993) 'Post-Fordism? Technology and New Forms of Control: The Case of Technology in the Curriculum', *British Journal of Sociology of Education*, 14 (3), 227–44.

Silver, H. (1988) *Intentions and Outcomes: Vocationalism in Further Education*. London, Further Education Unit.

Smithers, A. (1993) *All Our Futures: Britain's Education Revolution*. London, Channel Four Television Dispatches Report on Education.

Stark, S. (1992) 'Experiencing a Competence Based Teacher Training Programme in Further Education: Student Perspectives', *Journal of Further and Higher Education*, 16 (1), 74–83.

Stark, S. and McAleavy, G. (1992) 'Initiating a Competence Based Teacher Training Programme in Further Education: Staff Perspectives', *Journal of Further and Higher Education*, 16 (2), 80–9.

Steadman, S.D., Eraut, M.R., Cole, G. and Marquand, J. (1994) *Ethics in Occupational Standards, NVQs and SVQs*. Sheffield, Employment Department.

Stenhouse, L. (1975) *An Introduction to Curriculum Research and Development*. London, Heinemann.

Stuart, J. and Hamlyn, B. (1992) 'Competence-based Qualifications: The Case against Change', *Journal of European Industrial Training*, 16 (7), 21–32.

Tomlinson, P.D. (1995a) 'Can Competence Profiling Work for Effective Teacher Preparation? 1: General Issues', *Oxford Review of Education*, 21 (2), 179–94.

Tomlinson, P.D. (1995b) 'Can Competence Profiling Work for Effective Teacher Preparation? 2: Pitfalls and Principles', *Oxford Review of Education*, 21 (3), 299–314.

Toye, J. and Vigor, P. (1994) *Implementing NVQs: The Experience of Employers, Employees and Trainees*. Sussex, Institute of Manpower Studies.

Tuxworth, E. (1989) 'Competence Based Education and Training: Background and Origins', in Burke (1989b).

Twining, J. (1994) 'Vocational Qualifications: The European Dimension', *Competence and Assessment*, 27. Sheffield, Employment Department.

Tyler, R.W. (1949) *Basic Principles of Curriculum and Instruction*. Chicago, University of Chicago Press.

Watson, A. (1991) 'Competency-based Vocational Education: Is This the Answer?', *The Vocational Aspect of Education*, 114, 113–45.

Whitty, G. and Willmott, E. (1991) 'Competence-based Teacher Education: Approaches and Issues', *Cambridge Journal of Education*, 21, 309–18.

Winter, R. (1992) ' "Quality Management" or "The Educative Workplace": Alternative Versions of Competence-based Education', *Journal of Further and Higher Education*, 16 (3), 100–15.

Wolf A. (1989) 'Can Competence and Knowledge Mix?' in Burke (1989b).

Chapter 7

Reality testing in the workplace

Are NVQs 'employment-led'?

John Field

Work and the workplace play a central role in the new system of National Vocational Qualifications. For individual employers, trainees and workers, like all occupational qualifications, an NVQ only pays off when the owner is working at their job. Indeed, the design of NVQs makes the workplace the primary site of learning and assessment of the skills that the owner of an NVQ is deemed to possess. Those whose job it is to develop, promote and sell NVQs have consistently claimed that, unlike previous qualifications, the new system is 'employment-led'. The underpinning ideology of the NVQ system places great emphasis upon the workplace as a guarantor of relevance, reliability and demand. At the level of rhetoric, a contrast is frequently drawn both implicitly and explicitly between the kinds of skills and knowledge taught and examined within educational institutions (characterized as academic, abstract, impractical and knowledge-based) and those learned and observed within the workplace (characterized as useful, applied, practical and skills-based). The goal of the reform has been from the outset to shift the emphasis irrevocably from the former to the latter.

NVQs are, then, defined in all essentials as reflecting more reliably and accurately than in the past the demands of the workplace. This chapter takes that claim as its starting point. It deals with the concept of NVQs as driven by the requirements of the workplace, and more particularly as reflecting the needs of employers. The analysis is presented in four stages:

1 a brief description of the new system as it is now settling into shape;
2 analysis of conditions in the labour market, in order to judge how far they mirror the kinds of assumptions upon which NVQs are predicated;
3 an outline of the ways in which NVQs appear to be being received within the workplace; and
4 an indication of some possible explanations of the social determination of the NVQ system, and vocational qualifications systems more generally.

Underlying this critique is the belief that, whatever the merits or faults of NVQs in themselves, what counts is how they are received in actually existing workplaces, each of which has its own social relations and organizational cultures.

Much of the empirical research associated with the debate over NVQs has been frankly technical, and concerned chiefly with identifying, clarifying and resolving the practical problems of implementation. This is not meant to be a dismissive comment, but rather to indicate the limits of much of the empirical work undertaken to date. Typically, it has been concerned with such questions as the identification of task-related skills, the assessment of broadly applicable skills, and the best balance of competence with 'underpinning knowledge' in higher-level qualifications. Other interventions have been of three kinds. There has been some discussion of the psychology of learning which informs the NVQ system; a number of critics have suggested that NVQs are based upon a simplistic and outmoded behaviourism which has no place either for individual cognitive differences or for the context-specific nature of some human learning (Marshall, 1991, pp. 61–2). From a philosophical standpoint, it has been suggested that NVQs are narrowly utilitarian (Hyland, 1991), although this of course begs the question of what wider human qualities British vocational qualifications measured before 1986. Associated with the philosophical analysis of NVQs is a concern for terminology, with a number of attempts – not least by NCVQ – to define more precisely what is meant by 'competence' (Short, 1984; Ashworth and Saxton, 1990; Hodkinson, 1992).

By comparison, the social and economic analysis of NVQs remains in its infancy. As a result no serious challenge has been offered to the view that NVQs are 'employment-led'. This phrase, used both by NVQs' proponents and supporters and their critics, is understood by the system's enthusiasts to mean that it reflects the 'needs of the workplace', and by its neo-Marxist critics as confirming that it reflects capital's latest, post-Fordist mode of subordination of labour (Edwards, 1993). As a consequence, the relationship between NVQs and employment has been taken for granted by all sides. In particular, there has been relatively little study of the operation of NVQs in the labour market. This is understandable; much of the social and economic research into NVQs has concerned their impact upon training institutions, and chronologically it is at this end that the new system has been most noticeable. However, it is the labour market that forms the primary context of vocational qualifications. Yet, with the significant exception of Lorna Unwin's case study of NVQs in Courtaulds' Coventry fibre plant, this context has been largely taken as given (Unwin, 1991). I now propose to look underneath this particular stone.

In part, this chapter is research-based, drawing on evidence from a mixture of published material and original research collected during the course of a study of NVQs and the organization of work in contemporary Britain

(Field, 1991; Field and Weller, 1992; Field, 1993). Material is taken from interviews conducted during autumn 1993 with managers responsible for personnel and training issues in large and medium-sized enterprises; these followed on an earlier study of trade union officers' perceptions of the new system (Field and Weller, 1992). Published statistics are drawn on, in order to quantify the availability and take-up of NVQs. Other supporting evidence is drawn from analysis of published material, which can be used to shed light on both the real level and nature of the market demand for NVQs, and on the processes by which a particular definition of 'employment interests' has been constructed and inserted into the NVQ system. This arises from a long-standing interest in what I think of as 'the pedagogy of labour'. As I see it, the concept and practice of using work in itself as a didactic instrument has a history which has in modern times assumed a new character (Field, 1992). What is significant about the NVQ system is that it represents an attempt to construct at national level a rational, coherent and transparent system of qualifications, based on national standards which are drawn from social scientific methods of occupational analysis. Furthermore, its founding principles are designed in such a way as to uncouple the traditional association between qualifications and courses of training; rather, in principle at least, the link between qualifications and occupations is direct and potentially unmediated, so that an individual may work towards a qualification simply through the assessment of her performance in her job. This development has been tied in some critical accounts to the predominance of an allegedly 'post-Fordist' organization of work in the contemporary economy (Edwards, 1993). However, the evidence presented here suggests that NVQs have arisen less because of demand from those involved in managing labour than from the ideas and aspirations of a small coalition of modernizing civil servants and highly placed training professionals. In essence, the market for NVQs is largely confined to different arms of the Government.

National Vocational Qualifications: the implementation

Responsibility for the introduction of NVQs is usually accorded to the 1986 *Review of Vocational Qualifications* chaired by Oscar de Ville (MSC/DES, 1986). However, this is to foreshorten a more sustained reform effort. Quite aside from the election of the Thatcher Government in 1979, with its vigorous interest in youth training as an instrument for managing unemployment, the decline of the apprenticeship system throughout much of industry can be dated back to the later 1960s, with consequences in turn for the qualifications system which it had nurtured. One of the major concerns expressed by the Donovan Commission on industrial relations in its 1968 report was the apprenticeship system's 'failure to develop objective standards' (Aldcroft, 1992, pp. 57–8). Hints of reform in the vocational qualifications system came in 1982, with the publication of the *New Training Initiative* (MSC, 1981). As well as identifying priorities in youth and adult training, the report called for the establishment of clear occupational standards to guide the training system. These were introduced in the Youth Training Scheme as 'standard tasks' then grouped in 1984 into 'modules of accreditation'. *Training for Jobs* in early 1984 foreshadowed the creation of 'a coherent system of training standards and certificates of competence' (HMSO, 1984). In 1985, unit-based schemes were tried out in the catering and horse management industries (Marshall, 1991, p. 56).

Some years of criticism and experiment, then, predated de Ville's review committee, with its call for 'an effective national system for vocational qualifications' which 'recognises competence and capability in the application of knowledge and skills' (MSC/DES, 1986, pp. 16, 30). The *Review* criticized existing arrangements for identifying occupational standards; however, it was agnostic about precisely how these should be drawn up, and how individual attainment against them should be assessed, calling for a National Council for Vocational Qualifications to be created which should have oversight of these matters. The NCVQ was created almost immediately, and was set the ambitious target of putting NVQs in place covering 80 per cent of the workforce by the end of 1992. In the event, that broad target was apparently achieved, in that, according to government estimates, those occupations engaged in by some 76 per cent of the workforce were covered potentially by NVQs up to Level 4 by the end of October 1992 (*Times Higher Education Supplement*, 30 October 1992).

Why did NVQs emerge when they did and in the shape that they now assume? There seems little doubt that they were conceived and promoted as part of a wider strategy designed to encourage the creation of a more flexible, skilled and mobile workforce. Put at its crudest, the early designs for what later became NVQs were being drafted at a time when Government was expressing growing concern about the lack of flexibility of the British workforce. The resulting rigidities in the labour market could in part be corrected by forms of training which encouraged the acquisition of new skills, and by the development of a qualifications system which was both transparent and focused upon the demands of the workplace. A series of official reports published in the early 1980s linked Britain's 'training deficit' with her economic performance (Aldcroft, 1992), claiming that it was not only the possession of skills which counted but the capacity to carry skills between jobs. Flexibility and skill transfer therefore became important goals within wider fields of government policy on training and the labour market.

Much critical comment so far has tended to share the assumptions behind the official diagnosis, even if they do not endorse the prescriptions. If we start to question the underlying assumptions, though, two sets of questions arise. The first set concerns flexibility: is it true that there is a marked rise in the demand for greater flexibility in the workforce, and to what extent is this linked to the possession of portable qualifications as opposed to other factors such as physical and geographical mobility? The second set concerns the nature of the 'training deficit': what kinds of skills bottlenecks can be identified, and to what extent might they be alleviated by interventions in the qualifications system?

Vocational qualifications and the labour market

Occupational flexibility has been the subject of intense debate in recent years. On the one hand are those who argue that capitalism has surpassed its 'Fordist' phase, which was characterized by the aggregation of un- and semi-skilled labour in large units undertaking the mass production of standardized goods (Murray, 1989; Allen, 1992). In the place of the Fordist 'mass worker', contemporary capital is held to require an increasingly adaptable labour force, which can adjust (or be adjusted) to dramatic changes in increasingly global product markets. While the range of those who detect the presence of occupational flexibility range from the NCVQ and, of course, the Government through to neo-Marxists such as Robin Murray, there is considerable doubt whether they are right to detect a major, generalizable shift across the labour market as a whole, rather than a series of situationally specific transitions in particular segments of the labour market (Kern and Schumann, 1990, pp. 300–18). Thus, together with change and transformation we can also detect major continuities, such as the secular change in the economy and workforce which has led to the numerical dominance of white-collar occupations (Pollert, 1991). It is clear that some of the phenomena which were taken in the late 1980s as signs of enhanced flexibility were in fact relatively short-lived; thus the growth of the small-firm sector can be explained primarily through the job-shedding policies of large firms throughout the 1980s, rather than their collective impulse to subcontract parts of their operation to peripheral organizations (Johnson, 1991, p. 255). Similarly with the growth of part-time work, much of which can be explained through increased participation in the labour market among women; or multi-skilling, whose extent remains extremely small scale. Empirically, it is hard to determine the scale of flexibilization with any accuracy. Nor is it clear how far flexibilization is simply another way of describing ongoing managerial responses to uncertainty and competition in the product market. To the extent that product markets are increasingly subject to worldwide competitive pressures, flexibilization may indeed represent more of a return to the highly competitive capitalism of Victorian and Edwardian Britain – what might be called 'pre-Fordism' – rather than an absolute break with the past. As Hyman (1991, p. 282) has argued,

> the multiple sources of instability in national and international economic relations offer the prospect of a sustained phase of disturbance and

disruption. Flexibilisation is therefore not simply a one-off process of removing a set of entrenched rigidities, but also a means of adapting institutions and expectations to the certainty of uncertainty.

How particular managements respond to these uncertainties, Hyman (1991, p. 283) reminds us, is another matter; and each response selected carries with it the risk of introducing new rigidities, or of destabilizing those rigidities that were not on the agenda of management-led change. The point is, then, to emphasize that there is no single, abstract labour market in general; but rather a series of overlapping markets for labour, both internal and external, which are subject to a range of pressures for change, some long-term and some short-term. It is by no means clear that greater flexibility has as yet become a powerful requirement within these specific labour markets on any scale.

It is reasonable to suppose, then, that flexibility is more talked about than experienced. None the less, intensified competitive pressures have fostered at least a search for flexibility; to what extent can changes in the qualifications system support that search? Many of the features of NVQs – their unit-based structure, their transparency and their transferability – make them at least potentially a highly portable qualifications system. On the surface, then, they seem to display many of the design features which meet the requirements of occupational flexibilization. However, this is to overplay the significance which qualifications of any kind are likely to possess in the labour market.

A number of separate issues arise here. First is the question of whether or not vocational qualifications routinely play a significant role in employers' recruitment decisions. Empirically, there is abundant evidence that they do not; in general, formal qualifications are one of a number of variables involved in obtaining and advancing in a particular job (Dale and Pires, 1984). In the external labour markets for un- and semi-skilled occupations, for both workers and employers it costs more to seek to match each individual's formal qualifications with a job specification than the search yields in rewards; the more specialized the occupation, the more economical the search. Other than in more specialized occupations, only where there are other rewards – or sanctions – will both parties submit to this search. An example would be an enterprise that has adopted a policy towards equal opportunities which then requires both employer and job-seeker to scrutinize job specifications in the light of the applicant's proven capabilities. In internal labour markets, it remains the case that experience of a job is often deemed to be the strongest basis for career advancement; the internal information system, formal and informal, largely displaces the need for any formal certification. Hence the preference is for recruiting labour and then, if at all, developing a training plan, rather than rigorously seeking to recruit those with the best formal qualifications. Any attempt, for example by trade unions, to enhance the role of formal qualifications is likely, in my own findings, to be resisted by personnel managers as a contract upon flexibilization.

Second, there is the question of whether the information required in labour markets is supplied by the vocational qualifications system. This is particularly at issue if the flexibilization thesis does hold water, as many of the capabilities which employers are likely to seek are not likely to be categorized reliably by the qualifications system. Blackburn and Mann found in the 1970s that managers stressed such affective qualities as 'responsibility, stability, trustworthiness' in making their recruitment and promotions decisions (Blackburn and Mann, 1979, p. 280). More recently, a Dutch study found personnel managers identifying such 'social-normative' attitudinal requirements as 'responsibility, reliability, accuracy', communication skills and obedience to company norms (Ostenk *et al.*, 1991, p. 5). My own findings repeat those of Blackburn and Mann in the 1970s: 'From the employer's point of view, the internal labour market allows workers to demonstrate these qualities (if they have them) over a number of years before they reach jobs where mistakes would matter' (Blackburn and Mann, 1979, p. 280). Occupational qualifications which are necessarily silent on social-normative qualities will tend to be largely disregarded in the labour market.

NVQs and the labour market

Conceptually, changes in qualifications systems need to be distinguished from changes in skills outputs. What are the skills shortage areas in Britain, and how do changes in qualifications systems affect them? Considerable effort has been spent in recent years on the identification of skills shortage areas in Britain, especially in comparison with our major competitor nations, and the results appear to be reasonably consistent. A number of researchers have concluded that although there are question marks over Britain's performance in basic numeracy and communicating training, as well as over the economic relevance of the higher education system, it is at the intermediate skills level (i.e. those above routine skills but below professional ones) that there is a marked discrepancy between the British labour force and those of its major competitors (the research is summarized in Ryan, 1991; and Aldcroft, 1992). Yet despite this identifiable deficit at the intermediate level, there is strong evidence to suggest that the market for NVQs is confined mainly to rudimentary entry qualifications to low-skill-level occupations.

Stated bluntly, the NVQ system has failed to tackle this key skills problem. By the end of 1993, some 1,346 NVQs were in place, compared with 392 twelve months previously (see Tables 7.1 and 7.2). The 1993 list of NVQs in place was published approximately one year after the

Table 7.1 The scope of national vocational qualifications in place by autumn
1992

	Total NVQs in place (%)	Certificates awarded (%)
Level 1	23.9	18.6
Level 2	43.9	62.2
Level 3	18.1	3.7
Level 4	13.3	15.4
Level 5	0.8	0.1
Total	(392)	(92,905)

Source: The NVQ Monitor, September 1992, December 1992.

Table 7.2 The scope of national vocational qualifications in place by autumn
1993

	Total NVQs in place December 1993 (%)	Certificates awarded, September 1993 (%)
Level 1	16.1	34.3
Level 2	42.6	57.6
Level 3	28.0	2.8
Level 4	12.4	5.2
Level 5	0.8	0.1
Total	(1,346)	(341,812)

Source: The NVQ Monitor, Winter 1993/1994.

Government judged that some 76 per cent of the workforce was covered
by the new system. Of these qualifications, nearly three-fifths were at the
lowest two levels. Indeed, 16 per cent of all NVQs listed in late 1993 were
at Level 1; nothing corresponds to such an elementary skills level in either
the German or French vocational qualifications systems. The intermediate
skills level overlaps the upper part of Level 3, with just 28 per cent of the
NVQs in place, and Level 4, with a further 12 per cent. However,
the Level 3 NVQs, and to a lesser extent Level 4, are predominantly in the
areas of goods and services, construction and health care, rather than engineering and other manufacturing occupations. At this stage, the important
fact to note is that the vast majority of NVQs in existence were at an
elementary level.

Similarly with the NVQ certificates so far awarded. By the end of
September 1993, a grand total of 341,812 NVQ certificates had been
awarded (NVQ Monitor, Winter 1993/1994). While this represents a substantial rise on the total of 92,905 certificates awarded under the NVQ system

by September 1992, the proportion of certificates at the lowest skills levels, far from changing since September 1992, had in fact increased over the intervening twelve months: whereas four-fifths were at Level 1 or 2 in September 1992, by the autumn of 1993 the proportion at these levels had risen to 92 per cent! Meanwhile, while a mere 3.7 per cent were awarded at Level 3 in autumn 1992, twelve months later the figure had shrunk to 2.8 per cent. By far the largest single numbers of NVQs were at Level 2; almost one-third of the Level 2 certificates were issued in business administration and a further one-quarter were in hairdressing. At Level 1, one-half of the certificates awarded were in business administration and a further quarter were in 'public service (armed service)'.

Thus in the early years at least, the qualifications being awarded were almost entirely at the lowest levels of skill and competence envisaged. Furthermore, across the board they reflected skill areas with little or no connection with the manufacturing sector. If it would be wrong to make too much of these figures, they suggest that NVQs' contribution towards the identified shortages of intermediate skills, especially in technician and manufacturing occupations, is negligible.

Further evidence of the bias inherent in the system can be seen in the higher level of qualification. At the professional level, the impact of NVQs has mostly been indirect rather than direct. Few qualifications exist at Levels 4 and 5, and fewer still have been awarded. Indeed, the take-up at higher levels has grown much more slowly than at Levels 1 and 2, where the purchasing power of TECs and the Further Education Funding Council have made themselves felt. Almost all of the Level 4 certificates were in accountancy, involving chiefly such awards as those of the Association of Accounting Technicians. From 1993 on, demand for higher-level NVQs started to grow, albeit slowly. Demand is mostly from government agencies and departments such as Royal Mail and the Benefits Agency where the influence and support of the Cabinet Office has encouraged human resources managers to switch their purchasing to higher-level NVQs and away from more traditional forms of management development. In addition, the autumn 1993 Budget introduced tax exemptions for individuals' expenses incurred while working towards an NVQ, in an attempt to stimulate the market among higher-band tax-payers. While it was notable that demand for higher-level NVQs was, outside accountancy, minimal in late 1993, the momentum for higher-level NVQs in the public sector had started to rise by early 1994. In turn, providers had started to position themselves to compete in this new market, for example with the creation of the Management Verification Consortium by the Association of Business Schools. Once more, though, the main purchasing forces were Government-led.

It remains the case, however, that demand for professional-level qualifications is low. In the field of training and development, for example, 22 qualifications existed by the end of 1993, but a mere 49 had apparently been awarded *(NVQ Monitor,* Winter 1993/1994, p. 34). While it is true that much larger numbers are registered for NVQs, or are being assessed for single units within NVQs, the overall numbers completing are remarkably low. The largest single number of qualifications awarded at Level 4 is in Management, where 1,621 certificates had been issued at Level 5. This, however, reflected the peculiarities of a niche market within the wider management development market; in addition, the lead body for management (the Management Charter Initiative) is also an awarding body and a private company, and has managed to exert some independence within the broad NVQ framework. However, it was not to reform professional-level qualifications that NVQs were introduced, but to address the much broader challenges of upgrading the skills, flexibility and qualifications of the labour force as a whole, especially in those areas regarded as vital to national prosperity. The system that has emerged, however, has been heavily biased towards the lowest end of the range.

It is relatively simple to explain why this pattern has emerged. Typically, intermediate skills are costly to develop, and are likely to fall victim to market failure; they are at least potentially highly transferable across employers, thus providing an incentive to employers to poach rather than train wherever possible. This is therefore a field where state action is likely to prove both effective as an investment and to possess legitimacy amongst most major players. However, changes in the qualifications system are probably the least effective means of dealing with skills shortages at this level. For example, poaching has hardly been hindered by the absence of transparent, coherent, nationally determined occupational standards! On the other hand, the NVQ system has found a ready market among public purchasers of qualifications. In fact, the single largest market has been among colleges offering full-time training to young people; these are financed through the Further Education Funding Council, whose funding priorities – largely set by Government – favour the purchase of NVQs. The second major market has been among providers of training programmes for unemployed people; these are mainly financed through Training and Enterprise Councils and Local Enterprise Companies, whose government-set funding priorities also favour the purchase of NVQs. There is thus a powerful bias in the market towards the mass purchase of low-skill, entry-level qualifications.

Changes in the qualifications system are therefore unlikely to make much of a contribution towards the identified shortages in the labour market. When it comes to considering the actual role of NVQs within the workplace, it is also important to recall that they are, by international standards, relatively narrowly focused and have been developed chiefly at the most basic skills level. This skewed pattern suggests that the determining factors may lie at least in part on the supply rather than the demand side. This can be confirmed by such evidence as currently exists of the existing impact of NVQs within the workplace.

NVQs in the workplace

In November 1992, the Employment Secretary announced the launch of a campaign in the spring 'to put NVQs on the map' *(Times Educational Supplement,* 13 November 1992). A month later, a survey of 70 companies in the leisure industries with 260,000 employees concluded that employers were 'mainly unaware' of NVQs *(Times Educational Supplement,* 11 December 1992). Similar conclusions have come from HM Inspectors in their reports on NVQs in further education colleges, as well as from other surveys of industrial responses to NVQs including those carried out by employers' organizations (Maguire *et al.,* 1993, p. 23). These messages alone should cause some scepticism over the claim that the NVQ system is 'employment-led'. That claim will now be put under closer scrutiny.

The claim that NVQs are 'employment-led' relies largely upon the role of the industry lead bodies in determining the national standards frameworks for their respective industries. This is an area which deserves far closer study. Constitutionally, the lead bodies are dominated by employers' representatives. Superficially, then, employment interests do indeed lead the system. However, there are two intervening factors which shape the way in which that representation of the employment interest operates in practice. First, there is the question of which types of 'employer' actually sit on the lead bodies; although no comprehensive study of their membership has yet been carried out, my own preliminary investigations have led me to question how far we can describe the lead body membership as representing employers at all. Rather, they consist of a mix of particular types of managerial profession, the majority of whom have senior personnel responsibilities (usually in the larger companies) or work in training administration (for example, in TECs, training boards or the training departments of the larger firms). They also include a wide sprinkling of 'consultants', some of whom have a long history of involvement in the Employment Department and its quangos (the most visible of this group is Canon George Tolley, but he is far from the only example). These highly specialized professionals are far from the generalized 'employers' who are represented in the rhetoric as driving the system; rather, they bring their own organizational expertise and interests into the NVQ system. Second, there is the question of how the lead bodies have gone about the process of identifying the national occupational standards. In practice, most lead bodies have contracted the task out to consultants, and scrutinized the results through a series of small working groups, supported by advisers from the Employment Department. These working groups have commissioned consultants to produce the standards around which particular NVQs are organized; it is reportedly rare for the lead bodies to discuss the standards in any detail once they have been agreed by the working groups. This process casts further doubt upon the claim that the lead bodies are employer-led, at least in any straightforward sense of the term. Rather, as with many of the training innovations of the past decade (Shackleton, 1992), the initiative has lain very substantially with the professional training lobby, working through the MSC and its successor bodies.

Indeed, there is evidence that many general managers are suspicious of the new system. Their chief concern focuses around costs. Implementation costs are clearly high, largely because of the labour-intensive nature of the assessment process in NVQs. Most personnel managers complained that the NVQ process was 'bureaucratic' or 'time-consuming'. Such complaints emerge even in enterprises which are at an extremely early stage of development. A personnel development officer in an urban NHS trust, for example, stated that: 'it is time-consuming. . . . It takes time to get NVQs into the organization, and time is money, and there is the release of the assessor to be trained, that also takes time.' Almost all personnel managers interviewed also made critical comments over the volume of paperwork generated by the NVQ system once it was in place.

Particular criticism was levelled at the assessment procedure. Assessors tend to be drawn from the supervisory ranks, and their labour costs are therefore higher than the average; the assessment process rests upon repeated observation over time within the workplace, often requiring extreme detail. One training manager, working in a large public agency and otherwise highly enthusiastic about NVQs, said that 'we do have a responsibility to get the work done so we have to be careful that the tail isn't wagging the dog, and that our staff are actually working in the workplace.'

In another workplace (a Midlands pig station), it was clear that assessment by supervisors was functioning in quite a different way from that intended; so long as the supervisors were satisfied with trainees' performance at the level of overall output (in this instance, weaning piglets), they were simply ticking all the relevant boxes in the trainees' log books, with little concern for whether or not each particular unit of competence was being demonstrated in performance.

Flexibility of employment has been a hallmark of government policy towards training for those in work. However, personnel managers saw things rather differently. One pointed out that although the new system was unit-based, thus allowing consumer choice in principle, in practice qualifications were only available for those who followed centrally prescribed routes:

> NVQs are supposed to be flexible but I find them quite rigid. For example, the way that they group their awards, like in Care – if you can't get one of the units you cannot get an award, so you have got to be able to prove yourself in a certain area, even if you are not involved in it. . . . In Mental Health Care, for example, one of the units is maintaining and control of stock and equipment – how they decide upon that as a unit for a Mental Health Care award I do not know! . . . In

order for someone to pass that unit we are going to have to place them in a situation that they will never be in again in their job.

Another training manager was running simulation exercises in order to cover the range of competences required for the award. The phrase 'red tape' was constantly used to describe what most of our sample – admittedly very restricted – saw as needless rigidity in the system.

Finally, and ironically, personnel managers were concerned that the transparency of the NVQ system might encourage more labour flexibility than they deemed desirable. Underlying such views were two practical concerns. First, several interviewees said that the possession of NVQs might encourage employees actively to seek work elsewhere, contributing to a rise in labour turnover to damaging levels, particularly among the more motivated and highly qualified staff. Second, a number of interviewees feared that the NVQ system might foster 'unrealistic' expectations of promotion and career development among staff. One training manager argued that the nature of NVQs could be taken as encouraging stability rather than flexibility in the internal labour market, but he was alone in our sample in doing so. He expressed this view as follows:

> When people first came onto the scheme they thought they could aspire to a higher level and this isn't possible. The competence programmes are designed to enable people to demonstrate the competences in the job they are currently in, not for somebody to look higher because it just isn't possible if you haven't got the job role to demonstrate the competences.

More typical was the view that the possession of a transparent qualification encouraged staff to seek greater mobility; this was held to be undesirable, potentially creating conflicts over such issues as gradings of staff whose vocational qualification showed them to be working at a higher level than that at which they were paid.

As against the criticisms, there were of course also a number of perceived benefits. Those identified in the interviews included the fact that NVQs are workplace-based (and therefore subject to direct managerial control, as well as potentially facilitating cost-cutting); the quality assurance gains of training against defined national standards; the coherence of the new system; and NVQs' compatibility with modern strategies of human resource management (one public agency manager claimed that NVQs were a strand in the wider process of 'empowerment of field staff and the inversion of the pyramid', for instance). At the same time, no one had as yet been able to think of a way of quantifying the benefits; indeed, one manager – himself keen on NVQs – described his investment in the new system as representing 'a massive act of faith'. Thus the benefits remain to some extent uncertain and unproven; for most managers in our sample, NVQs are a 'motherhood' concept at the general level but this is hardly surprising given that the system was allegedly designed to meet their needs. What is more significant is the evidence that, even among this group who are actively involved in the NVQ system, the practical drawbacks are as salient as they are.

Given the nature of the NVQ system, it is reasonable to suppose that managers who express doubts are generally rational in their approach. Compared with time-based exams, NVQs are indeed an expensive process; moreover, the charge is made visible and is direct to the employer (or sometimes the candidate), rather than being absorbed by the public education system (which anyway relies on the availability of examiners willing to work for pin money). Costs can be avoided by short-circuiting the assessment procedures (like the pig station supervisor who assessed a trainee weaning every day for a week), but this then tends to devalue the currency. A study of companies in the leisure industry suggested that two-fifths of firms did not intend even to test the NVQ system because of the costs (*Times Educational Supplement,* 11 December 1992). Given the intensive nature of assessment and verification, there are economies of scale in principle (Hawes, 1990); but these can only be triggered where a substantial group of candidates are submitting simultaneously. Where NVQs have a role in firms, it is frequently as a screen for initial recruitment; the expectation that the new recruits will pick up the job as they go along is apparently as strong as ever. While there is some evidence that trade unions are keen to use NVQs as a bargaining lever, training still tends to be seen as a supplementary item which can be 'traded off' during negotiations (Field and Weller, 1992).

It appears that NVQs have a limited market among companies, then. In so far as there has been sufficient demand to keep the system alive, it has been almost entirely created by the state. Central Government has focused its purchasing power in the training market in order to create a viable demand for NVQs; for example, limits on the use of youth credits, TEC funding for Youth and Adult Training and public funding for further education colleges have all been focused in this way. This has had the effect of creating an enormous demand for entry-level NVQs for younger people and the long-term unemployed; naturally, these are at levels and in sectors where there is a demand for new, usually young entrants. The Employment Department has also sought to encourage other government departments to use NVQs in personnel policies, but with more limited success; the Department of Health was among those which withdrew from the pilot scheme, allegedly as a cost-cutting measure. Demand for NVQs consists, then, largely of what might be called 'quasi-markets', created largely by the focused purchasing power of the state. Like other quasi-market systems, the costs of introduction and maintenance can be high; in the case of the TECs there have been persistent complaints of the detailed administration required in order to achieve performance-related funding (see also Hudson, 1992). The consequences can also be seen in the existing shape of the NVQ system: a handful of higher intermediate level NVQs in areas where a particular lobby has made itself felt (such as management development), and a mass of lower-level NVQs for newcomers and re-entrants to the labour market.

Of course, there are employers who are positive about NVQs and see them as contributing greatly towards their human resource strategies. Unwin's case study of Courtaulds Grafil is a case in point: the switch to a company-based system, which cost some £500,000 as part of a shift in the reward system for process operators (Unwin, 1991, pp. 174–80). However, this requires a longer-term view of human resource investments than is common in the UK – a point made by the company's chief executive. It also rests upon a desire to separate out a relatively homogeneous operative-level workforce, a specific context which will only apply in similar circumstances. Against this must be set the far more frequent complaints of employers that NVQs are too expensive and too complex.

Vocational qualifications as a tool for political management

NVQS have developed, then, through a heavily sponsored quasi-market, and have been shaped in large part by the nature of that market. They are indeed driven by 'employment interests', but that broad term needs to be further defined. It is no easy matter to reconcile the abstract phrase 'employment interests' with the human reality of the industry lead bodies and the NCVQ. In practice, those who have led the system have been a very loose and broad coalition of enlightened civil servants, chiefly from within the Employment Department, together with professional training specialists, often with close commercial connections with the Employment Department, and with personnel managers in some of our larger companies. What this amounts to is a highly selective coalition which has sought to present itself as plausibly representing the interests of 'employment'. The system itself was created in a context of considerable concern over skills shortages, combined with politically driven attempts to erode Welfare State systems and increase the role of the market in the provision of services. Finally, it was created during the high point of the Manpower Services Commission's influence – an influence which has now itself been substantially, though far from fatally, weakened. It is against this background that the creation of the NVQ system must, I would argue, be understood, and its prospects for the future assessed.

In itself, the NVQ system represents an abstract design for a national standards-based qualifications system. Its design stage was undertaken in the relatively rarefied atmosphere of the hotel and seminar circuit, involving a number of highly specialized studies of particular occupational groupings which were then translated into a series of behavioural objectives. Once the design stage was over, the products had to be brought to market. This process was dominated, and continues to be dominated, by the purchasing power of the State; the consequence is that the actual demand for NVQs continues to be dominated by particular policy imperatives. The most significant of these is the need to manage unemployment; thus the main market for NVQs has been among those government agencies such as TECs and the Further Education Funding Council which provide full-time training for young people who are, or who would otherwise become, unemployed. Visibly, the consequence has been to skew demand towards those types of NVQ which are most in demand in that part of the market: essentially, lower-level NVQs in areas where the prospects of a successful outcome are highest. Demand among employers is higher in the public than in the private sector, and this too can be traced to government policy. Thus major government departments and agencies have been stimulated by advice and support from the development division of the Cabinet Office in elaborating their own proposals for introducing NVQs. Here there is more scope for widening the market for NVQs above Level 2, although it is notable that even in the public sector the largest market by far has been for Level 1 qualifications in the armed services. This downward drift may be helpful in political management in a number of ways, but it has little to do with generating a genuine demand for the product.

Rather, it seems that the market among employers for NVQs is limited because qualifications in themselves are the answer to a set of problems which employers neither recognize nor accept ownership of. This may well be inevitable: from the point of view of any individual employer, reform of the qualifications system may be a good thing in general, but in practical terms it has little to do with them in particular. Restructuring of the qualifications system may, by generating increased labour flexibility, even run counter to the wishes and aims of the individual employer; it is therefore only defensible as a public good, undertaken by the State as a counter-balance to the allegedly destructive consequences of an otherwise untrammelled market. The difficulty with NVQs is that they are presented as an employment-led qualifications system, which it is then claimed are offered on a market basis. In fact they are entirely a creation of the State. When implemented in actually existing workplaces, they therefore appear to function in very different ways from those intended in the abstract by their designers.

Where does all this leave professional trainers and educators? First, from a purely pragmatic perspective, it seems reasonable to expect that involvement in NVQs represents a worthwhile investment of time and energy, at least so long as Government continues to back the NVQ bandwagon. In particular, the purchasing power of TECs, government departments and the Further Education Funding Council is sufficient to ensure a market for

NVQs of very substantial size. Second, it then follows that the market will be a skewed one. Demand will continue to be buoyant in areas where government bodies make the purchasing decisions. Government will seek to influence the markets of individuals and private employers, for example by linking tax breaks for training expenditure to the purchase of NVQs; it remains to be seen whether these sweeteners will overcome the undoubted reluctance of these markets to purchase the product. Third, it also follows that the likely impact of NVQs upon the labour market will be to place limits on labour mobility and flexibility. In large parts of the labour market, and particularly the growth areas where polyvalency and multi-skilling are at a premium NVQs play a very limited role. NVQs will continue to be widespread among those who have been on unemployed training programmes, studied full-time in further education, or work for government departments and agencies, thus contributing further to labour market segmentation. Fourth, trainers and educators should be hard-headed about acquiring NVQs for themselves; while they may make for greater employability in certain labour markets at the present time, NVQs' association with low-level entry qualifications and training for the unemployed must ultimately affect their perceived status. Finally, it makes sense for educators and trainers to try to influence the content of NVQs, particularly where they impinge closely upon the fields of professional practice where trainers and educators are most directly involved. Given the dominance of professional trainers and modernizing civil servants in the construction of NVQs, it is not surprising that the system has proved itself open to influence from related groups such as academics or the management development industry to whom the NVQ movement sees itself as closely related. It is therefore reasonable to press for a more holistic and integrated concept of competence which would mark a further step away from the atomized, behaviourist and bureaucratic conception which so dominated the early thinking of the competence movement in Britain.

As things stand, current policy and practice in fact seem to have very little relationship with 'employment interests'. Rather, it seems that the main function of the NVQ initiative is to serve as a tool for policy management. Much as the training revolution of the 1980s was in fact concerned primarily with the political management of high unemployment levels, so the NVQ initiative appears to be chiefly an attempt to provide a visible response to poor economic performance and the associated public criticisms of the British training system. It is therefore not surprising that, in the early stages, NVQs found so few purchasers outside the quasi-markets created by the State.

References

Aldcroft, D. (1992) *Education, Training and Economic Performance, 1944 to 1990*. Manchester: Manchester University Press.

Allen, J. (1992) 'Fordism and modern industry'. In J. Allen, P. Braham and P. Lewis (eds) *Political and Economic Reforms of Modernity*. Cambridge: Polity Press.

Ashworth, P. D. and Saxton, J. (1990) 'On competence'. *Journal of Further and Higher Education*, 14(2), 1–25.

Blackburn, R. M. and Mann, M. (1979) *The Working Class in the Labour Market*. London: Macmillan.

Dale, R. and Pires, E. (1984) 'Linking people and jobs: the indeterminate place of educational credentials'. In P. Broadfoot (ed.) *Selection, Certification and Control: Social Issues in Educational Assessment*. Lewes: Falmer.

Edwards, R. (1993) 'The inevitable future? Post-Fordism in work and learning'. In R. Edwards, S. Sieminksi and D. Zeldin (eds) *Adult Learners, Education and Training*. London: Routledge.

Field, J. (1991) 'Competency and the pedagogy of labour'. *Studies in the Education of Adults*, 23(1), 41–52.

Field, J. (1992) *Learning through Labour: Unemployment, Training and the State 1890–1939*. Leeds: Leeds University Press.

Field, J. (1993) 'Developments in vocational qualifications: emerging implications for industrial relations'. *The Industrial Tutor*, 5(7), 5–14.

Field, J. and Weller, P. (1992) 'Trade unions and human resource development'. *The Industrial Tutor*, 5(6), 41–8.

Hawes, B. W. V. (1990) *Verification of Work-place Assessment: Cost Indicators and Organisational Implications*. Sheffield: Employment Department.

HMSO (1984) *Training for Jobs*. London: HMSO.

Hodkinson, P. (1992) 'Alternative models of competence in vocational education and training'. *Journal of Further and Higher Education*, 16(2), 30–9.

Hudson, P. (1992) 'Quasi-markets in health and social care in Britain: can the public sector respond?' *Policy and Politics*, 20(2), 131–42.

Hyland, T. (1991) 'Taking care of business: vocationalism, competence and the enterprise culture'. *Educational Studies*, 17(1), 77–87.

Hyman, R. (1991) 'Plus ça change. The theory of production and the production of theory'. In A. Pollert (ed.) *Farewell to Flexibility?* Oxford: Blackwell.

Johnson, S. (1991) 'The small firm and the UK labour market in the 1980s'. In A. Pollert (ed.) *Farewell to Flexibility?* Oxford: Blackwell.

Kern, H. and Schumann, M. (1990) *Das Ende der Arbeitsteilung? Rationalisierung in der industriellen Produktion*. Munich: C. H. Beck.

Maguire, M., Maguire, S. and Felstead, A. (1993) *Factors Influencing Individual Commitment to Lifetime Learning*. Sheffield: Employment Department.

Marshall, K. (1991) 'NVQs: an assessment of the "outcomes" approach to education and training'. *Journal of Further and Higher Education*, 15(3), 56–64.

MSC (1981) *A New Training Initiative*. Sheffield: MSC.

MSC/DES (1986) *Review of Vocational Qualifications*. London: HMSO.

Murray, R. (1989) 'Fordism and post-Fordism'. In S. Hall and M. Jacques (eds) *New Times: The Changing Face of Politics in the 1990s*. London: Lawrence and Wishart.

Ostenk, H. J., Moerkamp, T. and Dronkers, J. (1991) 'Broadly applicable occupational qualifications: a challenge for vocational education'. Conference on Learning Across the Life Span, University of Groningen.

Pollert, A. (ed.) (1991) *Farewell to Flexibility?* Oxford: Blackwell.

Ryan, P. (ed.) (1991) *International Comparisons of Vocational Education and Training for Intermediate Skills.* London: Falmer.

Shackleton, J. R. (1992) *Training Too Much? A Sceptical Look at the Economics of Skill Provision in the UK.* London: Institute of Economic Affairs.

Short, E. (1984) 'Competence re-examined'. *Education Theory,* 34(3), 201–7.

Unwin, L. (1991) 'NVQs and the man-made fibres industry: a case study'. In P. Raggatt and L. Unwin (eds) *Change and Intervention: Vocational Education and Training.* London: Falmer.

Chapter 8

A critique of NVQs and GNVQs

Alan Smithers

Ten years ago vocational education was like the scattered pieces of many different jigsaws. Although some of the individual qualifications were widely respected, they did not belong to any coherent picture. There were several hundred awarding bodies offering a great variety of qualifications, many of which led nowhere. The Rev George Tolley,[1] Principal of what was then Sheffield Polytechnic, was at the forefront of a campaign to introduce a national framework to rival the well-established academic ladder of O-levels, A-levels and degrees. The government heard the cry, set up the De Ville Committee (De Ville 1986), and accepted its recommendations for a National Council for Vocational Qualifications to oversee a national system.

A decade later, with at least £107 million of public money spent (see Robinson 1996), there is not only the former confusion, but adding to it we have NVQs and GNVQs. NVQs, which were intended to be National Vocational Qualifications, are at best Niche Vocational Qualifications, suitable mainly for assessing prior learning in the workplace. General National Vocational Qualifications are an odd variant of them for schools and colleges. Over two-thirds of vocational qualifications currently awarded are the old-style awards outside the ambit of NCVQ.[2] Both the school and further education inspectors[3] have severely criticised the contribution of NVQs and GNVQs to education 14–19. What went wrong?

It is clear – and not only with hindsight – that the fault lies in the way NCVQ interpreted its brief. The 1986 White Paper called, somewhat unfortunately in view of what happened, *Working Together – Education and Training* (DES 1986) put in train De Ville's recommendation that: 'a new National Council for Vocational Qualifications (NCVQ) should be set up to secure necessary changes, to develop the NVQ framework and to ensure standards of competence are set'.

The emphasis on standards was to ensure, quite rightly, that the system was to be employer-led, geared to the nature and levels of performance required by them. A qualification to be a qualification must be *in* and/or *for* something. Since the *raison d'être* of vocational education is to prepare for, or enhance performance in, work, it is essential that employers be involved in specifying what a particular qualification is to be about.

The National Council for Vocational Qualifications (NCVQ), however, interpreted 'standards of competence' literally and tried to turn every standard into a statement of competence. This led to an orgy of analysis resulting in highly fragmented, almost incomprehensible, qualifications. What NCVQ lamentably failed to do was to distinguish between, on the one hand, setting standards and, on the other, designing qualifications to enable those standards to be met. It tried to turn one directly into the other, missing out the vital stages of settling what was to be covered and the tests by which we would know that the standards had been reached.

This was no mere oversight, however. In Bees and Swords (1990), Gilbert Jessup, the chief architect of NVQs, proudly wrote of doing away with 'the syllabuses, the courses or the training programmes, i.e. the specification of the learning opportunities provided'. He also had particular views on assessment. In his book, *Outcomes NVQs and the Emerging Model of Education and Training* (Jessup 1991) he wrote, 'what I am proposing is that we forget about reliability altogether and concentrate on validity, which is ultimately all that matters', seemingly unaware that assessments which are not reliable cannot be valid. As might be expected, with foundations like these, the qualifications that emerged were idiosyncratic, but within NCVQ the approach became elevated to almost a religious faith, with all attempts at constructive criticism being brutally rebuffed.[4]

Belatedly, the government, through Dearing,[5] Beaumont[6] and Capey,[7] is trying to get to grips with the problem, but the flaw runs so deep that it will require a radical re-think to get us back on track. The extent of the damage can be gauged from the consequences of NCVQ's approach for the content and assessment of qualifications.

Content and assessment

Qualifications to be recognised by NCVQ have had to conform to its model. This involves breaking down the award into 'units' which are further subdivided into 'elements' which are based on lists of 'performance criteria'. The candidate has to collect 'evidence', usually in the form of a 'portfolio', that the performance criteria have been met over certain 'ranges'. Although superficially plausible, setting out the requirements this way means that the content of the qualifications is not clearly specified, nor is there any assessment of overall performance. More specifically, as regards content, the approach lacks precision, is fragmentary, does not prioritise, and devalues knowledge and understanding. Assessment is atomised, internal and bureaucratic, and is not robust enough to withstand payment by results.

Precision

NCVQ's analytical approach becomes in practice a search for the elusive irreducible building blocks of competence. The NVQ Level 2 Care (Residential/Hospital Support), for example, is set out as 11 units, 39 elements and 338 performance criteria. Although this detail is assumed to give precision, in fact the performance criteria come out as very generalised. In the unit 'Enable clients to eat and drink' the first element is 'Enable clients to choose appropriate food and drink', of which the first performance criterion is, 'The support required by the client is established with him/her'. Similarly, in the NVQ Level 3 in Engineering Assembly, the unit 'Produce assembled output by joining and fastening operations' contains the element 'Process materials to produce assembled output', which has as a performance criterion, 'Materials presented to the assembly operation are completely compliant with operational specification'.

Not only are the performance criteria generalised, but they hang in the air and are addressed to no one. If they had been written for candidates they would have said something like, 'In order to get this qualification you will have to show you can . . .', or if for employers, 'A person holding this qualification is able to . . .'. But they are written in an odd abstract language which has been shown to break the rules of grammar and therefore be very difficult to read (see Channell and St John 1996).

Fragmentation

The fault is, however, more than technical: it is fundamental. There is no guarantee that numerous individual competences – even if they could be identified, and simply and unambiguously stated – would amount to skilled overall performance. Being able to dribble and do headers do not make a footballer. It is the way they fit together that matters.

Prioritisation

NCVQ's lists of performance criteria are not only not integrated, they are not prioritised. In the NVQ Level 2 in Bus and Coach Driving and Customer Care, for example, the minutiae of customer care are treated on a par with keeping the vehicle safely on the road. NVQs take no account of time, and thus difficult decisions as to what is essential as opposed to being merely desirable do not have to be faced. This is claimed as a virtue (see Jessup 1991), an escape from the time-serving basis of old apprenticeships, but discounting time altogether conveniently side-steps difficult decisions about what can be fitted in.

Knowledge and understanding

The telephone directory approach also has profound consequences for the way knowledge and understanding are treated. It was first considered to be embedded in the performance criteria and implied by them. But even in the Revised Criteria (January 1995),[8] which are intended to lay greater stress on knowledge and understanding, it comes out as itemised and disparate 'knowledge specifications'. This means that NVQs are virtually useless as qualifications for 14 to 19-year-olds, or indeed adults preparing *for* work, since there is no coherent statement of content. Nor is there a reservoir of knowledge and understanding to enable people to cope with a changing working world or provide a platform for progression.

Assessment

The unsuitability of NVQs as qualifications *for* work, as opposed to accrediting prior learning *in* work, is underlined by the way they are assessed. NVQs were said to have been devised on the driving test model. That is, it does not matter how you have learned to drive – through a school or from a spouse or friend or any other way – what is important is that you can do it, and satisfy an independent examiner that you can. However, as they have emerged, NVQs have no equivalent of the driving test, but consist of long lists of performance criteria that have to be signed off. Given that there may be several hundred of them, the only practicable way of achieving this is to leave it to the teachers/trainers, whose main task becomes signing their name. There is some check through external verification, but that is based on inspecting portfolios of evidence rather than observing the candidate in action. Moreover, because the requirements are loose, the external verifiers are to some extent able to invent the qualifications by insisting that in the portfolio the candidate does or does not include printed material, uses 'I' or 'we' and so on. For the sake of their candidates, some private providers are having to deploy a member of staff specifically to get to know the foibles of particular verifiers.

NVQ assessment, instead of being based on tests of skilled overall performance, depends on collecting evidence in relation to checklists. It lacks the fairness, reliability and authenticity that would make it believable. Without trust the qualification cannot act as a passport between the training provider and employer. Increasingly, the only training that an employer can have confidence in is that provided in-house. Far from enabling education and training to work together, NVQs have driven a wedge between them.

Output-related funding

Not only is the assessment of NVQs intrinsically flawed, but it is not strong enough to bear the weight of the payment by results that is increasingly being adopted by Training and Enterprise Councils and, to a lesser extent, by the Further Education Funding Council. As the instances of malpractice that surface from time to time in the press illustrate,[9] the assessment arrangements leave a lot to be desired. There is ample scope to, in effect, sell NVQs or give them away if the state is paying. What NVQ assessment amounts to, in practice, is a bit like your driving being assessed by your trainer, with each item – gear changing for example – signed off as you achieve it, and the trainer only being paid if he/she passes you. No wonder most employers do not find NVQs credible.

General National Vocational Qualifications

At best NVQs accredit prior learning in the workplace. As such, they are claimed to have a motivational value for people who missed out on education first time around (see Jessup 1991). But there is also a dark side. The Beaumont Committee heard evidence that some employers have been using NVQs as part of their downsizing process by setting requirements for existing employees, in terms of being able to read and write, that they cannot meet and so leave to avoid embarrassment.

However, whatever their merits for accrediting people for the job they already have, NVQs are not, as we have seen, a good way of preparing people for work. This makes it even more bizarre that, in 1991, the government should give NCVQ the job of developing applied education in schools and colleges. The White Paper *Education and Training for the 21st Century* (HMSO 1991), introducing the new qualifications, reads as if the original intention was to build on the success of qualifications like those of the Business and Technology Education Council, but what emerged in response to the NCVQ credo was something quite different (NCVQ 1993).

The General National Vocational Qualification in Health and Social Care at intermediate level (said to be equivalent to five GCSEs at grades A–C) came out as four mandatory units, two optional units, and three core skill units comprising 31 elements and 129 performance criteria (for example, 'Key social factors which influence well-being are identified and explained'; 'Key lifestyle patterns which affect individuals are identified'). The advanced GNVQ in Leisure and Tourism (said to be equivalent to two A-levels) has eight mandatory units, four optional and three core skill units consisting of 52 elements and 310 performance criteria (for example, 'Situations when customer contact or service is commonly needed are correctly identified').

Originally NCVQ intended GNVQs to be assessed on a pass/fail basis through evidence collection in the way NVQs are, but the government insisted on some external testing, and grading of performance. Reluctantly, NCVQ introduced one-hour multiple choice tests into the mandatory units, but sidelined them from contributing to the grading which was carried out by inspecting the portfolios against the themes of data handling and evaluation, with quality only becoming a criterion later.

The weaknesses of the approach, well understood by bodies like BTEC,[10] were brought into sharp focus when NCVQ was obliged to co-operate with the School Curriculum and Assessment Authority (SCAA) in developing GNVQ Part Is. These were mooted by Sir Ron Dearing in his review of the National Curriculum (Dearing 1993) to make vocational education available to 14–16-year-olds in the time of two GCSEs. The two halves of the joint SCAA/NCVQ committee found themselves speaking very different languages. At one stage, each pilot GNVQ Part I was drafted with a line down the middle of the page, with NCVQ's performance criteria, range statements and evidence indicators on the left, and, on the right, SCAA's amplification, which amounted to a syllabus and test arrangements. It was only through SCAA's approach that it was realised that most of the biology was missing from the intermediate GNVQ in Health and Social Care.

Gradually, the SCAA view prevailed and it is beginning to suffuse the whole GNVQ structure, not just Part Is. In the latest thinking, the GNVQ requirements will include some specification of content and assessment involving substantial tests of knowledge and depth of understanding and externally set assignments. But what a lot of time has been wasted through starting in the wrong place.

Take-up

What has really forced a reappraisal of both NVQs and GNVQs has been the growing realisation that the people for whom they are intended are not using them and, even if they do, they drop out in unacceptable numbers. The Confederation of British Industry, a strong supporter of the vocational reforms, in 1994 published a report exposing the low take-up and high cost, and making 68 recommendations for improvement which amounted to a complete redesign (CBI 1994).

While John Hillier, the Chief Executive of NCVQ, was comfortingly reassuring the Education Committee of the House of Commons in January 1996:

> To refer to the low uptake of a qualification that has only existed since 1990, now has in excess of a million people holding the qualification, and over three million working towards it, and whose uptake has been increasing steadily at the rate of 30 per cent per year and is continuing to do so, does seem to me simply to fly in the face of the facts,[11]

Peter Robinson of the London School of Economics was beavering away checking all the publicly available figures. He found (Robinson 1996):

- 660,000 *not* 3 million working towards NVQs;
- against a target of 50 per cent of the workforce to be working towards NVQ Level 3 by 1996, only 2 per cent were doing so by spring 1995;
- of 794 NVQs on the books, 364 had not been completed by anyone and 43 had been completed by only one person;
- the NVQs that are taken are in the internationally sheltered service occupations – clerical, secretarial, personal service and sales;
- over two-thirds of vocational qualifications currently awarded are the old-style pre-NVQ awards;
- NVQs do not appear to have added to the total training taken but have increased the complexity of provision.

John Hillier has once more responded by attacking the messenger.[12]

Similarly, GNVQs have officially been presented as a great success story. In August 1995 the National Awarding Bodies brought out a confident press release[13] claiming, '100,000 GNVQs successes and still growing'. However, contained within the notice were figures which showed:

- the 100,000 was based on 61,604 completions and 41,378 who had only passed some units;
- the completions were only about a third of the students who had registered to take the award;
- that of the 13,165 advanced passes (compared with 64,000 BTEC National Diplomas), 6,651 were in business and 1,669 in art and design (compared with the 21,818 and 31,534 at A-level respectively); only Health and Social Care (1,936) and Leisure and Tourism (2,340) seemed to be breaking new ground.

The Joint Council of National Vocational Awarding Bodies followed up their '100,000 successes' a year later with a press release[14] in August 1996 proclaiming 'Record numbers of GNVQ awards'. But this time the registration figures were conspicuously absent. However, comparing the 1996 completions for the advanced GNVQ with the 1994 registrations (since the courses could be expected to take two years) shows at best a pass rate of about 40 per cent. Over 90 per cent of those awards were in business, leisure and tourism, health and social care, and art and design. Manufacturing, engineering, construction and the built environment, information technology and science contributed only 1,749 awards between them.

The existence of advanced GNVQs alongside A-levels in business studies, art and design, the sciences and technology does raise the question of their respective roles. Why should a student do an advanced GNVQ rather than an A-level in, say, science? Is it a case of those who can – do A-levels; those who can't – do GNVQs? Or do the awards serve different purposes?

If so, what are they? These were some of the issues addressed by Dearing's review of qualifications for 16–19-year-olds.

Reviews

In spite of the generally rosy picture of the progress of NVQs and GNVQs presented by NCVQ, the system has come under intense government scrutiny. Gordon Beaumont (1996), recently retired Corporate Development Director of Alfred MacAlpine plc, and former Chairman of the CBI Training Policy Panel, was asked to review the top 100 NVQs. Dr John Capey (1995), Principal of Exeter Further Education College, was asked to review the GNVQ assessment system. The ubiquitous Sir Ron Dearing (1996), on completing his review of the National Curriculum, was asked to consider and report on qualifications for 16–19-year-olds. But perhaps most important of all for the future of vocational education, NCVQ itself was subject to a quinquennial review.[15]

Beaumont

Beaumont's review of NVQs was originally intended to be an in-house affair with NCVQ operating under a contract from the then Employment Department, Beaumont advised by NCVQ's Evaluation and Advisory Group and his report to go first to NCVQ Council. In the event, Beaumont was encouraged by ministers to be more independent and several new members were added to the committee, including myself. His report also went directly to the government, with NCVQ Council allowed to comment on it subsequently.

Beaumont produced a potentially hard-hitting report:

- It suggested that setting standards and designing qualifications should be separated (p. 5: *'It is proposed that standards are written for employers. Qualifications, training and the development of assessment needs should be separately specified'*).
- It recognised that NVQs as presently framed are all but incomprehensible (p. 13: *'Standards are marred by complex jargon ridden language'*; p. 28: *'The complex and jargon ridden language used is universally condemned.'*).
- It identified a number of problems with assessment (p. 13: *'Assessors and verifiers are unsure of the standards they are judging and their views differ'*; p. 19: *'External verifiers suffer from combining incompatible roles'*).
- It found that the assessment system is not robust enough to withstand output-related funding (p. 7: *'Funding programmes and policy should be harmonised with qualification systems'*; p. 40: *'Funding by outputs brings a potential for conflicts of interest'*).

- It recognised that NVQs do not provide a training route for unemployed young people or adults (p. 26: '*The fact that NVQs are work-based prevents those not in work from obtaining the qualifications*').

But the edge is taken off of it by the claim, 'There is widespread support for the NVQ concept'. There is certainly widespread support for introducing good occupational awards but it is not clear that this is for NVQs as they stand.

For example, 'competence' is defined in the Consultation Document as 'The ability to apply knowledge and understanding in performing to the standards required in employment, including solving problems and meeting changing demands' ('skills' was added later). Most people, myself included, would have no difficulty in signing up to this.

But it is different from 'competence' as it is used in devising NVQs where 'functional analysis' seeks to arrive at numerous (often several hundred) 'competences'. Beaumont himself used competence in this sense on p. 13, where he wrote: 'Candidates are unsure of the competences they are trying to achieve.' So just what is 'the concept' for which there is apparently widespread support – capability or a competence catalogue?

The claim in the report that most employers are in favour of NVQs (the percentage is variously put at between 80 and 90 per cent) is based on a very shaky sample. In fact, fewer than one in five of the employers contacted bothered to respond in spite of boosting the sample and frequent follow-ups. Neither of the claims tallies with the CBI report (CBI 1994) expressing concern at the low take-up of NVQs. If employers were using them there would be no problem. They are not, so there is.

It gradually dawned on Beaumont that NVQs were not working, but what he saw as a language problem is a concept problem. This will become increasingly apparent as attempts are made to get NVQs into plain English (or plain Welsh as Beaumont disarmingly reiterates). So long as NVQs are frozen at the stage of fragmenting into competences there will be problems.

Capey

Capey had a specific remit: 'to review GNVQ assessment and grading'. His findings as encapsulated on page 22 were: 'the evidence presented to the review group was unequivocal in identifying the need for a further simplification of the GNVQ assessment and recording requirements'. But the recommendations are disappointing in that the review group seems to have got bogged down in NCVQ-speak rather than going to the heart of the matter.

Capey recognises (p. 23): 'the GNVQ differs significantly from the NVQ in its broader purpose and range . . . this in itself is sufficient to justify a different approach to the assessment of outcomes'. But this is not followed through by asking what good applied education should consist of, and how it should be assessed. NCVQ-speak tends to cause people, including Capey, to take their eye off the ball. Essentially, with applied education it matters *what* is being learned not *how* it is being learned. Curiously, this was one of the early tenets of NCVQ which seems to have got lost in the keenness to prescribe particular styles of learning.

Capey becomes enmeshed in learning styles and goes beyond his remit when in the executive summary he contends (p. 7): 'Many students are being motivated by the independent approach to learning that the GNVQ offers.' This does not square with the failure of two-thirds of registered students to complete. Moreover, the style of learning is largely irrelevant if the focus is outcomes. Crucial here is the credibility of the assessment process. This is likely to involve some external practical and written tests: just what Capey was set up to advise on and where notably he fails to give a clear lead.

NCVQ has attempted to put a gloss on both Capey and Beaumont. In the NCVQ's foreword to Capey it claims to have support for 'the characteristics of GNVQ' and 'the philosophy and structure' when neither was part of the remit. Nor are these claims sustainable when so many of those attempting to deliver GNVQs are gagged from commenting on them.'[16]

Dearing

Dearing asked Capey to consider some specific issues including:

- modifying the tests so that they contribute to grading
- introducing standard assignments
- the use of end-of-course externally set examinations or projects through which students could show they had integrated the knowledge and skills from the course

which indicate the kind of improvements to GNVQs that were being looked for. But Dearing's remit was far wider: to consider the whole range of qualifications for 16–19-year-olds. In doing so he addressed the thorny question of the respective roles of A-levels, GNVQs and NVQs.

Dearing recommended that:

- A-levels and GCSE should be for 'where the primary purpose is to develop knowledge, understanding and skills associated with a subject or discipline'.
- GNVQs should be for Applied Education 'where the primary purpose is to develop and apply knowledge, understanding and skills relevant to broad areas of employment'.

- NVQs should be for Vocational Training 'where the primary purpose is to develop and recognise mastery of a trade or profession at the relevant level'.

To underline the importance of the applied pathway he recommended renaming advanced GNVQs 'Applied A-levels', and transferring A-levels like business studies to become flagships of the new route. But this is seen by some as threatening the gold standard of A-levels and it may not be accepted by the government.

Quinquennial review

The largely unsung and unheralded review of NCVQ itself conducted by the Department for Education and Employment has thrown the future of the body into the melting pot. Although it was brought about as a regular five-yearly monitoring exercise, 'a prior options review' was added to determine 'whether the functions delegated to NCVQ remain essential to Government and Department objectives' and, if so, 'whether there is scope for merger with or transferring some or all of the functions to another body'. In other words, the future of NCVQ was up for grabs.

The review reported in two parts, in November 1995 and February 1996, with an Executive Summary added later (May 1996). It concluded that NCVQ 'has not been able to establish a national framework for all, or even a majority, of vocational awards', and 'despite all its achievements, there remains a negative perception of the organisation from some quarters'. The Executive Summary notes that 'The Review Team thought that NCVQ's marketing function might lend itself to separate contracting out. This would provide the solution to what some saw as a fundamental problem, that of the incompatibility of NCVQ's regulatory and promotional roles.'

Sir Ron Dearing, in his review of qualifications for 16–19-year-olds, considered regulation (the rough equivalent of Ofwat or Ofgas – Ofqual perhaps) and put forward two options:

- setting up two new bodies, one responsible for qualifications from 14+, the other responsible for the curriculum and for statutory assessment by national tests;
- replacing SCAA and NCVQ with one body to oversee qualifications, the curriculum and statutory assessment.

The government consulted on the two options in May 1996 (DfEE 1996), expressing a preference for a single body. This led, not unexpectedly, on the basis of about 75 votes for and 25 against, to a proposal[17] to establish a Qualifications and National Curriculum Authority (QNCA) to bring together the work of SCAA and NCVQ. It is intended to be in place for

September 1997 but it will require legislation. In 1997 the 'National' was dropped.

At best, the new authority could be just the shake-up vocational education needs. With NCVQ gone there would be room for fresh thinking. At worst, however, it could mean the take-over of SCAA and an undermining of the academic ladder through competence-speak.

What next?

Assuming that QCA comes into being, it will have the vital task of driving forward the follow-up to Dearing, Beaumont and Capey. The central issue facing it will be how to establish a truly national system of awards. The model devised by NCVQ became a Procrustean bed on which all other awards were going to be forced to lie: 'the Government intends that GNVQs, together with National Vocational Qualifications (NVQs), will replace other vocational qualifications and become the main national provision for vocational education and training.'[18]

In order to achieve a national framework, QCA will have to adopt a set of criteria for vocational awards which can accommodate the qualifications that employers value, whether old or new. The key to this is probably the distinction that Beaumont makes between setting standards and designing qualifications. It is for employers through their Lead Bodies to set the standards, and for the vocational awarding bodies to design appropriate qualifications. The role of the regulatory body then becomes to check that the award meets the standards.

It should not, however, attempt to do this through criteria which imply one-to-one correspondence, as with present NVQs, but by making sure that vocational qualifications have:

* appropriate content
* appropriate assessment.

It is likely, as Capey and Beaumont suggested, that there will be different models for preparing *for* work and upskilling *in* work.

GNVQs need to be properly designed as applied education. They are, if anything, further back than NVQs. At least with NVQs employers did attempt to set the standards even if they did not always recognise what the consultants wrote for them. But GNVQs have been largely left to the people contracted to write the specifications, without any high-level thought being given as to what their organising principles should be (as the organising principle of a subject is a distinctive way of making sense of the world).

Applied education is about practical organisations of understanding. The organising principle of a GNVQ should be the class of practical problems that it addresses, in the way that medicine in higher education is organised about health. Not enough thought has gone into the defining core of GNVQs. Leisure and tourism, for example, sit uneasily together, with would-be travel agents and swimming pool attendants sometimes unhappily getting their wires crossed.

Unless significant progress is made in the meantime, QCA will have to consider what distinguishes GNVQs from A-levels and GCSEs, what to call them, how they are to be set out and how they are to be tested.

Conclusion

Just over ten years ago the government took some bold decisions. It recognised that a crucial problem was how was Britain going to pay its way in the world and it has come to see an improved system of vocational education as making a major contribution towards increased competitiveness. It has also accepted that, in countries like Germany, Switzerland and Hungary, many young people who do not happen to like learning for its own sake are able to reach high levels of attainment in mathematics and their mother tongue through applied learning and vocational training.

These aims are no less important today. The fact that NCVQ went down the wrong path has set us back, but QCA gives us a chance to put things right. But will the government be prepared to grasp the nettle? It was aware that something was seriously amiss five years ago, but attempted to tough it out through the appointment of John Hillier as Chief Executive of NCVQ. It is to be fervently hoped that this time the realities will be faced and we will at last get a coherent set of pathways for 14–19-year-olds and a truly national system of vocational awards.

Notes

1 G. Tolley, 'Putting labels on people: the qualifications business'. *RSA Journal* no. 5363, October 1986.

2 DfEE, *Awards of Vocational Qualifications 1991/2–1994/5*, Statistical Bulletin 4, 1996.

3 FEFC, *NVQs in the Further Education Sector in England – National Survey: Report from the Inspectorate*, September 1994; FEFC, *GNVQs in the Further Education Sector in England – National Survey: Report from the Inspectorate*, November 1994; OFSTED, *GNVQs in Schools: Quality and Standards of General National Vocational Qualifications, 1993/4*, November 1994; 'OFSTED, *Assessment of General National Vocational Qualifications*, June 1996; Her Majesty's Chief Inspector, *Annual Report*, June 1996.

4 See, for example, 'Lecturers in row over academic freedom', *Financial Times*, 19 April 1996. 'Developing a framework for vocational qualifications is always going to be expensive', Letter from John Hillier, *TES*, 18 October 1996.

5 R. Dearing, *Review of Qualifications for 16–19 Year Olds* London: SCAA, 1996.

6 G. Beaumont, *Review of 100 NVQs and SVQs* London: NCVQ, 1996.

7 J Capey, *GNVQ Assessment Review* London: NCVQ, 1996.

8 *NVQ Criteria and Guidance*. London: NCVQ, January 1995.
9 See, for example, 'Colleges in scandal of exam passes', *Observer*, 27 March 1994; 'Inquiry set up into worthless qualifications', *Observer*, 3 April 1994; 'Second training scam alleged', Guardian, 27 May 1994; 'A vocational charter for cheats', *Daily Telegraph*, 14 December 1994; 'Sleaze and loathing in the classes of conflict', *Observer*, 12 March 1995; 'Fraud squads to root out phantom studies', *Independent on Sunday*, 28 May 1995; 'Minister acts on exams for cash scandal', Evening News, 2 May 1996; 'Arrests in £1m NVQ "fraud"', *TES*, 18 October 1996.
10 P. Rogers, Chairman's Speech, Launch of BTEC Annual Report, 27 May 1992.
11 J. Hillier, Oral evidence to the Education Committee of the House of Commons, 17 January 1996.
12 J. Hillier; 'Misleading view of NVQ progress'. Letter to *Financial Times,* 9 October 1996.
13 National Vocational Awarding Bodies, '100,000 GNVQ successes and growing'. Press release, 21 August 1995.
14 Joint Council of National Vocational Awarding Bodies, 'Record number of GNVQ awards in 1995/96', press release, 28 August 1996.
15 DfEE, *NCVQ 1995 Quinquennial Review,* Stage One Report, November 1995; DfEE, *NCVQ 1995–96 Quinquennial Review',* Stage Two Report, February 1996; DfEE, *NCVQ 1996 Quinquennial Review',* Executive Summary, May 1996.
16 See, for example, 'Lecturers loath to report on GNVQs'. Letter to *THES,* 11 November; 1994: 'Colleges impose sound of silence'. *Guardian*, 15 November 1994: 'Quango blunders'. Letter to *Guardian,* 29 November 1994.
17 DfEE. 'Top advisers join forces to raise standards'. *DfEE News*. 281, September 1996.
18 *GNVQ Information Note*. London: NCVQ, 1993.

References

Beaumont, G. (1996) *Review of 100 NVQs and SVQs*. London: NCVQ.

Bees, M. and Swords, M. (1990) *National Vocational Qualifications and Further Education*. London: Kogan Page and NCVQ.

Capey, J. (1995) *GNVQ Assessment Review*. London: NCVQ.

CBI (1994) *Quality Assessed: The CBI Review of NVQs and SVQs*. London: Confederation of British Industry.

Channell, J. and St John, M.J. (1996) 'The language of standards', *Competence and Assessment*, no. 31, February.

Dearing, R. (1993). *The National Curriculum and its Assessment: Final Report*. London: SCAA.

Dearing, R. (1996) *Review of Qualifications. for 16–19 Year Olds*. London: SCAA.

DES (1986) *Working Together: Education and Training*, Cmnd, 9823. London: HMSO.

De Ville, H. G. (1986) *Review of Vocational Qualifications in England and Wales: A Report by the Working Group*. London: HMSO.

DfEE (1996) *Building the Framework. A Consultation Paper on Bringing Together the Work of NCVQ and SCAA*. London: DfEE.

HMSO (1991) *Education and Training for the 21st Century*, Cmnd 1536, vol. 1. London: HMSO.

Jessup, G. (1991) *Outcomes: NVQs and the Emerging Model of Education and Training*. Lewes: The Falmer Press.

NCVQ (1993) *GNVQ Information Note*. London: NCVQ.

Robinson, P. (1996). *Rhetoric and Reality: Britain's New Vocational Qualifications*. London: Centre for Economic Performance, London School of Economics.

Chapter 9

Ideology and curriculum policy

GNVQ and mass post-compulsory education in England and Wales

Denis Gleeson and Phil Hodkinson

Introduction

For the first time in Britain, a large majority of young people are now staying in full-time education and training for at least one year after the end of compulsory education at 16. This significant reversal has coincided with the introduction of a major new qualification – the General National Vocational Qualification (GNVQ). The GNVQ has had an immediate impact on the 16–19 system in England and Wales. Original expectations of 50,000 enrolments have been outstripped, with an estimated 80,000 students currently on GNVQ nation-wide. A key attraction of GNVQ is its dual role as a route towards both employment and Higher Education. Moreover, what was originally known as level 3 GNVQ has been recently given new status as 'GNVQ Advanced' or a vocational A level. This chapter analyses the ideological rationale for and consequences of GNVQ as a means of restructuring mass education and training in England and Wales.

There have been numerous recent studies pointing out that English post-16 education and training lag behind equivalent systems in most other developed countries, summarised by Green and Steedman (1993). At long last, partly driven by this comparative evidence, there is now a consensus that post-16 education and training provision in England and Wales has not worked either for a majority of young leavers or in meeting the perceived need for a better workforce. Some, including the present British government, see A levels successfully facilitating HE entry, but a problem in developing a vocational qualification of similar status. A majority of academics follow Finegold *et al.* (1990) in viewing the long-standing division between high status academic courses and low status vocational courses as at the root of the problem. In apparent response the government has, following on the White Paper *Education and Training for the 21st Century* (ED/DES, 1991), introduced GNVQs as an attempt to solve these problems. Their hope is that GNVQs will have equivalent status to A levels, encourage staying on and achieve reskilling, thereby bridging the academic/vocational divide. But can GNVQ fulfil these multi-functions?

The positioning of GNVQs can only be understood through a complex combination of perspectives that are often treated separately. In this chapter we focus on four: the ideological tensions and ambiguities within government policy and English cultural values surrounding GNVQ; the relationship between GNVQ development and the new managerialism which is currently rampant in British post-16 education: the relationship between the knowledge and content of GNVQs, the labour market and notions of upskilling the workforce; and the importance in GNVQs, as in all post-compulsory education, of addressing wider educational issues beyond current obsessions with economic rationalism.

GNVQ, ideology and tripartism

In promoting GNVQ as an 'alternative route' through post-16 education and training, the British government has boxed itself into a corner. On the one hand, rejection of the Higginson report (DES, 1988), which proposed radical changes to the long established and repeatedly criticised A levels, legitimated continued pressure from right wing groups for the retention of A level essentially unchanged. On the other hand, the government remained committed to the continued development of competence driven, essentially work based NVQs as the central basis for its vocational training reforms. With a growing, if belated, recognition that these two radically different types of qualification did not add up to an appropriate post-16 provision, GNVQ has taken on the appearance of a political solution, designed to satisfy the different requirements of employers, labour markets and post-compulsory education itself. Failure to respond to calls for a unified system of qualifications, across the 14–19 age range, has resulted in GNVQ filling the gap controlling both the supply and demand side of post-16 expansion.

Though both the TVEI and subsequently the National Curriculum emphasised curriculum breadth and a technical/vocational perspective for all young people, the White Paper (ED/DES, 1991) sought to establish a three-track system for academic and vocational guidance and progression post-16, redrawn in Table 9.1.

Though this chapter deals with tripartism in an English and Welsh context, it should be remembered that most continental education systems also have or had a tripartite structure, in the sense that vocational provision is divided either between technical and vocational or between school-based and alternance-based approaches. Part of a widespread 'commonsense' belief in tripartism is the division of people into Plato's men of gold, bronze and iron. The history of English education in the twentieth century can be seen as various ill-fated attempts to reproduce these 'natural' divisions in the educational system. Coffey (1992) shows that a tripartite hierarchy of educational provision in Britain was explicitly linked to class divisions

Table 9.1   Three parallel pathways in post-16 education and training

Academic	GNVQ	NVQ	Equivalent job level
Postgraduate		Level 5	Professional, middle management
Degree		Level 4	Higher technician, junior management
A/AS level	GNVQ Advanced	Level 3	Technician, advanced craft, supervisor
GCSE (grade C or better)	GNVQ Intermediate	Level 2	Basic craft
	GNVQ Foundation	Level 1	Semi-skilled

in the late nineteenth century. There was professional education in the public schools which stressed leadership, general education for the middle class and skilled working class in grammar schools, and job-related training for the rest in the elementary schools, with an explicit reference to 'obedience' rather than leadership. By the twentieth century, the divide between grammar schools and public schools had narrowed, at least in curriculum terms, as the growing middle classes sought the same academic education as had developed originally for the sons of the aristocracy. Tripartism by then had become the division between academic, technical and practical. This is seen most clearly in the Norwood report of 1943, which was the precursor of the 1944 Education Act and the political settlement that followed it, a central principle of which was the British secondary tripartite system of grammar, technical and modern schools.

A belief in three clearly differentiated types of people is fundamental to one of the dominant ideological belief systems in British educational politics ... which Skilbeck (1976), following Williams (1965), called 'classical humanism'. For those whose views are close to this ideal-type, such tripartism is seen as the natural order of things. There are four logically separate but commonly conflated assumptions within this tripartite 'common sense'. First, that people fall naturally (socially and genetically) into three distinct types, academic, technical and practical. Second, that these are closely correlated with 'ability' as it is generally understood. Thus the most able are naturally academic, the least able are practical and the technicians fall in the middle. The third assumption is that schooling and the curriculum should similarly be divided into different types of provision, to correspond to these different types of people and ability. The fourth assumption is that the opportunities and needs of the labour market also fall into the same neat divisions. None of these statements stands up to logical and empirical examination when taken in isolation, let alone together, but such ideological beliefs are notoriously resistant to rational challenges.

Once even a cursory examination is made of twentieth-century English educational history, there is a glaring paradox. Despite the dominance of this tripartite perception, the middle strand of the three has always had a troubled and low-key existence. Until the 1960s, the focus was on three types of schooling. The 'top' and 'bottom' of the system are well known – the grammar schools that developed out of the public school tradition, and the various schools that evolved from the elementary school into the secondary modern schools of the 1950s and 60s. There have been several attempts to develop technical high schools in the middle. Sanderson (1994) describes the growth of the junior technical schools (the term 'Junior' is misleading, for they mainly recruited at 13+) and he and McCullough (1989) both describe the post-1944 secondary technical schools. Sanderson is an enthusiast, eulogising what the schools could do, despite an often hostile environment. McCullough is more critical, suggesting that, in general, the technical schools never really established a coherent and credible vocational curriculum. Both agree that these schools were always few in number and never catered for more than the tiniest fraction of children. In effect, the tripartite system was a myth, rhetorically labelling what was, in reality, dual provision. Whitty et al. (1993) show how the latest rebirth of the technical school, the CTCs, has largely repeated these earlier experiences.

Following comprehensivisation in the 1970s and with the later exception of the CTCs, the focus largely changed from separate technical schools to technical curriculum provision. McCullough (1989) argues that the initial conception of the TVEI was also originally aimed at this middle group of 'technical' young people, though as the initiative developed, the objective became one of providing technical education for all. GNVQ can be seen as the latest in a long series of attempts to establish this middle, technical/higher vocational track, now seen as lying between A levels and NVQs.

McCullough (1989) and Sanderson (1994) demonstrate the dangers of attributing simplistic explanations for the failure of technical education in Britain, and both list a range of inter-related, complex factors. We argue that part of this complexity can be explained by (i) an inevitable internal tension within classical humanist tripartism and (ii) conflicts between this widely held classical humanist ideology and other equally deeply held, though possibly less dominant, educational ideologies within English society.

The internal tensions in classical humanism arise because, in English society, very few people aspire to the technical route. As people strove for what Bourdieu (1984) called 'distinction', both technical schools and secondary modem schools began to ape the grammar school curriculum long before comprehensivisation became the norm, whilst parents wanted their offspring to attend grammar, not technical, schools if they passed the 11+. In essence, middle-class families saw anything other than grammar (or public) school as inappropriate, seeing both technical and modern schools as for the working class. In this context, the upwardly mobile working class were also more likely to aspire to the academic grammar school route than to a technical career that kept them firmly below the class equivalent of the glass ceiling.

This was reinforced by the common system of taking the young people with the best 11+ passes for the grammar schools, giving the technical high schools (where they existed) those who were left. Thus, a technician was identified not through a positive interest in or aptitude for technical studies, but simply as someone who was not judged capable of an academic career. This partly explains the lack of investment in technical schools, which were more expensive than grammar schools, for in such an elitist system, 'common sense' and the self-interest of the dominant groups suggest that most should be spent on the top level, not the middle.

Late twentieth-century post-16 tripartism in England focuses on separate institutions as well as a separate curriculum. This is because of the anomalous position of sixth form colleges. These had been originally set up within school regulations, to provide the traditional academic education based on A levels, as part of a reorganised comprehensive education system. It was often an old grammar school that was transformed into a sixth form college. The new post-16 funding arrangements abruptly moved them from the school sector in 1993, giving them independence from LEAs with funding provided by the FEFC. They exist alongside the predominantly vocational FE colleges, which have a very different history and ethos (Smithers and Robinson, 1993). Research by Robinson and Burke (1995) suggests that many sixth form colleges are striving to preserve their elitist, academic ethos, based around provision of A level to full-time 16–19-year-old students. Many will not offer more than a token GNVQ curriculum in one or two occupational areas. The risk is that if high status institutions like public schools and sixth form colleges do not take GNVQ seriously, the new middle vocational track will be squeezed every bit as effectively as were technical schools in an earlier age. Furthermore, a belief in a technical strand, for other people's children and for other educational institutions, reinforces the status and sense of well-being of those who have succeeded on the academic route. From this point of view, a middle stratum that is weak in practice but strong in rhetoric meets the status needs of the academic elite. To succeed where technical schools failed, GNVQ must break out of this ideological closed circle.

One of many other ideological conflicts relevant to GNVQ lies between classical humanism and what Skilbeck (1976) called reconstructionism. Within a reconstructionist ideology, the educational system is seen as a means of restructuring society, normally for economic ends. This can be

seen in the repeated calls for more or better vocational or technical education, in order to close the skills gap between Britain and her rivals, to make
industry more competitive and to ensure future prosperity. Such beliefs are
almost as strong as classical humanism in Conservative government thinking,
and are advocated by the influential CBl, amongst many others. Such a
reconstructionist argument is frequently restated in the official rationale for
GNVQ, which stresses the need to raise the standards of education and
training across the board. Hence the National Targets for Education
and Training (NTETs) express government commitment to 50 per cent of
any year group achieving NVQ level 3 equivalence by the turn of the
century, and these targets are likely to be increased upwards in the immediate future (NACETT, 1994).

Such universalist views of attainment run counter to the classical humanist
view that a norm-referenced, hierarchical distribution of ability and
therefore appropriate qualifications is part of the natural order of things.
Paradoxically, the British government can, at the same time, proclaim
NTETs as official policy and create new A* (starred) grades for A level and
GCSE because 'too many people are getting an A'. Constant talk of A level
as the gold standard has set GNVQ a difficult cultural and educational
task. To succeed, at least in the terms of those government directives that
brought it into existence, GNVQ must establish a credible vocational middle
track whilst simultaneously raising levels of education and qualification
in ways that are acceptable to the mass of the English public, be they
parents, young people, teachers, employers or politicians. It is our belief
that success will be more likely if the rigid three-track system is abandoned, in favour of the type of unified curriculum structure advocated by
Finegold *et al.* (1990).

Quality and managerialism in the post-16 curriculum

Another key question relates to the nature of learning experiences in GNVQs
and what counts as quality learning. 'Quality' is the buzz word of the
currently dominant 'new managerialism' in British education. As attempts
are made to import industrial procedures, such as Total Quality Management, into schools and colleges, there is a widespread assumption that what
counts as quality in education is straightforward and unproblematic. Thus
the FEFC or OFSTED inspectors read mounds of documentation, watch
some classes, talk to staff and ascribe a teaching quality rating to a course,
department or institution.

What is more, the income of English and Welsh educational institutions
is being ever more closely linked to simplified and unexamined assumptions of quality, measured through performance indicators. Two approaches
to funding are currently dominant. First, income follows students, so schools

and colleges are rewarded for recruiting. Marketing and the hard sell become more important than either good teaching or good student relations in determining success and defining 'quality'. To balance such distortions, increasing proportions of funding are now being awarded only on successful course completion and student certification. In this way, 'quality' becomes synonymous with passing and the intrinsic value of the course followed becomes marginalised. From this perspective, all that matters about GNVQ is (i) how many young people can be persuaded to enrol and (ii) how many of them can achieve successful completion. While such measures might satisfy some politicians and policy makers, they at best deflect attention from the really important issues about educational quality within GNVQ and at worst undermine it (Gleeson, 1993).

Yet the reality is that educational quality, far from being simple, agreed and measurable, is problematic and highly contested. Once more, Skilbeck's analysis of ideological positions helps make the point, for the nature of quality varies between each. Skilbeck (1976) identifies three conflicting ideologies, 'progressive', 'reconstructionist' and 'classical humanist'. Progressivism is well known as a label, drawing on a student-centred and individually developmental view of education. For progressives, the process of learning, assessment and decision-making should be shared by student and teacher, so that negotiation becomes a central concept. Progressive views of education have influenced post-16 provision in Britain in two ways. There has been a growth of student-centred approaches in many A level subjects, with a greater emphasis on learning processes, group work, project-based course work and the like. In parallel, prevocational education has developed similar approaches, with an explicit work preparation focus. From either progressive viewpoint, the test of educational quality is the developmental needs of individual young people.

As we have seen, reconstructionism is arguably the dominant ideology in the development of GNVQ. From this perspective, the test of quality is the value of educational provision to employers and the economy. Since Skilbeck wrote, this reconstructionist approach to education has developed a radical formulation, worthy of the separate ideological label of 'market forces'. Numerous variations of this ideology have developed, but in the post-16 context, the ideas of the CBI (1989, 1993) are dominant. They argue for individual students to become the purchasers of education and training, through the issue of a voucher. In such a market system, quality would be defined by the choices made by the purchasers, as colleges and schools are supposedly forced to improve in order to compete.

In contrast, the classical humanist position on educational quality supports high academic standards for the more able elite and better quality vocational training for the rest. This view of quality can be seen in the fight to preserve A levels, insistence on written external examinations and the development of separate vocational and academic educational pathways. Our main point here is not to debate the relative merits of these ideological positions, but to demonstrate that the new managerialism is based on a fallacy, for there is no agreed, unproblematic notion of what educational quality is. The inevitable result is that, despite the broad overall consensus about the need for change in post-16 provision, the nature, purpose and content of education remains contested and the subject of struggle.

As we have seen, one result of such conflicting pressures, in the English context, has been the repeated failure to establish a credible middle road between high status academic education and low status vocational preparation. Can GNVQ succeed where other initiatives failed? For Halsey *et al.* (1991) the danger is 'academic drift', whereby provision originally designed as vocational copies the higher status academic curriculum in order to acquire some of that status for itself. If this happens to GNVQ, driven by the ever elusive parity of esteem with A level, the practical and technical will remain marginalised in English and Welsh education.

There are two further problems. The current obsession with outcomes and qualification achievement means that the explicit focus on learning processes within GNVQ specifications may be lost. The worries of Smithers (1994) and others about the reliability of GNVQ assessment reinforce the marginalisation of educational experience *per se*, so that measurable attainments become all-important. But many of the most important aspects of (vocational) education are not directly measurable.

Also, current managerialist approaches to education risk reducing teachers to technicians, who simply 'deliver' the official curriculum to young people. This ignores the fact that

> teachers don't merely deliver the curriculum. They develop, define it and reinterpret it too. It is what teachers think, what teachers believe and what teachers do at the level of the classroom that ultimately shapes the kind of learning that young people get.
>
> (Hargreaves, 1993, p. ix)

If GNVQs are to be successful, ways must be found reinforcing and protecting the professionalism of teachers rather than attempting to control their actions through inspections and performance-related funding.

GNVQ, upskilling and economic rationalism

In looking at the relationship between GNVQ and post-compulsory education, we also need to consider the connection between employers, labour markets and the knowledge content of the vocational curriculum. Essentially, two competing perspectives circumscribe the English and Welsh debate: the need to provide young people with high quality education and training to improve their job prospects, and the question of whether employers have an equal need to employ highly educated and trained young people. Three further policy implications arise: the first is that without adequate inducement in the form of tax breaks or tax levies (depending on political viewpoint) employers may remain committed to training only those already in work. The second is that the longer and further removed young workers become from the workplace, either through unemployment or off-the-job training, the less employable they may become. The third concerns the content and underlying assumptions of the GNVQ curriculum which on the one hand promises parity, progression and reskilling while on the other it is locked into a youth labour market characterised by unemployment, casualisation and low pay. In such circumstances, the danger is that GNVQ will become either another substitute for employment or a conduit to service-sector employment. Traditionally, industries such as engineering, construction and energy had the highest concentrations of young people with formal recognised qualifications. With the decline of such industries, the need for formal training may increasingly be determined by the demands of the expanding, mainly casualised, service sector (Gray *et al.*, 1993). If this bodes well for improving training levels in a sector with the lowest incidence of high quality training, it may well fail to address national and local skill shortages.

There is an assumption in much writing about post-16 education and training that better skilled and qualified young people are a necessary condition for economic prosperity. Implicit in such a view is the belief that, if young people become better skilled and qualified, they will be more able to acquire good jobs. For many, this notion is linked to views of a supposedly post-Fordist labour market, where both core and periphery workers require higher levels of skill and flexibility than in the past. While there remains disagreement about the extent to which a shift from Fordism to post-Fordism has taken place, there are those who see radical potential for education in such change (Brown and Lauder; 1992, Young, 1993). The argument runs that increasingly hierarchical systems of managerial control and surveillance are being replaced by flexible organisational structures, involving adaptable machinery, flexible workers, flatter hierarchies and the breakdown of the division between mental and manual labour It is argued that, in the twenty-first century, new skills of learning, abstraction, teamwork, independent thinking and experimentation will be required by increasing numbers of workers (ED/DES, 1991).

It is not difficult to see how this radical and universal conception of the knowledge worker, for which the GNVQ has been ostensibly created, finds appeal across a broad and diverse spectrum including government, opposition, CBI, Trades Union Congress and examination bodies. For different ideological reasons, each retains different interpretations of what post-Fordism will bring in terms of innovation, profit, change in work organisation, labour and self-development. Such is the flexibility of the post-Fordist vision of society that it has become highly chameleon-like. For the Left it legitimates critiques of old models of hierarchy which offered false promises of choice, classlessness and freedom. For the Right it legitimates market-led reforms in modernising Britain's work and education institutions on more flexible and competitive terms. In so doing, both perspectives are able to idealise education and the quality of teaching and learning as a necessary co-determinant of economic change. Moreover, modernisers (of all political persuasions) anticipate a progressive and humane conception of the worker, as an autonomous rather than as an alienated being. Thus, not only does the post-Fordist vision of society suggest that education and work are synonymous, but also that the creation of the knowledge worker implies radical changes in both the content and form of the curriculum. For Young (1992) this necessarily involves challenging divisive specialisation associated with academic–vocational divisions, insulated subject boundaries and the separation between education and training. However, it is also the case that successful 16–19 education and training provision is dependent on a buoyant youth labour market. The commitment of young people to the explicitly vocational curriculum offered within GNVQ will be strongly linked with their perceptions of the likelihood of a good job at the end of it. Currently, the reality of high youth unemployment and job chasing in Britain contrasts sharply with the rhetoric of post-Fordist curriculum planning at ED, DFE and NCVQ level.

GNVQ, progression and careership

Most current research on the transition from school to work stresses the stratification of inequality (Furlong, 1992; Banks et al., 1991; Bates and Riseborough, 1993; Kerckhoff, 1993). This contrasts sharply with policy assumptions based on individualism and free choice (CBI, 1989, 1993; Bennett et al., 1992; ED/DES, 1991). Ostensibly, GNVQs are designed with the intention of enabling young people to progress either to HE or into employment, allowing virement and freedom of movement between academic and vocational courses. Yet both routes and virement are problematic.

Despite a recent report that 90 per cent of universities have accepted GNVQ as the equivalent to A level for admission purposes (Nash, 1994), it is unlikely that GNVQs will provide ready access to popular, high status HE courses. Currently, over 70 per cent of the year group are now entering full-time post-16 education, and funding for FE colleges is designed to expand that percentage rapidly. At the same time, intake into HE has been capped at around 33 per cent. It is, therefore, unlikely that more than a third of GNVQ Advanced students will progress to university. For the majority of students recruited to GNVQ, the enormous efforts currently being devoted to ensuring progression to HE may be largely irrelevant.

However, the progression routes direct to employment via GNVQ are also problematic and plagued by uncertainties. Traditionally, most British employers looking for school leavers took them at 16+, whilst a small group of major employers, such as banks, recruited at 18+. Recently the 18+ recruitment has largely dried up, partly in response to recession and partly as employers react to the recent expansion of HE by recruiting exclusively from that sector. Moreover, traditional 16+ recruiters are being forced to change because there are fewer young people looking for jobs and training places at that age. Even if, in future, employers recruit at 18 or even 19+, there remain progression problems for those leaving with GNVQ. Many employers traditionally disregarded qualifications altogether (Moore, 1988). Furthermore, many small and medium-sized employers are unlikely to know what GNVQ is.

These difficulties are exacerbated by a growing gulf between GNVQ and NVQs (Hodkinson and Mattinson, 1994). Unless students have topped up GNVQ with NVQ units, they may have little relevant work-based skill. This means that many young people leaving at 18 or 19 with GNVQ Advanced may need to take NVQ level 2 once they start work. This contradiction calls into question the official pattern of three equivalent pathways post-16, where the normal progression would be from any level 3, including GNVQ Advanced, to level 4 or its equivalent (Table 9.1). Furthermore, many of the young people with GNVQ Intermediate or Advanced will have turned down opportunities to train at NVQ level 2 when they were 16+. They may see a move into this type of training, following two or three extra years of full-time education, as a step backwards and consequently as undesirable.

Because the launch of GNVQ has been so closely linked with supposed employment needs, it is likely that many of the young people flocking to take these new courses are doing so in the hope of getting into HE and/or of getting a good job. But education does not create jobs for students. Unless there are widespread changes to the ways in which labour markets, industry and the city are organised, progression for many GNVQ students will be undermined no matter how good the actual course provision may be (Finegold and Soskice, 1991). There is a serious risk that the GNVQ bubble will burst if, regardless of the quality of actual provision, inflated expectations of progression are dashed, to be replaced by disillusion. Mass post-16 educational provision must be based on wider and more substantial foundations than this.

The wider purposes of education

From being a relative backwater of research and education policy, post-compulsory education and training has become strategic in the official discourse of social and economic reform. If from the 1950s to the 1970s research and policy emphasised investment in human capital in determining both comprehensive and flexible determinants of labour (Newsom, 1963; Crowther, 1959; Robbins, 1963), that situation has since changed, with the influence of unemployment, markets, changing technology and work organisation, global and geopolitical factors. Such factors have brought into question traditional distinctions between schooling, education and work, academic and vocational knowledge, and mental and manual labour in work and education. International comparisons associated with a knowledge revolution have exposed weaknesses in post-compulsory education and training in England and Wales. These include overly behaviourist models of training, lack of investment in intermediate skills, and an inability to translate knowledge and innovation into growth. Such factors, often overlaid with traditional suspicions about theory and thinking skills in Britain, have maintained narrow and arbitrary distinctions between academic and practical modes of thought. Increasingly, there is a need to challenge the dependency culture engendered by instructional discourse in favour of a pedagogy of work and self-learning, embracing what has recently been described as the predeterminants of a knowledge based society (Reich, 1991). According to Lyotard (1984), '. . . the old principle that the acquisition of knowledge is indissociable from the training (Bildung) of minds, or even of individuals, is becoming obsolete and will become ever more so'.

In England and Wales, the tension within a policy which encourages prescriptive pedagogical discourse and at the same time demands a pedagogy of empowered self-learning has been a major obstacle to progress. Is there a unifying way forward? There is a need to go beyond both the 1944 and Thatcherite settlements: the challenge is to generate a new 'third education settlement' which combines conceptions of social unity with competitiveness and productivity. According to Donald (1990), such a settlement should be based on '. . . participation and distributive justice rather than simple egalitarianism and on cultural heterogeneity rather than a shared humanity'. For Whitty (1993) the new settlement should combine conceptions of unity and a common good with differentiation and recognition of individual needs. This not only has crucial implications for the future of mass schooling and vocationalism, exemplified in GNVQ, but also for the nature of knowledge which underpins new policies and practices of teaching and learning. If Donald's and Whitty's accounts challenge both the 1944 and 1988 settlements, the emphasis on equality and civic restructuring retains much in common with earlier post-war policy assumptions (Newsom 1963; Crowther 1959; Robbins 1963). The difference lies in the determination and transition from an instructional pedagogy to a learner oriented pedagogy which, though still circumscribed by economic rationalism (after all, capitalism hasn't changed that much), radically redefines the social relationship between learning, earning and competitiveness (Husen, 1986).

Perhaps now is the time to address long overdue questions about the nature and purpose of education in a social democracy. In the rush to increase staying-on rates post-16 and thus effectively raise the school-leaving age to 18 for most young people, we need to revisit the difficult problem of past educational failures. From the 1960s onwards, study after study showed the educational system, be it based on grammar and secondary modern schools (Hargreaves, 1967; Lacey, 1970) or on comprehensive schools (Ball, 1981; Hargreaves, 1982; ILEA, 1984), failing large numbers of young people, especially the less able of working-class origins. More recently, the focus has shifted to problems for young women and young people of minority ethnic origins (Arnot and Weiner, 1987; Troyna, 1987). Contributors in Bates and Riseborough (1993) paint graphic pictures of inequality in post-16 education just prior to the introduction of GNVQ. Though we are in favour of expanding educational provision post-16, more does not necessarily mean better. It is interesting that in the USA, where staying-on rates are much greater than in Britain, similar concerns about poor quality provision are frequently expressed (Brause, 1992).

Missing in current policy discourses in England and Wales is any broader vision of citizenship and learning – in terms of the kind of people the new post-16 education system is designed to produce – including images of 'human nature' which GNVQs (or A levels) presume to develop. The question arises: is there a way of rescuing the reform process from itself, and in what direction should we be looking for a broader vision of post-16 education and training?

Genuine alternatives must embrace a socially constructed view of education and citizenship which inter-links partnership and empowerment in personal, education and economic relations, beyond market, qualification and employer-led considerations. For example, Hodkinson (1994) suggests that education for all young people should include three overlapping dimensions – personal effectiveness, critical autonomy and community. By personal effectiveness he means the ability to do things for oneself and with others. The emphasis is on being practically proactive, be it running a play group, making jewellery, or raising funds for a charity. Critical autonomy refers to the importance of thinking for oneself, including the ability to critique common assumptions. Community is about developing one's place in a diverse society – about understanding conflicts of interest and struggle, about recognising and respecting the rights and opinions of others, and about contributing to society, through individual and communal effort. Too often educational provision has fallen well short on some or all of these, as when vocational courses were/are typically uncritical, so that important issues of social justice and inequality were/are not even discussed. Education should include attention to economic and commercial issues. However, analyses such as this demonstrate the narrowness and sterility of basing a curriculum exclusively on the economic agenda. As ever, principles of democracy and justice are involved here, which render holistic conceptions of education and training a right and precondition of all citizens.

According to Tomlinson (1993), the new model must necessarily offer the development of intellectual capacities, economic skills and personal qualities that every individual has a right to acquire and the obligation to put these to the service of society. This not only demands rethinking teaching and learning, but also the content and process of the curriculum as it affects knowledgeable adult development in a learning society. As Lee *et al.* (1990) point out, leaving youth training to market forces has resulted in under-provision, skill shortages and a waste of young people – tantamount to their civic exclusion. This phenomenon, recently associated with cuts in benefit, and with homelessness, poverty and single parent families, has further marginalised some young people, in both societal and educational terms. The danger here is that alienation and anomie become overlaid, effectively creating an underclass.

Conclusion

Despite the inherent pessimism of much of our analysis, there are hopeful signs for the future. The increasing importance of post-16 education and training is inevitably opening up new possibilities for change across schools and FE which, at local level, have proved remarkably resilient in the face of external criticism and constraint. Much of this has been due to the collective professionalism of teachers, who have made considerable successes out of GCSE and TVEI, and, with some rationalisation from Dearing (1993), may still rescue the National Curriculum from total disaster The same professionalism provides hope for the rapidly developing GNVQs though, as Hatcher and Troyna (1994) remind us, 'to be effective, opposition to government education policy has to extend beyond the level of pragmatic micro-political action at the level of the individual and the school and take more collective, active and strategic forms' (p. 168). In the meantime, there are aspects of GNVQ design which promise considerable improvement on what went before. The crude, work-based, competence focus of NVQs has been avoided. The unitary structure of GNVQs offers the potential of choice and negotiated curriculum pathways for many young people, where colleges or groups of schools can provide a genuine variety of options. Alongside all this, A level reform continues apace, even if only within individual subject syllabuses, and modularisation continues. It is possible that we are slowly and erratically moving towards a structure that will enable some of these deeper educational questions to be addressed, though we are convinced that a final break with tripartism must be part of the ultimate goal

However, challenging tripartism is not just a technical curricular matter It would be naive, for example, to regard GNVQ as an isolated policy incident disconnected from broader educational policy. The current policy discourse which surrounds GNVQ and the plethora of other recent English educational initiatives, is positioned within several favoured projects central to the Conservative government's overall social and economic strategy. These projects include broader social, economic and welfare policies for restructuring the workplace, for controlling the inner cities, for trade union and industrial relations reform and for replacing planned education, housing and welfare with market-orientated provision. Increasingly, related policies associated with marketisation, competition and corporate status for schools and colleges are having marked educational effects: first in ensuring selection to match a hierarchical society and, second, in bringing forward uncomfortable decisions about how institutions should compete rather than co-operate in the marketplace. Such factors not only reinforce and reproduce principles of inclusion and exclusion associated with tripartism, but they also underpin a political system which encourages passivity rather than active participation and learning in the public domain. Thus, in challenging tripartism, it is necessary to address a broader vision of citizenship and learning, in fact a different polity (Ranson, 1994), which will sustain the personal development of all. In addressing this issue, four preconditions are essential.

First, the professionalism of teachers and lecturers needs to be enhanced rather than destroyed, as a lethal combination of school-based Initial Teacher Training, growing centralised government control of education and, ironically, repressive Fordist school and college management approaches threaten it. Second, the FEFC needs to re-examine its funding regime in terms of the broader educational issues addressed here. The current obsession with performance-related funding, focused on student numbers and completion rates, reinforces a narrowing of choice, removal of flexibility and loss of unfunded 'curriculum extras' such as non-examination adult and general education studies. Third, educational purpose must range beyond economic performance and markets. This is not a matter of either/or. Ironically, the much cited evidence from our European partners also suggests that a broader, more general education might also better fit the economic imperative (Green 1995). Even some advocates of a three track system (Smithers and Robinson, 1993) see a need for a broader general technical/vocational education, with a greater emphasis on mathematics and science education to underpin practical skill development. Finally, the issue of inclusion and exclusion which has bedevilled British education must he abandoned in favour of a unified approach to 14–19 education and training. Recent recommendations to improve GNVQ assessment, quality and curricular procedures, on the lines advocated by Smithers (1994), actually reinforce academic–vocational, divisions. This, coupled with the Tory Reform Group's conclusion that 'historians may attribute the failure of National Vocational Qualifications to narrow the skills gap with our competitors in Europe to a Whitehall turf fight between civil servants in two government departments' (Tory Reform Group, 1994) acknowledges deeper splits between education (DfE) and training (ED) within English culture and the policy making process itself.[1] A common certification for years 14–19, along the lines outlined by the National Commission on Education (1993), is a necessity. The introduction of a General National Diploma in Education might make parity of esteem or A level and GNVQs as 'alternative routes', redundant concepts (Sweetman, 1994). The types of curriculum approach advocated by Young (1993) would be valuable in providing a general education that is flexible and less divisive, broader whilst still specialised. Given some or all of these changes, GNVQ may yet play a part in the reconstruction of post-16 educational provision. Without them it offers little hope of real and lasting reform and, like so many previous attempts to redefine the middle ground of tripartism, may well wither on the policy vine. In the meantime, Crowther's (1959) recommendations for universal post-school provision remain on the table, unaddressed.

Note

1 Since this chapter was written, the ED and DfE have been combined into the new Department for Education and Employment. It is too soon to identify what effect this will have on the issues raised here.

References

Arnot, M. and Weiner, G. (eds) (1987) *Gender and the Politics of Schooling.* London: Hutchinson.

Ball, S.J. (1981) *Beachside Comprehensive: A Case Study of Secondary Schooling.* Cambridge: Cambridge University Press.

Banks, M., Bates, I., Breakwell, G., Bynner, J., Elmer, N., Jamieson, L. and Roberts, K. (1992) *Careers and Identities: Adolescent Attitudes to Employment, Training and Education, their Home Life, Leisure and Politics.* Milton Keynes: Open University Press.

Bates, I. and Riseborough, G. (eds) (1993) *Youth and Inequality.* Buckingham: Open University Press.

Bennett, R., Glennester, H. and Nevinson, D. (1992) *Learning Should Pay.* Poole: BP Educational Service.

Bourdieu, P. (1984) *Distinction. A Social Critique of the Judgement of Taste.* London: Routledge and Kegan Paul.

Brause, R.S. (1992) *Enduring Schools: Problems and Possibilities.* London: Falmer Press.

Brown, P. and Lauder, H. (1992) Education, Economy and Society: An Introduction to a New Agenda. In P. Brown and H. Lauder (eds) *Education for Economic Survival.* London: Routledge.

CBI (1989) *Towards a Skills Revolution, Report of the Vocational Education and Training Task Force.* London: CBI.

CBI (1993) *Routes for Success – Careership, a Strategy for All 16–19 Year Old Learning.* London: CBI.

Coffey, D. (1992) *Schools and Work: Developments in Vocational Education.* London: Cassell.

Crowther Report (1959) *15–18: Report of the Minister of Education's Central Advisory Committee.* London: HMSO.

Dearing, R. (1993) *The National Curriculum and its Assessment.* London: School Curriculum and Assessment Authority.

DES (1988) *Advancing A Levels,* The Higginson Report. London: HMSO.

Donald, J. (1990) Interesting Times, *Critical Social Policy* 9 (3): 39–55.

Donald. J. (1992) Dewey-Eyed Optimism: The Possibility of Democratic Education, *New Left Review* No. 192.

ED/DES (1991) *Education and Training for the 21st Century.* London: HMSO.

Finegold, D. and Soskice, D. (1991) The Failure of Training in Britain: Analysis and Prescription. In G. Esland (ed.) *Education, Training and Employment, Volume 1: Educated Labour – the Changing Basis of Industrial Demand.* Wokingham: Addison-Wesley.

Finegold, D., Keep, E., Milliband, D., Raffe, D., Spours, K. and Young, M. (1990) *A British 'Baccalaureat': Ending the Division between Education and Training,* IPPR Education and Training Paper No. 1. London: Institute of Public Policy Research.

Fullan, M. (1991) *The New Meaning of Educational Change.* London: Cassell.

Furlong, A. (1992) *Growing up in a Classless Society? School to Work Transitions.* Edinburgh: Edinburgh University Press.

Gleeson, D. (1993) Legislating for Change: Missed Opportunities in the Further and Higher Education Act, *British Journal of Education and Work,* 6(2) 29–40.

Gray, J., Jesson, D. and Tanner, M. (1993) *Boosting Post-16 Participation in Full Time Education: A Study of Some Key Factors,* ED Research Series, Youth Cohort Report No. 20. Sheffield: Employment Department.

Green, A. (1995) The European Challenge to British Vocational Education and Training. In P. Hodkinson and M. Issitt (eds) *The Challenge of Competence: Professionalism through Vocational Education and Training.* London: Cassell.

Green, A. and Steedman, H. (1993) *Educational Provision, Educational Attainment and the Needs of Industry: A Review of the Research for Germany, France, Japan, the USA and Britain,* Report No. 5. London: National Institute of Economic and Social Research.

Halsey, A.H., Postlethwaite, N., Prais, S.J., Smithers, A. and Steedman, H. (1991) *Every Child in Britain,* Report of the Channel 4 Commission on Education. London: Channel 4 Television.

Hargreaves, A. (1994) *Changing Teachers, Changing Times: Teachers' Work and Culture in the Postmodern Age.* London: Cassell.

Hargreaves, D.H. (1967) *Social Relations in a Secondary School* London: Routledge and Kegan Paul.

Hargreaves, D.H. (1982) *The Challenge for the Comprehensive School* London: Routledge and Kegan Paul.

Hatcher, R. and Troyna, B. (1994) The Policy Cycle: A Ball by Ball Account. *Journal of Education Policy,* 9(2): 155–70.

Hodkinson, P. (1994) Empowerment as an Entitlement in the Post-16 Curriculum, *Journal of Curriculum Studies,* 26(5): 391–508.

Hodkinson, P. and Mattinson, K. (1994) A Bridge Too Far? The Problems Facing GNVQ, *Curriculum Journal*, 5(3): 319–32.

Husen, T. (1986) *The Learning Society Revisited*. Oxford: Pergamon Press.

ILEA (1984) *Improving Secondary Schools*, The Hargreaves Report. London: Inner London Education Authority.

Kerckhoff, A.C. (1993) *Diverging Pathways. Social Structure and Career Deflections*. Cambridge: Cambridge University Press.

Lacey, C. (1970) *Hightown Grammar*. Manchester: Manchester University Press.

Lee, D., Marsden, D., Rickman, P. and Duncombe, J. (1990) *Scheming for Youth: A Study of YTS in the Enterprise Culture*. Milton Keynes: Open University Press.

Lyotard, J.F (1984) *The Post-Modern Condition: A Report of Knowledge*. Minneapolis: University of Minnesota Press.

McCullough, G. (1989) *The Secondary Technical School*. London: Falmer Press.

Moore, R. (1988) Education, Employment and Recruitment. In R. Dale, R. Ferguson and A. Robinson (eds) *Frameworks for Teaching*. London: Hodder and Stoughton.

NACETT (1994) *Review of the National Targets for Education and Training: Proposals for Consultation*. London: National Advisory Council for Education and Training Targets.

Nash, I. (1994) GNVQ Falls Victim to Its Own Success, *Times Educational Supplement*, 11 March.

National Commission on Education (1993) *Learning to Succeed: A Radical Look at Education Today and A Strategy for the Future*. London: Heinemann.

Newsom Report (1963) *Half our Future*. London: HMSO.

Ranson, S. (1994) *Towards the Learning Society*. London: Cassell.

Reich, R. (1991) *The Work of Nations*. London: Simon and Schuster.

Robbins Report (1963) *Committee on Higher Education Vol. 1*. London: HMSO.

Robinson, J. and Burke, C. (1994) Tradition, Culture and Ethos: The Impact of the Further and Higher Education Act (1992) on Sixth Form Colleges and their Futures. Mimeo.

Sanderson, M. (1994) *The Missing Stratum: Technical School Education in England, 1900–1990s*. London: Athlone.

Skilbeck, M. (1976) Three Educational Ideologies. In The Open University *E203 Curriculum Design and Development, Unit 3: Ideologies and Values*. Milton Keynes: Open University Press.

Smithers, A. (1994) *All our Futures: Britain's Education Revolution*. Dispatches Report on Education. London: Channel 4. TV.

Smithers, A. and Robinson, P. (1993) *Changing Colleges: Further Education in the Market Place*. London: The Council for Industry and Higher Education.

Sweetman, J. (1994) Examining New Options, *Guardian Education*, 1 April.

Tomlinson, S. (1993) No Future in the Class War, *Times Educational Supplement*, 20 August.

Tory Reform Group (1994) *The Great Jobs Crisis: Mobilising the UK's Education and Training Resources*. Cambridge: Sheraton House.

Troyna, B. (1987) *Racial Inequality in Education*. London: Tavistock.

Wexler, P. (1992) *Becoming Somebody: Toward a Social Psychology of the School*. London: Falmer Press.

White Paper (1994) *Competitiveness. Helping Business to Win*. Cmnd 2563. London: HMSO.

Whitty, G. (1993) New Schools for New Times? Educational Reform in a Global Context. Unpublished paper presented to an International Conference on Educational Reforms: Changing Relationships between the State, Civil Society and the Educational Community. University of Wisconsin – Madison, USA, June.

Whitty, G., Edwards, T. and Gewitz, S. (1993) *Specialisation and Choice in Urban Education – the City Technology College Experiment.* London and New York: Routledge.

Williams, R. (1965) *The Long Revolution.* London: Pelican Books.

Young, M. (1992) A Curriculum for the 21st Century. Paper presented at the International Workshop on Mutual Enrichment and Academic and Vocational Education in Upper Secondary Education, Institute for Educational Research, University of Jyuaskyla, Finland, 23–26 September.

Young, M. (1993) A Curriculum for the 21st Century? Towards a New Basis for Overcoming Academic/Vocational Divisions, *British Journal of Educational Studies* 41(3): 203–22.

Chapter 10

The implementation of GNVQs in further education

A case study

Margaret Bird, Geoff Esland, Jane Greenberg, Sandy Sieminski and Karen Yarrow

To meet the changing requirements of the labour market in Britain in the last decade 'massive' innovations have taken place in the programmes and assessment procedures within colleges of further education (FE). Alongside the resulting changes in qualifications, the 'incorporation' of the colleges in 1992, creating a marketplace for the funding of courses, has had profound ramifications for the organisation, management and delivery of the new qualifications. This case study is concerned with the effects of the changes in two areas of the vocational curriculum: business studies as well as health and social welfare. In interviews with key people concerned, it explores the very substantial changes that have taken place in the FE sector and the impact which these changes have had on the role of professional educators. It questions whether or not an unreformed GNVQ programme is likely to provide the adaptable workforce which is seen to be required.

Any changes which have been instituted in the field of education and training must necessarily be viewed within the wider societal context. No more so than when examining the implementation of new curricula in colleges which, traditionally, have bridged the transition for 16–19-year-olds from school to the labour market and, more particularly in recent years, have provided an alternative route to higher education (Raffe, 1979). Increasingly, too, the colleges of further education have fulfilled an important role for the adult population in providing for adults' re-training and re-entry to employment.[1] Helpful in providing a wider framework in which to understand these developments is the model developed by Esland (1999), discussed below. This model enables us to identify the political and economic agendas which influenced the formulation of the policy and the managerial and institutional agendas which have responsibility for its implementation. Useful in relation to the latter are theories concerning the implementation of policy more generally (Bird, 1998). It is believed that locating the curriculum initiative within the broader social context and theoretical framework prompts questions as to its likely efficacy in the longer term. We begin, therefore, by examining the rationale for the development of the General National Vocational Curriculum (GNVC) employing Esland's model.

The policy framework

Economic agenda

It is some time since it was first recognised that improvements in the quality of the labour force could influence economic growth (Blaug, 1968). This identifiable link has led to much of the blame for the downturn in the British economy in the 1970s being directed at the educational establishment for failing to produce a sufficiently highly skilled workforce. It is nonetheless evident that, in comparison with other advanced industrial countries, Britain, until quite recently, had a much smaller proportion of young people entering higher education.[2] As Finegold and Soskice (1988) observed, it has been trapped in a 'low skills equilibrium'. Meantime, technological innovation and the power of the multinational corporations have created a global marketplace. The effect of this is two-fold: first, it requires that Britain compete on the world stage and that due attention be paid to the value of the currency through monetary policy; second, it necessitates that the country increases its investment in the education and training of its workforce, to be sufficiently adaptable to meet new technological exigencies.

First, therefore, consider the economic cycle of activity depicted in the Esland model (Figure 10.1). This can either be a virtuous circle (clockwise movement, where, for example, low interest rates encourage investment, economic growth, exports, profitability, etc.) or a vicious circle (anti-clockwise movement, whereby, when an 'overheating' of the economy occurs, for example, increased consumption increasing imports and creating a balance of payments deficit). Public services such as education, particularly, are affected by both the monetary and fiscal policies of the government. One question, therefore, to address in this study was whether there were any signs that the government was making the resources available to finance curriculum innovation to provide for an increased student intake in the post-school sector.

Second, consider the wide-reaching nature of the changes taking place in the labour market. (The concepts encapsulating the nature of the changes taking place in the labour market are depicted in italics in Figure 10.1.) To be economically successful, post-industrial societies are seen to require a high level of investment in human capital. Ideally, workers, in what has been termed a post-fordist labour market, have essentially to be prepared for flexibility in their roles and for occupational mobility. In his 1989 speech, Kenneth Baker said:

> We want to equip young people with knowledge and skills so that they have greater chances. In the changing employment world they will need broad-based qualifications. They will want to show their employers flexibility. They will need to think and act independently. Otherwise the next wave of technology will leave them stranded.

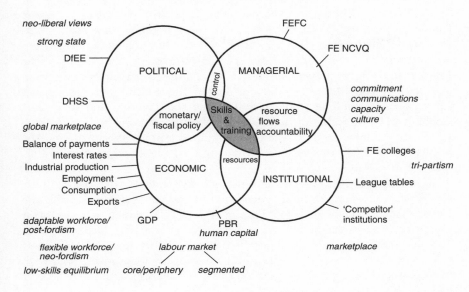

Figure 10.1 The policy framework of the implementation of GNVQ

More recently, the notion of flexibility has become associated with a deregulated labour market and has connotations of a neo-fordist labour market.[3] Hence, perhaps, the notion of adaptability is to be preferred[4] Evaluating the new curricula in relation to the perceived needs of the labour market prompts critical questions about its likely efficacy in the longer term in providing for the desired comprehensivisation of the post-school sector. Can it provide a national qualification which has parity of esteem with Advanced Level (AL) and thereby an alternative vocational route into higher education? Will it develop young people's generic skills sufficiently to facilitate access to higher education for an increased number and furnish the more adaptable labour force required or, will it simply facilitate a more 'flexible' labour force, so perpetuating the 'low-skills equilibrium' noted above, and the segmentation of the labour market as described by Hutton (1995)?

Political agenda

The political rationale for the development of NCVQ could be identified in that 'wing' of the Conservative Party, the 'modernisers', who believed in a strong state which favoured the establishment of a national framework for vocational qualifications together with central control over a system of funding the FE sector. Another identifiable strand, however, in the Conservatives' ideology of the 1980s was the neo-liberal view that education was a marketplace like any other and competition between colleges would result in a more efficient use of resources.[5] Hence, the passing of the Further and Higher Education Act in 1992 established further education and sixth form colleges as corporate bodies funded through the Further Education and Funding Council (FEFC) and the Training and Enterprise Councils (TECs), each institution responsible for its own budget. It was, therefore, pertinent to note when conducting this study the impact on the implementation of the GNVQ programme of these other very radical changes in policy.

Figure 10.1 depicts the two government departments with responsibilities which influenced the implementation of the new curricula in FE: the Department for Education and Employment (DfEE) which was the main source of finance channelled through the FEFC; and the Department of Health and Social Security (DHSS) which was the department which operated rules in relation to social benefits and hours of study for students who were unemployed. It was, therefore, pertinent to note what impact financial factors had on GNVQ course provision.

Managerial agenda

The medium through which the changes in curriculum were implemented by central government was the Further Education and Funding Council (FEFC) and the Training and Enterprise Councils (TECs) which determined the funding of colleges of further education and the National Council of Vocational Qualifications (NCVQ) which was charged with the task of designing, trialling and implementing the new qualification. (See the managerial agenda in Figure 10.1 which depicts the bodies which have a managerial function in relation to the FE curricula and the concept of 'control' which denotes their function.) The incorporation of the colleges in 1992 meant that they were no longer democratically accountable to their local communities and their governing bodies were 'dominated by a self-perpetuating oligarchy of business people' (Reeves, 1997).

An explicit intention of the ideology of the hybrid of Conservatism described above, which was came to be known as the 'New Right', was that education and training should be more responsive to the needs of the labour market. Hence, government had sought to wrest control of the curricula and assessment from the validating bodies and professionals and set up quangos such as the Training and Development Lead Body (TDLB), where employers were the main representatives (Chown, 1996; Hodkinson, 1995). The role of teacher was perceived to be more that of a technician. 'The presumption is that "they" will do what they are told . . . They are meant to be impotent, and it is assumed that they have nothing to contribute to workplace organisation' (Millward, cited in Hutton, 1995). Most particularly, therefore, the study undertaken was concerned to explore how the new curricula were managed by the NCVQ and what impact this had had upon the professionals involved in the programme's delivery.

Institutional agenda

Within the colleges, another aspect of the new managerialism at the time of the study (1997) was the institution of new contracts of employment for the lecturers employed. This was thought to be an important consideration when the impact of the changes in curricula on the professionals involved was being explored. The people responsible for delivering the new programme, in Lipsky's terms the 'street-level bureaucrats' (1980), were at the critical interface of policy implementation. Their commitment was very important. But so too were good communications, both within the organisation (in terms of professionals sharing a 'common definition of the situation' (Young and Mills, 1980) but, also, the all-important role of two-way communication (of 'feed-back' from the 'street-level' to those at the NCVQ whose function it was to interpret policy decisions and to implement them) (Williams, 1980). Hence, information relating to factors influencing implementation – the professional culture and commitment of the staff involved, the financial factors influencing the institution and the student population, the extent of communications (as defined above), and the various forms of control exercised by NCVQ – were explored in the interviews undertaken with staff.[6]

Research methodology

Five FE colleges were selected as sites for the study: three were located in the Greater London area (two of which were in the inner city), one in a city suburb, one in a metropolitan county and one in a 'greenfield' site in the Home Counties.[7] Within each institution two members of staff were identified, one who was involved in the co-ordination of the GNVQ in Business Studies and the another who was involved in the co-ordination of the GNVQ in Health and Social Care. Each respondent was asked to compare the GNVQ course which they were delivering in 1996 with a course in the same field which they had delivered for another qualification some five years previously. The interview focused on comparisons of the two courses identified in terms of: their content; student-selection criteria; resources as indicated by the course length and staff–student ratios; teaching delivery; assessment practice; moderation and validation procedures; and the lecturers' observations of student recruitment, retention and progression. Further, views were elicited as to whether or not the change to GNVQs had impacted on the lecturer's work role. Details of the colleges' location, the courses selected for study and the professional background of those interviewed is given in Table 10.1. The findings are presented below.

What changes have there been in FE colleges as a result of the implementation of GNVQs? What impact have these had on the professionals involved?

Two-thirds (6) of those interviewed chose to compare the GNVQ programme with their prior experience of a course on the same subject at a similar level for the Business and Education Council Qualifications (BTEC). Of the others, where a comparison of a course was possible in the same field at a not dissimilar level, one chose to compare GCSE and GNVQ Intermediate in Business Studies, one the Preliminary Certificate in Social Care (PCSC) and the GNVQ Intermediate in Health and Social Care and the other the course for the Nursery Nurses Educational Board (NNEB) with the GNVQ Intermediate in Health and Social Care. In one case there was no suitable course for the purposes of comparison.

Course content and structure

Prior to the advent of NVQs and GNVQs the expectation of the providers' courses leading to a recognised qualification was that there was a syllabus which detailed the areas and specific content of the course to be covered by the teacher. The assessment procedure(s) adopted, whether the use of an oral or written examination and/or the assessment of course work, tested the student's capabilities. But how teachers structured the work, which teaching strategies were adopted, the textbooks employed, what assignments and tasks were set, was entirely in their hands. The syllabus and the mode of assessment were prescribed; the structure and the process of learning were not.

In contrast, the courses leading to a GVNQ did not have a syllabus *per se* but instead were very prescriptive as to: the outcomes to be assessed; and the structuring of relevant information as 'evidence indicators' for that purpose. Thus, the process of learning was very much determined by these requirements. All GNVQs, Foundation, Intermediate and Advanced, had a unit structure comprising mandatory units, optional units and core skills (see Appendix 10.1). To get a GNVQ certificate, at whatever level, students had to pass all the units. Each unit was made up of 2–5 elements, or state-ments of ability, and students had to demonstrate that they were competent in all of the elements that made up the unit to obtain a pass. Each element was broken down further into a number of performance criteria which indi-cated what sort of things students had to understand to show mastery of the elements and units. All performance criteria had to be covered before

Table 10.1 Sample of colleges/courses/professionals involved in study

	A/FE		B/FE		C/FE		D/FE		E/FE	
Catchment area	Metropolitan County		Outer London suburb		Central London urban		West London urban		Home Counties 'greenfield'	
Subject	Business	H&SC	Business	H&SC	Business	H&SC	Business	H&SC	Business	H&SC
Qualification level	BTEC GNVQ Ad.	BTEC GNVQ	GCSE 'O' GNVQ Int.	NNEB GNVQ Int.	BTEC GNVQ Ad.	PCSC GNVQ Ad.	BTEC GNVQ Ad.	BTEC GNVQ Ad.	BTEC GNVQ Ad.	GNVQ Ad.
Professionals' qualifications/ background	HND, DMS BA B.Ed. regis. MA	CQSW Cert. Ed.	Cert. Ed.	SRN/HV Cert. Ed. MA Ed.	History regis. MBA	Cert. Ed./FE Voc. Qual. 'Working with children'	MIPD former Personnel Manager	B.Sc. Soc. MA	Cert. Ed. TDLB	SRN/ TDLB/ D32/33/ 34 former Nursery Nurse
Years in teaching	–	–	20	8	20	18	12	7	10	1
Contract	Negotiated	Negotiated	'Silver Book'	CEF contract	Negotiated	Negotiated	Negotiated	'Silver Book'	'Silver Book' Negotiated	
Interview no.	1	2	3	4	5	6	7	8	9	10

Note
BA   Bachelor of Arts
B.Sc.   Bachelor of Science
BTEC   Business Technical Education Council
CQSW   Certificate Qualification in Social Work
DMS   Diploma Management Studies
GCSE   General Certificate Secondary Education
GNVQ Ad.   General National Vocational Qualification – Advanced
GNVQ Inter. General National Vocational Qualification – Intermediate
H&SC   Health and Social Care
HND   Higher National Diploma
HV   Health Visitor
MA   Master of Arts
MBA   Master of Business Administration
MIPD   Management Institute Personnel Diploma
NNEB   Nursery Nurses Education Board
PCSC   Preliminary Certificate in Social Care
SRN   State Registered Nurse
TDLB   Training Development Lead Body

a GNVQ certificate was obtained. For a Foundation/Intermediate GNVQ there were about 100 performance criteria and for an Advanced GNVQ there were about 200 performance criteria. Whilst teachers could still employ which texts they chose and adopt whatever teaching strategies they deemed appropriate, with one exception, the lecturers interviewed expressed frustration at what was perceived to be the very prescriptive nature of the GNVQ course.

The main criticism expressed of the GNVQ was that, because the information obtained by students was so fragmented, students failed to get an overall view of the subject. Thus, it was felt that they lacked a conceptual framework and their understanding of the subject matter was very superficial. One teacher on the GNVQ Advanced in Business Studies gave an example of the unit on the business environment which was seen as:

> a mixture, a bit of economics, a bit of business studies, a bit of the old commerce and everything is put together with very little thought. So you know the teachers don't like teaching it very much, their unit. . . . For instance, there is supply and demand and elasticity, they are quite deep concepts, they need a lot of background but we haven't got the time. And we introduce them in a very simple way, really I don't see the point.[8]

Another tutor on a Health and Social Care, Intermediate, also felt constrained by the way in which the GNVQ impacted on the mode of learning adopted:

> it is different. Some say [there are] opportunities for creativity but it is clearly defined what you have to teach and you don't have time to deviate from that really, so it is really very very specific and that is something I have never been used [to]. I have had the subjects laid down in the syllabus, obviously, what you have to cover, but this is very prescriptive, GNVQ, it is very rigid . . . students are not bringing knowledge together in any holistic way, [they] do not leave the course with a coherent block of knowledge.[9]

All the lecturers who had been involved in delivering the forerunner to the GNVQ appeared to feel a loss of professional autonomy in delivering the GNVQ. The one exception was the person who was responsible for the GNVQ, Advanced, at E/FE who would appear to have been a recent recruit to the role, having spent twenty years previously working in a nursery.

Financial factors: student recruitment, staff–student ratios, student retention, course duration

In all the interviews conducted there were a number of issues arising in relation to the implementation of the GNVQ qualification, with regard to student recruitment, staff–student ratios, and the length of the course, which had financial implications for the institution. The incorporation of the colleges in 1992, prior to the first presentation of GNVQs in 1993, had the effect of bringing all the FE colleges into one marketplace in which they had to bid for resources.[10] If they failed to recruit and meet their quotas they suffered financial penalties. Moreover, as the GNVQ was a qualification which school sixth forms could offer, FE institutions were not only in competition for students with both neighbouring FE institutions but also with secondary schools in their locality.

Student recruitment and selection: As with the entry to established BTEC and 'A' level courses there were qualification entry criteria (4 GCSEs at grade C or above, or the GNVQ Intermediate) specified in college brochures with regard to GNVQ Advanced. There was an indication in one college (C/FE) on the GNVQ Health and Social Welfare course that the criteria for entry had been lowered in order that the student target be reached. The GNVQ Foundation/Intermediate course did not require formal qualifications. This aided recruitment but resulted in some instances of poor matching of students with the course requirements. As the tutor on the GNVQ Intermediate in Health and Social Care commented:

> [We] are under pressure all the way through – pressure to recruit students – so you may well take on to GNVQ – I think you have also got to look at the sort of students who come on to the GNVQ at Intermediate level. They tend to be students who haven't done well academically at GCSE and aren't that sure that they want to be in an academic environment but don't know what else to be doing and maybe GNVQ picks up more people who think 'well I'm not sure but I will give it a try, because it could lead to all sorts of things because it has a broad base'. . . . And I think that one of the difficulties that the group you get in aren't necessarily positive that this is where they want to be and that accounts for some of the drop-out. And the difficulty is retaining – completing. We pick up students – you take them in even if you are not sure that you think they will complete the course.[11]

Most conscious of the importance of student recruitment was the relatively new appointment on the GNVQ Advanced course at E/FE. She said she was under pressure to increase student enrolment because 'it is business at the end of the day and [you] have to justify your wages basically'.

Staff-student ratios: A comparison the staff–student ratios on the GNVQ courses with those which obtained on the BTEC courses previously showed that among the courses in the study the proportion of students to tutors was not dissimilar. However, in three of the five colleges in the sample it was said that the ratio of students had been increased to allow for the increase in the number of students who 'dropped out'.

Student retention: This issue is clearly linked to those detailed above. And, given the FEFC criteria for funding at different stages of the course, the loss of students had differing cost implications. A very substantial 'drop-out' in the first year of a two-year course could threaten its financial viability. In making comparisons with the situation on the GNVQ Advanced course at C/FE with the former PCSC, the co-ordinator said:

> You can't run a course now without about twenty to start. PCSC always recruited well, until . . . the last couple of years, but we continued to run it. In the current climate we'd no more be allowed to do that than fly to the moon . . . now you'd start at twenty to one, assuming that you would lose about four in the first year. We've lost more in previous years and there's a real implication in two-year GNVQs. The first year we ran an Advanced we were down to seven at the beginning of the second year and five actually passed. Now in that climate we made a tremendous financial loss to the department.[12]

In four cases the rate of retention on the GNVQ Advanced had been substantially less than that on the former BTEC course. (At FE/C completion rates in Business Studies had dropped from 85–90 per cent to 60–70 per cent and at E/FE, also in Business Studies, completion rates had dropped from 75 per cent to less than 50 per cent.) One of the four colleges experiencing low retention had opted to revert to BTEC.

The substantial drop-out, however, has to be seen in relation to the high proportion of students who are registered as unemployed or in receipt of other social benefits. As one tutor commented:

> We have got young people who are 16, parents who are on benefit living in hostels. We have all sorts of students and it is difficult for them because I find myself asking, 'Well, why weren't you here?' And they say, 'Well, I haven't got the bus fare.' What can you do?[13] It was possible that there were more people taking courses in FE in 1997 who were technically unemployed and seeking work than five years earlier when the financial incentive (the top-up to unemployment benefit given to those taking a training course) was not available.[14]

Course duration: Whilst the BTEC and the GNVQ Advanced courses were both delivered over a period of two years, the amount of time given to some subject areas was much reduced. For example, at A/FE the lecturer commented that, whereas previously on the BTEC his subject, Social Policy and Administration, had been delivered over the two-year period, on the GNVQ it was an option unit and the time reduced to 12/14 weeks. He felt it was an 'impossible task' to cover the massive changes that had taken place in social policy – the National Health Service (NHS), community care and the Children's Act. The limited amount of time meant that there was no opportunity for analysis and theoretical perspectives. Another constraint on the weekly number of contact hours was the rules governing unemployment benefit. A very high proportion of students were in receipt of this. At C/FE the courses in Business Studies had been reduced successively from 23 to 21 to 16 and at the time of the study stood at 14½ hours. This reduction in hours was to enable students to claim benefit while studying because, technically, they were available for work. It was commented that the reduction in teaching time had led to much 'cutting of corners'.[15] The net effect of the reduction in hours on the staff concerned was that they felt more pressured. As one commented, 'it is like a factory, rush, rush . . . time is money'.[16]

Assessment

Whereas students on BTEC courses had been assessed on their course work through their undertaking of some twenty integrated assignments, the students on GNVQ courses were assessed on each element within all the units undertaken. To pass a unit they had to show that they were competent in all the performance criteria that made up a unit. As one tutor remarked, 'it's totally unforgiving this course, you've got to pass everything'.[17] Further, students had to gain over 70 per cent on the multiple choice tests which were set for the mandatory units. They could sit the tests when they were deemed to be ready and if they did not achieve a high enough mark the tests could be retaken at a later point in the course. The rigorous testing procedures required for assessment for the GNVQ were seen by the majority of lecturers as 'mountains of paperwork' and 'onerous'. It resulted in their spending less time teaching and more time 'cramming' in preparation for the tests. There were two alternative views expressed among the staff interviewed. One was the relative newcomer to further education who had no experience of the predecessor course in E/FE. On the GNVQ Advanced course in Health and Social Care she had found it helpful to base the assignments on the students' work placements. The other was a tutor on a GNVQ Intermediate Business Studies at B/FE who had found that the model of assessment could be quite empowering of students who had a learning disability or behavioural problem. These students, she commented, had

> probably failed in the secondary sector and have actually come here for a second bite of the apple . . . on the GCSE it was pass or fail whereas

on the GNVQ you are either not ready for approval or you have achieved. So you don't have this stigma of having failed yet again. You are not ready for approval.

Much use was made of 'workshops' to develop study skills, time management skills and how to make effective use of a library. The system of assessment was also seen as advantageous in creating a 'fast track system' for the able students who had underachieved earlier:

There are some students who have not succeeded in the secondary sector because they have been bone idle, troublemakers or whatever, but they are bright, so we try and encourage them to complete in 20 weeks. If they complete in 20 weeks, they progress to the Advanced course. This year we had 11 students completing in 20 weeks.

In general, however, those interviewed felt that the very strict assessment procedures which had to be adhered to on the GNVQ programme detracted from their satisfaction in the job. The focus on assignments, it was felt, as the 'be all and end all' was alienating.[18]

Verification/moderation procedures

The changes that had taken place in the process of assessment were mirrored in the monitoring procedures which had been instituted with the GNVQ programme. With the former BTEC course, when it worked well, the moderation process, it was observed, could be both very effective and supportive of the teaching staff concerned. First, it involved some 'cross marking' within the college, a form of internal standardisation, and then there was the 'external moderator who came in two or three times a year and he or she would look at the work of the students . . . talk to the staff, talk to the students and that was that'.[19] In another institution, the former arrangement was described as a much more leisurely process taking place over two days.

[Moderators] were reasonably rigorous . . . there was a variety of evidence provided, lots of students self-assessment, they saw all the students, they saw them as individuals and they saw them as groups . . . the value is in what it does for the students in terms of them feeling important and feeling involved. I think there was a feeling of involvement with the moderation process.[20]

In engaging with the staff, in commenting on the materials and making practical suggestions, the moderator was providing professional support and development for those in the department.

In contrast, the experience of verification with the advent of GNVQ, in the way in which it was described, appeared to be a much more impersonal experience, more akin to a 'policing' of the system.

> Now the focus seems to be much more, the basics are always there, the schemes of work, the difference being the concentration. Have you got the PCs, have you got the assignments that covered all the elements, or are you internally verifying the assignments? Have you got the records or a tracking system for students, have you got boxes to tick to show if all the PCs are covered? Now it seems to be an examination of the administrative mechanisms we use to track these students. That seems to be the focus and verification seems to be the big focus. So testing, verifying, having evidence that something is there, that it's been achieved, that seems to be the focus. All of which is away from teaching, all of which is even away from knowledge, all of which is towards bureaucracy.[21]

One of the reasons why the experience of the GNVQ system of verification appeared so alienating was that the external verifier did not necessarily come from the same field as the course which he was verifying. He/she was 'just looking at systems'. In some cases, therefore, this led to a certain amount of 'nit-picking' and there was not the same engagement with the lecturers, an exchange of ideas and opportunity for rapport.

The process of verification, however, needs to be seen in the wider context of changes that had taken place in the employment situation in colleges of FE. The 'turnover' of staff, it was noted, had increased.[22] It was acknowledged that a national programme had to establish national standards. As one respondent remarked:

> I'm not sure it's the perfect thing to rely on tutor integrity, tutor honesty and all the rest of it, and that's fine when you are working in a team that operates on those lines, the internal verification can become a doddle in that sort of case. But when you've got a constant turnover of staff, or staff that are not competent, or just not doing their job, there is a place for an external verification system I think.[23]

Further, the increase in the number of teaching hours with the 'negotiated contract' had meant that staff were under more pressure and accepted that they no longer had the time to give to a two-day visit by an external verifier/moderator.

Teaching delivery

One of the main differences between the BTEC and the GNVQ, it has been noted, was the nature of assessment. This had important implications for the teaching approach adopted. The integrated nature of the BTEC assignments encouraged co-operative working between tutors and between students, whereas the fragmented nature of the GNVQ method of assessment discouraged co-operative working and students worked much more on their own. Moreover, the pressure to meet all the performance criteria in the limited time available led some tutors to teach almost by rote or in the easiest possible way. As one described:

> I think the style of delivery is more didactic, to start with anyway, to get the basics in for any unit. The sheer volume means there's far more handouts given now, less discussion. We'd like to make it more discussion because that's what we need but we can't always do that. Just to get through the amount there's an awful lot of up-front teaching goes on to get started. It's not what it's supposed to be. The theory is that there is much more freedom to do research and what have you. But the practice, particularly at the beginning I think, is that you have to find methods that allow you to do that but at the same time allow you to get the information in more rapidly at both levels.[24]

Some tutors seriously questioned whether they were teaching in any real sense. They felt that they had become managers of learning resources: if they were in a class they were either giving specific instructions for a test, constantly checking on assignments or helping individuals. As one said:

> So you are more of a facilitator . . . you've got to get them through the assignments. It is almost a by-product if I stand there and do a beautiful lesson, which I must do at least once a year. It's almost a by-product to do good teaching because the emphasis is on good learning.[25]

Another limitation of the mode of individualised learning which resulted from the demands of assessment process for a GNVQ was that there were fewer opportunities than on the BTEC course for group discussion or critical challenging of other people's assumptions. Students who had come from schools it was noted by one tutor:

> have become more adjusted to this educational approach of not being so analytical but they are happy to sit there in splendid isolation in a room copying out work and writing it down. And I think it is sometimes, you know, a bit of a shock if you try to challenge them, then they don't feel comfortable with it in terms of having to analyse and having to think.[26]

The BTEC curriculum, it was felt, had offered tutors more opportunities to be more spontaneous and responsive in their teaching style. Reflecting on the very different requirements of the two modes of learning, one tutor remarked:

> the GNVQ . . . I find it a compatible way of working . . . my style, because I like order and the organisation it brings and I like to know I am being objective . . . but perhaps you don't see the rising stars that perhaps you saw on the National in terms of creativity, coming to you with things they have found out. You are not able [now] to take time out to debate an issue that perhaps you hadn't planned because the 'evidence' [required] is so demanding, the 'range' [stipulated] is so demanding and working towards the test that we have to go with that, there is no sidetracking to explore anything else.[27]

Work placement was not an essential requirement on the GNVQ course but some FE colleges 'fought hard to keep it'. One tutor was able to facilitate five placements in five different parts of the health and welfare services for each student on the GNVQ Advanced Health and Social Care course. She used the opportunities that placements offered to provide the material for some of the assignments. For example, one had been undertaken on issues on the structure and funding of the Health Service. Another had required a group to write a short piece on what the political parties were offering. Placements were used effectively, 'so that [the students] begin to think about what is going on in the real world'.[28] They were the one area where the professionals felt they could still exercise some autonomy.

Student progression

Eight of the ten courses investigated in the study were at GNVQ Advanced level. Although the rate of retention was lower on the GNVQ course than on the former BTEC course, the rate of progression to higher education, it was noted, had increased. But there were reservations expressed by some tutors that the GNVQ Advanced was as suitable a preparation for degree level work as in so far as it didn't

> teach them to analyse and think as the old BTEC National did. The pressure of work is that they're . . . gathering evidence for their portfolio or they're preparing for a test as opposed to analysing a set of information, finding different routes through it and options, so that when they get to degree work there's a gap in their preparation for doing higher level [work].[29]

On the other hand, the tutor of the GNVQ Advanced course in Health and Social Care from the college on the 'greenfield' site in the Home Counties commented on ways in which the GNVQ course did prepare students for university-level work in the emphasis that was placed in GNVQ on planning and the investigative approach. Students were expected in this institution to write essays as well as undertake projects. (Because she had not taught on a BTEC course she drew comparisons between the GNVQ and traditional 'A' level courses.) A number of students from the course at this institution went into higher education through Project 2000 (Nursing), others had degrees in Physical Therapy, Chiropody, Psychology and Community Work. Some of those who had not taken the route into HE had become health and social care assistants.

Two of the courses investigated were GNVQ Intermediate, one in Business Studies and the other in Health and Social Care, both at B/FE. The Intermediate level course appeared to be a vocational course without an immediate vocational outcome; it did not lead to employment. It allowed for progression from Foundation level for those coming into college without GCSEs (some of whom, with special educational needs, may have taken a pre-Foundation course). Hence, it could be seen as a stepping-stone either to vocationally specific courses such as the NNEB or to the GNVQ Advanced. It was seen as 'perhaps attractive to people who wouldn't have come in before'. Some students, however, had been disappointed in that they had taken the course thinking that it would enable them to get a job. There were some instances of students from the GNVQ Intermediate in Business Studies who had progressed to the GNVQ Advanced and to university, most often to local HE institutions.

> They were below average students who kept at it and got there in the end. [Interviewer: Rewarding?] . . . Yes, well I think it is constantly encouraging them and they actually come back after the first block like homing pigeons and after that you didn't see them and then you get asked for a letter of reference.[30]

One effect, therefore, of the lack of employment possibilities for young people at the age of leaving school was that they continued and succeeded in education when in earlier years they would have left education for unskilled/semi-skilled employment.

The impact on the professional's role

Let us now consider what impact this new programme has had on the working lives of the lecturers concerned. In addressing the specificities of the GNVQ, in particular the prescriptive requirements of the curriculum and the rigidities of the assessment and, in some instances, placed alongside coping with students with special learning difficulties and/or limited resources, one has already gained an insight as to demands which have been placed upon the staff involved in the colleges. The imposition of uniformity had often acted to stifle the creativity and spontaneity of their teaching role, with the result that there was a strong sense of their having suffered a loss of professional autonomy. It was, perhaps, most noticeable among lecturers who had a particular identification with an academic subject and less so among those who had a specific occupational training background. As one remarked,

> I've lost the autonomy over my subject. . . . I don't think the profession of lecturer is respected in GNVQ, the nature of the qualification takes away something from the lecturer, it's prescribed, it . . . doesn't allow you the flexibility that I think you need and what gives me my job satisfaction.[31]

There were a number of factors which, cumulatively, had detracted from people's job satisfaction. Almost two-thirds of those interviewed commented on the fact that they had fewer opportunities to collaborate with colleagues. Where it had been possible to maintain a team approach, it had clearly been beneficial to those concerned. Even the undertaking of the training in verification, the much derided D32/33/34s, when taken as a team, had helped to overcome some of the perceived futility of the exercise.[32] There was also a sense of loss expressed that there was less contact with other professionals working in the same field in other colleges. In part, this resulted from the administrative demands of the GNVQ but it was also perceived as one of the effects of 'incorporation'. One lecturer commented on the benefits which he had earlier experienced in being a member of an active professional association concerned with social care.

> Particularly with the National Association you just saw people from all over the country and compared experience. You got the same idea of what was going on. At the moment you feel as though you are all in separated little fish tanks basically. We weren't in competition with our neighbours and we are now, so you don't see them . . . you just got a much wider overview I think, and those conferences that we run weren't just factual they were fun as well. All that's gone now.
>
> [Then] there was the London Boroughs Group . . . that used to meet three or four times a year . . . there was some sort of mutual interest. Whereas now, the way it's all been split up and you're in competition you don't feel that, well one we don't meet, but also you feel like you're in competition with all your local colleges as well. Fighting for the same fish.[33]

Whilst the GNVQ was largely seen to have detracted from the co-operative working with other staff and the opportunities to develop fruitful contacts in the wider professional network, it was also seen to have led to less satisfying personal contact with the students on the course, which was perceived to reduce not only the tutor's job satisfaction but also detract from the student's educational experience. Previously, one tutor said:

> I would know about them, I knew if they played in the bands, I'd know what they did up to about ten years, if I see people I recognise them. Now I just don't know them, the same detail . . . it's easier to teach them if you know them, you understand them and it's a different way of working. If what you are doing is going in and you're filling in bits of paper and you're processing them . . . it's like this idea of *individualised learning*, there's a process, the product is this bit of paper at the end and they feed it through. It's much less satisfying and it's much less effective, particularly with our student base.[34]

An important element in the loss of job satisfaction was a concern over the diminution of the quality of the education which the lecturers felt they were delivering. With one exception, the person who was relatively new to teaching, there was a sense in which the staff involved in GNVQ felt that the emphasis on uniformity had been undermining the quality of what was provided. As one tutor said:

> I think there's a false perception that for there to be quality education it has to be screwed down to the floor and have everything monitored and assessed and I don't think that does give you good quality education, what it gives you is a standard that is uniform, but having uniformity doesn't necessarily mean good education because people are different and have different needs and different backgrounds and perceptions and a quality education would take account of that, whereas if it's about producing a record and a portfolio of evidence and a common standard process then it doesn't meet that need.[35]

The other factor which impinged upon the lecturers' satisfaction in the job and which cannot be separated from either the impact of 'incorporation' or the implementation of GNVQs was the change in the lecturers' work contracts. The move from the 'Silver Book' to the 'Negotiated Contract' had entailed an increase in number of teaching and contact hours for those employed in colleges of further education.[36] This move had impaired relations in many colleges between the management and the teaching staff. As one of the respondents remarked:

> I have to try very hard to keep myself motivated. I feel the management style has changed and it's like – more for less. They want more from us and we are getting less and there's not the commitment. We are expected to give 100 per cent commitment but there's not 100 per

cent commitment from the management, therefore it is very difficult to be motivated.[37]

This response came from a lecturer who had both taken a course in customer care, with a view to the greater retention of students, and was interested to pursue her own personal professional development by undertaking an MBA. She did not feel personally undervalued by management but, she said, there were others who did. Further, she recognised that the reason for the constraints which the staff felt were due to the criteria for funding determined by the FEFC.

> It's just the funding and we are a lowly funded college and they have cut our funding yet again and they, the management, I suppose have got to think of ways of staying afloat basically. So, in that sense, I suppose it's difficult. But I wish there were more interaction. I feel it is very much 'them and us'. . . . If I were a manager I would lay my cards on the table. Okay you can't tell everyone everything, but I would appeal to their better nature because I do feel with goodwill you can say 'this is it' and after all it's our livelihood isn't it? If we are all working in the same direction but I don't think that people – they just come here to do twenty or whatever hours.

In spite of the frustrations with management and the lack of resources which hindered her work, this tutor had developed a team approach with her colleagues and still derived satisfaction from her tutoring role. She said it came from:

> seeing [students] achieve. They come and they – some of them are very reluctant, truculent, and then they actually achieve and they say thank you. That's really wonderful . . . they pretend to give me a hard time, but they do care. When the parents actually write and say thank you I feel as if I have done something good.

Conclusions

In drawing conclusions from this case study undertaken in five institutions, reference will be made to the results of other studies (Hyland and Weller, 1996; Wolf, 1997). Initially, let us make some judgement as to whether the GNVQ curricula, as they are currently constituted, are likely to provide the wide range of skills and adaptability in the workforce which is seen to be required for the twenty-first century. Subsequently, we will examine the factors which influenced the programme's implementation in order that the programme's shortcomings might be addressed.

First, there were positive factors to note: most notably, the increased number of young people who were reported initially as 'staying on' in education. The nature of the GNVQ programme offering Intermediate and Advanced courses has provided post-school education for students with a wider range of academic ability than hitherto. Important features which were valued were: the modular nature of the programmes; the involvement of students in planning their work; the use of an investigative approach; the attention given to study skills and the facility to 'structure in' work placements into the programme. In addition, the radical change in the method of assessment avoided the stigma of failing and was found to be empowering of some sections of the student population who had become alienated from their former secondary schools and an academic curriculum. As a result, there were some able young people for whom GNVQ provided access to HE who might not otherwise have had that option. In principle, therefore, one can argue that the introduction of a national vocational qualification, which is recognised by HE as an alternative, albeit not rated equivalent to 'A' Level,[38] has furthered the comprehensivisation of post-school provision and provided for the expansion of HE, as well as preparing other teenagers for employment. It has, therefore, increased post-school participation and furthered National Education and Training Targets (Macfarlene, 1993). But, it is important to note from a recent national survey of GNVQs (Wolf, 1997) that GNVQ students are largely concentrated in four subject areas (Art and Design, Business, Health and Social Care and Leisure and Tourism).[39] Moreover, it would appear that GNVQ has done little more than match the numbers taking the range of courses it replaced. Further, only about a half complete the qualification (Wolf, 1997). This leads one to question whether the current focus on a limited range of subjects is likely to meet the future needs of the labour market.

However, there were more than a small number of criticisms expressed of the GNVQ programme as it was presented in 1997. Problems associated with the new curriculum have also been noted elsewhere (Utley, 1993; Spencer, 1994; OFSTED, 1996; Spours, 1997). Whilst the GNVQ rhetoric centred on the notion of 'student-centred' learning, the reality for those who delivered the programme was that their 'teaching' had become very didactic in order that they were able to assess the students on all the necessary performance criteria. Moreover, in 'teaching to test' it was felt that students were not developing a conceptual framework or engaging in any critical debate/dialogue. The quality of the programme had also been undermined by a reduction in the course length, which had led to a superficial treatment of issues. The 'drop-out' rate was also high.[40] This leads one to question whether the programme, as it is currently constituted, is an adequate preparation for students who are seeking entry to higher education, who need, it is argued, both an adequate knowledge base and a questioning approach. In its existing format the GNVQ would appear to provide more for a 'neo-fordist' flexibility and a segmented workforce (Hutton, 1995), than for a 'post-fordist' adaptability in the labour market.

Let us now review the factors which have been identified earlier as influencing the efficacy of the implementation of policy in order that the shortcomings of the implementation of the GNVQ programme might be identified and addressed. First, in relation to 'capacity', one has to note that FE colleges, following incorporation, have been placed in direct competition with one another and have been obliged to cut their costs in order that they can survive in the market place.[41] Hence they have tended to promote the lower per capita cost courses, which has led to a concentration on the 'big four' GNVQs to the detriment of courses in science, manufacturing, technology, etc. Further, changes in the rules relating to students drawing unemployment or social benefits has led to a reduction in course hours in order that these students could continue to study. Hence, the quality of the GNVQ programmes has been undermined. Second, in relation to the professional 'culture' and the 'commitment' of the teachers involved, it was observed that the staff concerned had invested a great deal of time and effort in delivering the new programmes but expressed frustration at the shortcomings of the mechanistic approaches of competence-based education.[42] Morale was also undermined in some colleges as a result of the imposition of new contracts of employment.[43] Third, in relation to 'communication', it was evident that there were limited opportunities for the professionals involved to feed back their evaluation of GNVQ to those who had designed the programmes and assessment procedures. Moreover, the new contracts and the competitive situation facing colleges had seriously curtailed their opportunities to work with colleagues within and between institutions, which had previously been such a valued form of staff development. Finally, it was evident that the pressure resulting from excessive control of the assessment procedures was actually undermining of the educational process. In reviewing and revising the GNVQ programme, the newly constituted Educational Excellence Foundation (Edexcel) needs to listen to the 'front-line' professionals who have experience with more structured, knowledge-based programmes such as BTEC. These courses have incorporated broader assessment techniques and have a proven record in preparing young people both for higher education and for entry to the labour market.

Notes

1 The numbers of adults returning to full- or part-time education increased by 40 per cent between 1994/5 and 1995/6 (FEFC). *TES* 2 Dec. 1997.

2 'In 1979 about one in eight young people entered full-time Higher Education (HE). By 1993, the proportion was one in four' (EC Memo on HE in the EC, 1993, para 6).

3 For a discussion of neo-fordism see Avis *et al.*, 1996.

4 For a discussion of this point see Will Hutton's article, 'Let's not get too rigid about flexibility' in the *Observer*, 13 July 1997.

5 For a discussion of the differing Conservative ideologies influencing the educational agenda in the 1980s see R. Johnson (1990) 'A new road to serfdom? A critical history of the 1988 Act' in Education Group II, *Education Limited: schooling, training and the New Right* London: Unwin Hyman.

6 For a more extensive review of the literature relating to the implementation of policy see Bird (1998).

7 In technical terms the sample of institutions is an 'opportunity' sample, i.e. the choice of cases is not selected to be representative of the total population in numerical terms, as in a survey, but cases are selected to test out a number of theoretical propositions.

8 Interview No. 5 with the co-ordinator for GNVQ Business Studies at C/FE, 6 May 1997.

9 Interview No. 4 with the co-ordinator for HSW at B/FE, 20 May 1997.

10 For a discussion of the impact of the changes in the funding mechanisms in FE, see Spours and Lucas (1996).

11 Interview No. 4 with the co-ordinator for HSW at B/FE, 20 May 1997.

12 Interview No. 6 with the co-ordinator for H&SC at C/FE, 14 March 1997.

13 Interview No. 3 with the co-ordinator for Business Studies at B/FE, 20 May 1997.

14 To qualify as a full-time student, a student must attend an average of 15 hours' lessons a week.

15 Interview No. 6, with the co-ordinator for H&SC at C/FE, 14 March 1997.

16 Interview No. 8 with the co-ordinator for H&SC at D/FE, 22 May 1997.

17 Interview No. 9 with the co-ordinator for Business Studies at E/FE, 19 May 1997.

18 Ibid.

19 Interview No. 5, with the co-ordinator for GNVQ Business Studies at C/FE, 6 May 1997.

20 Interview No. 6 with the co-ordinator for H&SC at C/FE, 14 March 1997.

21 Interview No. 9 with the co-ordinator for Business Studies at E/FE, 19 May 1997.

22 'The switch to a revolving-door labour market for teachers has been most marked in further education and sixth-form colleges, which have suffered four years of deep cuts and a huge growth in part-time and temporary contracts'. (*TES*, 2 May 1997).

23 Interview No. 6 with the co-ordinator for H&SC at C/FE, 14 March 1997.

24 Ibid.

25 Interview No. 9 with the co-ordinator for Business Studies at E/FE, 19 May 1997.

26 Interview No. 1 with the co-ordinator for Business Studies at A/FE, 14 February 1997.

27 Interview No. 7 with the co-ordinator for Business Studies at D/FE, 13 March 1997.

28 Interview No. 1 with the co-ordinator for Business Studies at A/FE, 14 February 1997.

29 Interview No. 3 with the co-ordinator for Business Studies at B/FE, 20 May 1997.

30 Ibid.

31 Interview No. 2 with the co-ordinator for H&SC at A/FE, 14 February 1997.

32 Interview No. 3 with the co-ordinator for Business Studies at B/FE, 20 May 1997.

33   Interview No. 6 with the co-ordinator for H&SC at C/FE, 14 March 1997.
34   Interview No. 1 with the co-ordinator for Business Studies at A/FE, 14 February 1997.
35   Ibid.
36   Following incorporation, the College Employers' Forum (CEF) advised college managements to introduce a new contract, replacing the Silver Book contract with one which would increase the number of teaching hours and reduce holidays. Strike action ensued in a number of colleges. Some senior managements sought to negotiate their own terms with staff, offering better conditions than were available under the CEF contract, although worse conditions than existed under the Silver Book. Others have refused to negotiate and at the time of the study (1997) were still insisting on the CEF contract. Table 10.1 indicates that staff were often on different types of contract even within one college.
37   Interview No. 3 with the co-ordinator for Business Studies at B/FE, 20 May 1997.
38   'A national survey of teachers, college principals and 1,300 Year 11 pupils showed that virtually all those planning academic studies were aiming for university, compared to one in four of those opting for vocational courses. . . . They see them as second-rate qualifications, citing A-levels as the gold standard and the natural route to a degree.' ('Pupils shun GNVQ degree path', *TES*, 10 May 1996).
39   Five subject areas were generally available in 1993/4. Ten others have been added since but the GNVQ programmes are dominated by four of the original five, which recruit three-quarters of GNVQ students.
40   Similar findings are reported elsewhere. See Spours, 1997.
41   'A shortfall in funding for FE was announced in April 1997. Colleges were expected to make savings of 7.6 per cent after inflation.' ('Post-16 places lost in budget bombshell', *TES*, 11 April 1997).
42   The positive commitment of the post-16 staff was also noted in a national survey (Hyland and Weller, 1996).
43   In 1995/6 the chief inspector's report for the FEFC stated that an increasing reliance on part-time staff and short-term contracts was threatening standards (Spours, *TES*, 2 May 1997).

References

Avis, J., Blommer, M., Esland, G., Gleeson, D. and Hodkinson, P. (1996) *Knowledge and Nationhood*, London, Cassell.

Bird, M. (1998) 'The implementation of an "equal opportunities" policy: a case study of an "open college" ' unpublished paper.

Blaug, M. (1968) *Economics of Education I*, Harmondsworth, Penguin Modern Economics.

Chown, A (1996) 'Post-16 teacher education, national standards and the staff development forum: time for openness and voice?' *British Journal for In-Service Education*, 22(2).

Esland, G. (1998) Agenda's paper in E837 Reader 1, *Education, Training and the Future of Work: social, political and economic contexts of policy development*. EB37 Study Guide Section 2, Milton Keynes: Open University.

Finegold, D. and Soskice, D. (1988) 'The failure of training in Britain: analysis and prescription', *Oxford Review of Economic Policy*, 4(3).

Hodgson, A. and Spours, K. (eds) (1996) 'From the White Paper to the Dearing Report: a conceptual and historical framework for the 1990s', *Dearing and Beyond: 14–19 qualifications, frameworks and systems,* London, Kogan Page.

Hodkinson, P. (1995) 'Professionalism and competence', in P. Hodkinson and M. Issitt (eds) *The Challenge of Competence: professionalism through vocational education and training,* London, Cassell.

Hutton, W. (1995) *The State We're In,* London, Jonathan Cape.

Hyland, T. (1996) 'Professionalism, ethics and work-based learning', *British Journal of Educational Studies,* 44(2).

Hyland, T. and Weller, P. (1996) 'Monitoring GNVQs: a national survey of provision and implementation', *Educational Research* 38(1).

Lipsky, M. (1980) *Street-Level Bureaucracy,* London, Sage.

Macfarlene, E. (1993) *Education 16–19 in Transition,* London, Routledge.

Office for Standards in Education (1994, 1995, 1996) *GNVQs in Schools: Quality and Standards of General National Vocational Qualifications,* London, HMSO.

Raffe, D. (1979) 'The "alternative route" reconsidered: part-time further education and social mobility', *Sociology,* 13.

Reeves, F. (1997) 'The alienation of the college from the community', *Social Science Teacher,* 26(2).

Spencer, D. (1994) 'GNVQs need immediate improvement', *Times Educational Supplement,* 4 November.

Spours, K. (1997) 'Too much too soon squeezes standards', *Times Educational Supplement,* 2 May.

Spours, K. and Lucas, N. (1996) 'The formation of a national sector of incorporated colleges: beyond the FEFC model', *Working Paper 19,* London, Post-16 Education Centre.

Utley, A. (1993) 'Tests spoilt for choice', *Times Educational Supplement,* 7 January.

Williams, W. (1980) *The Implementation Perspective: a guide for managing social delivery programs,* Berkeley, University of California Press.

Wolf, A. (1997) *GNVQs 1993–1997: a national survey report,* London, Development Agency.

Young, K. and Mills, L. (1980) *Public Policy Research: a review of qualitative methods,* London, Social Science Research Council.

APPENDIX 10.1

GNVQ structure

All GNVQs have a unit structure consisting, at Foundation and Intermediate levels, of 9 units and at Advanced of 15 units. It is possible to take additional units also.

	Mandatory Units	Optional Units	Core Skills
Foundation Business/L&T etc.			
Intermediate Business etc.			
Advanced Business etc.			

Notes:
- Core Skills: Communications, Application of Number, Information Technology. At Foundation level core skills must be achieved at Level 1; at Intermediate at Level 2; and at Advanced Level 3.
- Optional Units at Foundation level may be chosen from units of any other vocational area whether mandatory or optional.
- Additional units at all 3 levels can be taken from any other vocational areas.

To get a GNVQ certificate you have to show you are competent in all the units – in other words, you have to 'pass' each and every unit.

To pass a *unit* you have to show you are competent (or able to do) all of the *elements* that make up a unit. Each GNVQ unit is broken down into 2–5 elements, or statements of ability, that you must be able to show.

To make it easier to understand what is expected of you, these elements are broken down further into a number of performance criteria. These performance criteria spell out in more detail what the element means and what sort of things you have to understand to show complete mastery of the elements and units.

All performance criteria have to be covered before you can get a GNVQ certificate.

For a Foundation/Intermediate GNVQ this means you have to cover about 100 performance criteria. For an Advanced GNVQ there are about 200 performance criteria.

Chapter 11

The politics of training in Britain

Contradictions in the TEC initiative

Jamie Peck

In the biggest shake-up of Britain's training system since the 1964 Industrial Training Act, the Conservative government has created a new set of institutions, the Training and Enterprise Councils (TECs), to take over the delivery of training and enterprise development programmes, such as Youth Training (YT) and Employment Training (ET). With TECs, the government has handed over the 'ownership' of the training system to employers: almost £3 billion of public funds and in excess of 5,000 civil service jobs are being transferred to the private sector TECs in one of the Conservatives' most ambitious privatisation initiatives. *Employment for the 1990s,*[1] the White Paper in which the TEC initiative was launched, stipulated that these locally based institutions are to be controlled by private sector-dominated boards – two-thirds of TEC directors must be senior figures from the business community. In contrast to this privileged role for the private sector, trade unions, voluntary groups and local authorities have been purposely marginalised within the new training system by a government committed to removing the last vestiges of the corporatist state.

A network of 82 TECs is currently being established across England and Wales, with 20 similar bodies, the Local Enterprise Companies (LECs), being formed in Scotland. Progress has been rapid. The first ten TECs came on stream in April 1990 and the entire network is expected to be fully operational by the end of 1991 – a rate of formation twice that anticipated by the Training, Enterprise and Education Directorate (TEED) the arm of the Employment Department Group whose local-level operations are to be taken over by the TECs.[2] Portrayed in the business press as no less than a 'skills revolution', the TEC initiative is being sold to employers as an opportunity to restructure the training system largely on their own terms. Little wonder, then, that the initial response of the business community has been enthusiastic.

Even at this early stage, the cracks in this 'post-corporatist' partnership between the state and big business have already begun to appear. In the TECs, the government has created – perhaps inadvertently – a most powerful training lobby whose first action has been to bite the hand which feeds it.

Business leaders lured onto the TEC boards quickly found that they have taken charge of a training system which is grossly under-funded, which is geared towards the production of low-grade skills and which remains inextricably linked to the suite of 'make work' programmes hurriedly deployed to cope with the unemployment crises of the 1980s. Far from being given an opportunity to design new training packages, tackle skills shortages and create a workforce 'fit for Europe', the TECs seem to have inherited a poisoned chalice: the chance to operate a local branch of the civil service with its collection of discredited and largely ineffective 'training' schemes. Not surprisingly, this has resulted in some disillusionment – and many threatened resignations – amongst private sector TEC directors.

Matters were only made worse when, with classically ill-advised timing, swingeing cuts in the training budget were announced on the heels of the launch of the TEC initiative. The Employment Department's budget is to be cut by £300 million in 1991, with the most drastic reductions occurring in the funding of adult training through ET.[3] To many, the government's motives in creating TECs were now becoming apparent: anticipating falls in unemployment during the early 1990s, the opportunity was being taken to transfer back to the private sector the costs of training. The TECs reacted pugnaciously to this development, enjoying substantial press coverage.[4] They argued that funding levels have to be maintained. But more than this, if they were to respond to their remit of creating an effective, locally tuned training system then a greater degree of *flexibility* was required both in funding and in the design of the training programmes themselves.

Anxious to retain the commitment of the private sector TEC members, so important to the viability of the new training system and now a powerful lobby in their own right, it was necessary for the government to respond positively to the TECs' demands. Only minor concessions, however, could be granted at this stage: financial restrictions have been relaxed and increased discretion allowed in the design of programmes. While TEED continues to insist that it is committed to achieving increased local discretion for TECs, it is clearly proving difficult to convince Treasury colleagues that TECs will not simply become an unaccountable drain on the public purse. The likely trend is for TECs to be afforded slightly increased flexibility, but at the expense of over all budget reductions.

In this way, the tensions and contradictions which are inherent in the TEC initiative have already begun to emerge. Some have been quite explicit, such as those surrounding the issue of the TEC funding framework, while others are rumbling beneath the surface. The remainder of this chapter discusses the contradictions with which the TEC initiative is shot through, beginning with the issue which first came to the surface which is in many ways central, that of local discretion.

Contradiction I: direction vs. discretion

While the rhetoric surrounding the TEC initiative is about the delegation of decision-making powers to the local level, the reality clearly is that the TECs are operating to a tightly defined central government agenda. Indeed, one of the hallmarks of the Thatcherite project has been the *superficial* devolution of power to the 'consumer' – in this case, the consumers of training are deemed to be employers, not trainees[5] – underpinned by the firm hand of centralised control. Institutional devolution under the Conservatives has typically been associated with the centralisation of power.[6] But the powerful lobby that the government has created in the TECs has made it clear that it is not content to have Whitehall setting all the rules. If so, why have TEC boards in the first place? So far, the TECs have enjoyed some success in their lobbying of central government, establishing a permanent lobbying forum – the so-called Committee of the Ten TEC Chairs. This comprises representatives of TECs from every region of the country, its purpose being to deliver the 'TEC line' directly to the Secretary of State for Employment.

The problem for the Conservatives is that if the TEC initiative is to have any credibility at all then some degree of local discretion must be conceded. But the extension of TEC autonomy inevitably implies slackening the reins of central control. This would be problematic for the Conservatives on two counts. First, the TECs are already showing the potential to become a volatile political force in their own right. This raises the possibility that TECs, in researching and seeking to understand the problems of their local economies, may arrive at policy prescriptions quite different from those of central government. Having the ear of the press, TECs in say, the north of England or south Wales may reopen many of the debates over economic regeneration which the Conservatives have sought to stifle throughout the 1980s. While the Conservatives may have been partially successful in muzzling the likes of GLEB (Greater London Enterprise Board), they would face quite different problems in responding to calls for change from an empowered and effectively government-endorsed, business elite.

A second and potentially more serious problem arising from TEC autonomy is that employers are not interested in running unemployment schemes; they want TECs to move into the provision of what they see as 'real' training for the employed labour force. In order to address these issues, TECs require budgetary flexibility and discretion over the design of programmes. The cost, for the government, of giving TECs this freedom has to be counted its terms of the way in which it would compromise the viability of their unemployment programmes, YT and ET. Through their continual massaging of the unemployment statistics and through the wide-scale deployment of special employment measures dressed up as training schemes, the Conservatives have been relatively successful in smothering unemployment as a political issue. This of course does not alter the simple fact that mass unemployment not only persists but is again rising. The management of mass unemployment remains a critical political imperative. If the Conservatives do not retain a firm grip of their special employment measures, mass unemployment could again emerge as a highly visible and potent political threat. The Conservatives, then, simply cannot afford to allow the TECs too much scope to prune unemployment programmes in favour of locally designed training-packages, designed in the first instance to meet some manifest skill need, rather than to bring about an unemployment register effect.

Contradiction 2: policy vs. purse-strings

These issues surrounding the potential restructuring of TEC programmes relate to another key contradiction in the initiative, that between stated TEC policies and the financial restrictions imposed by central government. Close to 90 per cent of the funding that many TECs receive will be earmarked for the mainstream unemployment programmes, YT for young people and ET for the long-term unemployed. In spite of the rhetoric about the 'skills revolution', TEC budgets – and therefore TEC activities unless other sources of funding can be secured – remain tightly constrained to a set of programme areas defined not by the TECs but by central government. TEC budgets are divided into funding blocks, each allotted to a particular programme area. The TECs' scope for virement is minimal. The only scope that the TECs have for designing genuinely local programmes is afforded by a tiny Local Initiatives Fund. TECs receive £250,000 in this fund in their first year, followed by an average of £40,000 per annum subsequently. The fund may be topped up by performance bonuses and through the pound-for-pound matching by TEED of private sector funding earned by TECs. Despite the tax breaks announced in the 1990 Budget, the optimism of central government over TECs' ability to generate private sector funds is not shared by the TECs themselves. Few expect to achieve more than 5 per cent of their funding from private sources. Interestingly, the US Private Industry Councils (PICs), upon which TECs have been modelled, have fared no better in this regard. The private sector certainly does not want to pay for what are seen as unemployment measures.

Contradiction 3: public vs. private

The fact that TECs straddle this public–private interface will be a source of recruiting problems for the TECs. While the underlying logic of TECs is presented by the government as one in which the control of training is being 'returned' to the private sector, to the market, in reality the bonds with the public sector – although restructured – remain strong. The argument seems to run: Britain has a skills crisis; this is due to institutional 'interference' its the labour market by the state the answer lies in the state's withdrawal, enabling market forces (read: employers) to prevail. Thus, a common theme in public policy debates around the labour market re-emerges: when the labour market is not working properly, this must be due to problems associated with the 'interventions' of the state. This circular argument leads to old labour market institutions being replaced by 'new and better' ones – and in these days of deregulationist rhetoric, we must also pretend that the new institutions are not in fact state institutions at all. In this way, debates over labour market policy rarely even address the taboo question of whether the labour market actually works as a 'market' in the first place.

In the case of skill formation, it is quite clear that the labour market does not work. The economically rational actions of individual actors in the labour market do not constitute the basis for an adequate and self-sustaining system of skill formation. Firms are inclined to poach skilled labour rather than to make long-term and risky investments in training. Individual workers, on the other hand, are often reluctant to forgo earnings in the short term in order to acquire skills which are only saleable, and there is never anything certain in this, in the medium to long term. Even the most cursory examination of historical evidence or of other countries' training systems reveals that there is no such thing as a 'free training market'.[7] State intervention in crucial areas such as the funding of transferable skills training and the establishment, accreditation and maintenance of skill standards is a typical, one hesitates to say necessary, feature of training systems throughout the world.

The evidence for a structural requirement for state intervention in support of the training process sits uneasily alongside the British government's analysis. Here, a government which puts great faith in free market forces has created a training system which, although based on public funding, is ostensibly driven by employers (held to be custodians of the market logic) in accordance with market-type principles. The response to chronic market failure is not to explore which, necessarily *non*-market, system constitutes the most effective alternative, but to create a new market using public funds! This is a 're-regulation' not a deregulation, and an ill-advised re-regulation at that.

Contradiction 4: strategy vs. short-termism

A consequence of the reliance upon pseudo-market principles in the design of the TEC initiative is that strategic considerations are likely to be subordinated to short-term imperatives. This is ironic given that, even in the government's own analysis, the training problem itself is one of the more serious by-products of the short-termism of British industry.[8] Market-driven initiatives such as TECs are inevitably prone to short-termism. This is evident in the TECs' mission to shape training provision to meet local labour market needs expressed in the form of 'skill shortages'. The channelling of training provision into such areas not only ignores the fact that 'skill shortages', as reported by employers, are rarely due to a lack of training (typically being a result of low pay, poor working conditions or inadequate childcare facilities), it also represents a knee-jerk response to the recruitment problems of today rather than a strategic approach to the anticipated skill needs of tomorrow.

The chronic short-termism of the new training system is also reflected in the TEC funding regime, one which will be increasingly based on performance- or output-related funding. The funding of the TECs themselves, and of the plethora of training organisations which deliver training on contract to the TECs, will increasingly be linked to output measures, such as the proportion of trainees entering jobs at the end of the programme.[9] Schemes which fail to place trainees immediately in jobs will lose funding. Not only is this problematic for special needs training for disadvantaged groups (see below), it also militates against training in skill areas where vacancy turnover rates are comparatively low, which, generally speaking, tend to be high-skill occupations.[10] On the other hand, the training deemed to be most successful in the TECs' terms will be that associated with high turnover, relatively low-skill areas of the labour market with a high vacancy generation propensity, such as retailing. Importantly, training providers in such low-cost areas will also fare better on the 'value for money' criteria that the TECs are being implored to develop, relative to comparatively 'expensive' capital-intensive training such as in mechanical and electrical engineering. The outcome of these factors will be that TEC-funded provision is more likely to be characterised by induction training with a view to immediate vacancy-filling than by speculative, high-skill training in *anticipated* growth areas.

Contradiction 5: workers vs. workless

The government anticipates that the TECs will, on the one hand, be able to restructure TEED's current unemployment programmes in line with 'market needs' and, on the other hand, be able to develop innovative responses to training for those already in employment, the latter being supported by private funding. Implicit here is the view that, while it may rightly fall to the government to design and fund unemployment programmes, the training of those in employment is the responsibility of the private sector. This analysis differs significantly from that of many TECs, who seem to see their mission as the appropriation of public money earmarked for unemployment programmes and its redeployment in new training schemes for the employed labour force. Perhaps not surprisingly, the TEC publicity material is sufficiently vague as to encompass both views, being studiously ambiguous on the hard issues of funding.

An issue which is throwing these questions into high relief, though, is that of geographical differences in TEC funding. In straight cash terms, TECs in the depressed areas of England and Wales are markedly better off than those in the buoyant South East.[11] This may come as a pleasant surprise to those familiar with the debates over the North–South divide. It has been decidedly less popular, however, with TEC directors in the South East, many of whom are having understandable difficulty in reconciling their apparent under-funding with the fact that their region is characterised by the most serious skills shortage problems in the country. The plain fact is of course that TEC funding is a function of the underlying local unemployment rate, not of the level of training which is required.

The question of whether the TEC initiative is about training the employed or the unemployed stands set to divide the TECs and the government over and over again. While the TECs will be focusing their efforts on restructuring provision in favour of the employed, the government is likely stubbornly to insist that this be privately funded. In areas where the unemployment rate begins to fall – a fact which the TECs may well want to boast in their role as economic regenerators – TEC budgets will be cut. The impact of this on the motivation and morale of TEC directors is entirely predictable. But more serious questions surround the future of provision for the unemployed. Now such provision is at arm's length from the government, the door may have been opened to a whole variety of draconian practices. In particular, the emergence of work-for-the-dole schemes on the lines of the US Workfare system, several of which are already being mooted, seems a depressingly distinct possibility. Worse still, if the government responds to TEC pressure for increased flexibility by removing or 'relaxing' its guarantees of training places for the long-term unemployed,[12] this most disadvantaged group may find itself disenfranchised from the training system altogether.

Contradiction 6: efficiency vs. equity

Many local authorities and voluntary groups which have traditionally played a key role as both advocates for and providers of special needs training within government programmes are concerned that such provision may be compromised under the market-driven TEC initiative. The reliance on output-related funding, the emphasis on 'value for money' and the general drift to impose a 'market logic' on training programmes for the unemployed raise serious questions about the future viability of special needs provision. The use, for example, of the job placement rates of trainees as a performance measure for training providers takes no account of the quite different needs of disadvantaged trainees. Such crude measures say nothing about the value of training programmes for, say, disabled youngsters which should not be deemed less effective because they suffer a high post-scheme unemployment rate than a scheme which, 'working with the grain of the market', trains young white women in low-grade office skills for a hungry market. A similar argument would also apply to those schemes that seek explicitly to train women for non-traditional occupations, which also cannot be judged on simple job placement rates.

Special needs training providers are currently facing some difficult decisions over their future direction. There are essentially three options. First, schemes can raise their job placement rate and their level of achievement of vocational qualifications (another widely deployed output indicator) by simply raising their entry standards. This strategy, which has been termed 'creaming', clearly entails a partial or complete abandonment of the special needs client group and is a decision which no provider in this area could take lightly. Second, the training provider can accept a reduction in TEC financial support and subsidise the shortfall from its own reserves. Such an approach, while not uncommon amongst non-private sector training providers during the 1980s, is becoming less viable in today's straitened financial environment. Many voluntary organisations have no such back-up funds to turn to, while local authorities are also finding such cross-subsidisation increasingly difficult. These harsh realities are forcing many special needs providers to resort to their third option – to withdraw from training provision altogether. A rash of scheme closures have already been announced, as special needs trainers have reluctantly decided that they cannot operate under the new TEC funding regime.[13]

Contradiction 7: board vs. bureaucracy

Special needs training providers faced with closure have perhaps one last chance: an appeal to the TEC board. One of the more intriguing consequences of the TEC initiative is that in some areas it has brought forth a group of relatively liberal-minded employers, whose attachment to the ethos of special needs provision and equal opportunities often bears much more substance than that of the government. In such, admittedly exceptional, circumstances, such provision may win a reprieve. In doing so, however, it will be going against the grain of the entire TEC regime, one which by design constructs such provision as inefficient and irrelevant to the needs of the labour market.

Significantly, the 'character' of TEC boards stands likely to vary considerably from place to place, a fact which is in turn linked to the variable character and political capacity of local business elites.[14] Not only does this endow the TECs with a degree of political volatility *vis-à-vis* central government, it also stands set to create local tensions between the TEC boards and their own full-time staff. Already there is much talk of a clash of styles between the private sector-dominated TEC boards and the civil service secondees who have been transferred – some less than willingly – from the now defunct TEED Area Offices to staff the TECs. in some areas, the entire Area Office hierarchy is being transferred, virtually intact, to the TEC, which may even inhabit the same building. For many TEC directors, this does not amount to the significant break with the past which they had been told the TEC initiative was all about.

Many TECs have sought to assert their authority in what they see as a less than satisfactory situation by appointing a non-civil service chief executive to take charge of the day-to-day operations of the TEC. Many others have simply inherited the civil service Area Manager. Just how far the TECs will be successful in their quest to radically reorientate local training systems from the supply-driven, programme-led mentality of the MSC/Training Agency/TEED to a much more dynamic, service-driven, customer-led approach remains to be seen. While many TEC boards will push hard in this direction, they may find it difficult to enlist the hearts and minds of their full-time staff, many of whom will be disgruntled about the erosion of their employment security, the dilution or removal of trade union protection and the truncation of career paths which has been associated with their secondment to the TECs. It will be interesting to see, on the other hand, how successful these full-time staff are in manipulating the TEC boards, through their control of information channels, to their own ends. In the longer term, it is quite conceivable that the *real* control of the new training system will be vested in the bureaucracies of the private sector TECs. To be sure, there will be a clash of styles here which will impart its own unpredictable dynamic to the TEC initiative.

Contradiction 8: autocracy vs. accountability

Another set of tensions will arise from TECs' relationships (or lack of them) with their local community. At one level of analysis, it is clear that TECs are thoroughly unaccountable organisations. As private companies limited by guarantee, the TECs have a board of directors formally bound by commercial confidentiality rules. Strictly interpreted, this means that TEC directors are barred from 'reporting back' to their respective organisations, be these other private companies, local authorities or whatever. There are, moreover, no rules governing the selection of TEC directors: directors are effectively selected by the small group of employers who form the initial nucleus of the TEC board. The process of selecting TEC directors tends to go on behind closed doors: the inner circle of employers not only selects the other private sector directors (by whatever means and using whatever channels it sees fit), it also has the power to choose which 'representatives' from the voluntary organisations, trade union movement and local authority sector it wishes to join the board. TEED acknowledges that 'it takes time to get the right people', stipulating that non-private sector directors – as if the TECs needed to be reminded – must 'support the aims of the TEC'.[15]

Under these circumstances, there is no guarantee that the TEC even represents the local business community, let alone the community as a whole. Indeed, the process of TEC formation has only served to reopen rifts in the business community in many areas. The exclusion of small business representatives has been a common cause of friction, an issue which has been taken up nationally by the Association of British Chambers of Commerce. TEC boards also often fail adequately to reflect the industrial mix of their localities.[16] More seriously, both women and ethnic minorities are chronically under-represented on TEC boards. The representation of 'wider' community interests is yet more problematic. Most TECs have appointed a director from the local authority sector, although this will typically be a senior officer rather than a councillor. The degree of contact with 'the public' – the people who ultimately provide the TECs' funds – is minimal, being limited typically to an annual public meeting. While many TECs are making efforts to reach out into their local communities through the establishment of a subcommittee network (which is not restricted to the two-thirds private sector requirement), the fact remains that these organisations are, *by design,* undemocratic. 'Outside' voices may be listened to but certainly need not be heeded.

Contradiction 9: participation vs. peripheralisation

Those organisations marginalised or completely excluded from the new training system – trade unions, local authorities and voluntary organisations – also face a series of dilemmas in establishing relationships with the TECs. For many of these organisations, the talk of complete boycotts has subsided as it has been reluctantly decided that the TECs are too powerful to ignore. Most of those heavily involved as training providers in government schemes have had to accept the imposition of a new regime and, if they can, accommodate to it. Perhaps the greatest amount of soul-searching has surrounded the question of whether or not to pursue the option (where it has been extended) of board membership. The choice between the formal acceptance of a subordinate and inevitably marginal role through board membership or self-imposed exclusion from the TEC decision-making process is inevitably a difficult one. Formal participation in TECs, particularly by local authority and trade union representatives, of course only lends legitimacy to these undemocratic organisations and credibility to their programmes. For those local authorities and trade unions active in the boycott of ET, this decision has been a particularly trying one. It is in this quarter that the most critical stances on TECs remain.

Several Labour-controlled local authorities have sought to resolve some of these conflicts of interest by adopting a position of 'principled participation' in TECs: board membership is taken up on the understanding that the TECs abide by an agreed set of local authority principles relating to such areas as equal opportunities, community consultation and trade union recognition. It has to be said that few local authorities are in a sufficiently strong position to negotiate such agreements. Moreover, only time and experience will show whether those TECs which have been party to such local bargaining, having the power to vote them down at any time, will continue to abide by them. At best, these agreements must be considered precarious.

It is to be regretted, needless to say, that such 'partnership' approaches, albeit highly *unequal* partnerships, are the exception rather than the rule in Britain's new training system. There are as many cases at the opposite extreme, where TECs are controlled by a maverick employer group, suspicious and mistrustful of the public sector and of the labour movement, whose stewardship of public funds is likely to leave a lot to be desired. The naive reliance upon such 'private sector dynamism' within the TEC initiative – an act of blind faith even for the Conservatives – is almost certain to lead to some highly uneven, and highly undesirable, outcomes.

Contradiction 10: rhetoric vs. reality

One of the greatest challenges facing the TEC initiative is that of bridging the enormous gulf which exists between the rhetoric and the reality. Given the Herculean rhetoric which surrounds TECs, this will not be easy: Secretary of State for Employment, Michael Howard, recently enthused, for example, that TECs are 'the vanguard of a national movement which will bring unprecedented change in the way we develop the skills of our people, stimulate business growth and regenerate our communities'.[17]

The average TEC, with its limited lines of communication with the community and its staff of civil service secondees, with its suite of unpopular 'make-work' schemes and its rigidly 'ring-fenced' budget, is to say the least a long way from realising this vision. Indeed, the seeds of self-destruction for the TEC initiative may already have been planted, as its directors begin to comprehend the scale of the credibility gap between the glossy discourse and the down-to-earth reality of the new training system. Critical here will be the TEC funding formula, which at the moment, with its link to the underlying unemployment rate, means that TECs successful in stimulating local economic growth will be rewarded by a cut in budget.

The TEC initiative has got off to an unpromising start. The employers who have been invited to run TECs are not sure whether they have been given the tools to carry out the task set them by central government. Local authorities, trade unions and voluntary organisations have been marginalised and alienated. The future of the TEC initiative – and with it the British training system as a whole – seems to be tied up with, on the one hand, the evolving framework for the TECs' activities being hammered out in negotiations between the TECs and central government, and on the other hand, by a set of particularly *local* influences, as TECs begin to position themselves in their respective local political arenas. Together, these factors will condition the way in which the TEC system begins to unravel, or buckle under the pressure of its many internal contradictions. The future of the British training system is consequently a highly uncertain one. Given the critical importance of a robust skills base for the country's future economic well-being, this is a worrying situation indeed.

Notes

1 Department of Employment (1988) *Employment for the 1990s* Cm 540. London: HMSO.
2 TEED's corporatist origins in the Manpower Services Commission are now hardly distinguishable. The MSC was restructured into the Training Commission in 1988, an organisation which immediately collapsed following TUC opposition to ET. The Training Commission's replacement, the Training Agency, was to survive only until September 1990, when it was replaced by a more 'stream-lined' organisation, ostensibly more appropriate for the TEC era, TEED (see *Working Brief* November 1990).
3 *Financial Times,* 26 November 1990.
4 See, for example, *Financial Times,* 12 February 1990; *Guardian,* 17 March 1990, 22 March 1990, 4 April 1990; *!ndependent,* 10 May 1990, 8 August 1990.
5 One of TEED's justifications for the in-built employer dominance on TEC boards is that it is employers who are the consumers of training. See Main, D. (1990) Training and Enterprise Councils: an agenda for action', *Regional Studies* 24 pp. 69–71.
6 See Bob Jessop, Kevin Bonnett, Simon Bromley and Tom Ling (1988) *Thatcherism.* Oxford: Basil Blackwell.
7 For a thorough discussion of these issues, see David Ashton, Francis Green and Martin Hoskins (1989) 'The training system of British capitalism: changes and prospects' in: Green, Francis (ed.) *The Restructuring of the UK Economy.* Hemel Hempstead: Harvester Wheatsheaf, pp. 131–54; see also Streeck, Wolfgang (1989) 'Skills and the limits of neo-liberalism: the enterprise of the future as a place of learning' in: *Work Employment and Society* 3 pp. 89–104.
8 See Department of Employment (1988) *Employment for the 1990s* Cm 540. London: HMSO; Training Agency (1990) *Training in Britain.* London: HMSO; Manpower Services Commission and National Economic Development Office (1986) *A Challenge to Complacency.* Sheffield: MSC; National Economic Development Council and Manpower Services Commission (1985) *Competence and Competition.* London: MSC and NEDC.
9 Some training providers are already being funded entirely through such mechanisms under new TEC contracts. See *Financial Times,* 19 July 1990.
10 This tendency for ostensibly market-led training to become in effect 'vacancy-led' has for some time been a feature of YT and its predecessor the Youth Training Scheme. See Jamie Peck (1990) 'The state and the regulation of local labour markets: observations on the geography of the Youth Training Scheme' *Area* 22 pp. 17–27. Impacts of the TECs' market-led approach are discussed in Jamie Peck and Mike Emmerich (1991) *Challenging the TECs.* Manchester: Centre for Local Economic Strategies.

11 See *Personnel Management* May 1990 p. 15; *The Economist* 21 April 1990 pp. 33–4; see also evidence in Peck and Emmerich (1991, p. 31) cited in note 10.

12 For proposals on this, see Peter Ashby (1989) 'Training and Enterprise Councils: assessing the gamble'. *Policy Studies* 10 pp. 31–40.

13 Voluntary sector training providers have suffered a wave of scheme closures in the process of 'recontracting' for the TEC funding regime, with many more predicted to follow (National Council for Voluntary Organisations (1990) 'ET trainers face cuts'. *NCVO News* 14 p. 1).

14 This is discussed further in Jamie Peck (1990) 'Post-corporatism' in practice: TECs and the local politics of training' *SPA Working Paper* 9. Manchester: SPA, School of Geography, Manchester University.

15 Quotations from Catherine Stratton (1990) 'TECs and PICs: the key issues which lie ahead' *Regional Studies* 24, p. 72; Department of Employment (1988) *Employment for the 1990s* Cm 540. London: HMSO p. 41.

16 *Financial Times,* 6 December 1990.

17 Quoted in *Personnel Management*, May 1990 p. 15.

Chapter 12

Markets, outcomes and the quality of vocational education and training

Some lessons from a Youth Credits pilot scheme

Phil Hodkinson and Heather Hodkinson

Introduction

In Britain in the 1990s, a new paradigm for the management of Vocational Education and Training (VET) is emerging, based on market forces and payment by results. Though seldom challenged at the level of policy making, this new paradigm is largely untested empirically. Rather it depends on a 'common sense' belief in a highly problematic ideology, where the metaphor of production is assumed to apply to education, as to other public services. One of the purest forms of the paradigm that has been introduced thus far lies in the field of youth training, where a voucher or Youth Credit (YC) scheme has been piloted for three years and is being introduced nationally from 1995. Based on a detailed case study of one of the earliest YC pilot schemes, we argue that the supposed controls of training quality in the new paradigm are nothing of the sort. We begin by outlining the features and origins of the new paradigm, followed by a brief discussion about what is meant by education or training quality.

The new paradigm of quality management

There is broad agreement that British industry requires a much more highly skilled workforce than in the past. Numerous comparisons of education and training levels between European and Pacific rim countries all show Britain lagging behind (Green and Steedman, 1993). In order to meet this perceived need, the new management paradigm assumes that the quality of VET can be improved through the measurement of outcomes and payment by results within a market context. Thus, it is claimed, if customers (parents, young people or sometimes employers) make informed choices of provision, then providers will have to improve their performance in order to sell their services (CBI, 1989, 1993; ED/DES, 1991). To create such a market, most funding for colleges or other training organisations is derived from recruitment. To mitigate against the hard sell, customers are to be given 'objective' information to use for comparison, such as examination results and completion rates. Increasingly, either under Youth Training (YT) or Further Education Funding Council (FEFC) regulations, a significant proportion of the funding is held back until the young person has completed the course and achieved a qualification. This is intended to prevent inappropriate recruitment, reduce wasteful drop-outs (Audit Commission, 1993) and to encourage higher levels of achievement. In youth training, funding is provided via a voucher or Youth Credit (originally called Training Credit), owned by the young person and spent on training of their choice. In a recent White Paper, *Competitiveness: helping business to win* (White Paper, 1994), the government committed itself to the serious consideration of widening this credit system into 'learning credits' which could be used for any type of post-16 education and training.

As training providers respond to this new policy environment, management of quality is increasingly set against measurable performance indicators. This trend is reinforced at a national level through the National Education and Training Targets (NETTS). These targets quantify a major government policy objective, which is to increase the numbers of young people achieving specified levels of qualification and thus, it is assumed, raising VET standards to meet international competition.

Within full-time education and training, markets and outcomes are reinforced by inspections of quality. Institutions are to be inspected frequently, by the Office of Standards in Education (schools) or the FEFC (colleges). There is no equivalent inspection system for part-time vocational training, possibly because this could be seen as interfering with the freedom of employers, who provide most of the training, especially on the job. However, most Training and Enterprise Councils (TECs) have systems for approving training organisations.

Behind this seductively simple model lie three theoretical assumptions which are held as self-evident truths by many. They are rational choice theory, a belief in market forces, and the quality assurance procedures of the new managerialism, derived from an emasculated form of Total Quality Management (TQM). Rational choice theory (Elster, 1978, 1986) suggests that human behaviour can be best explained as the outcome of individual rational decisions. Such a belief is fundamental to a market model of VET, for customer control only works if customers are making rational decisions to choose high quality provision. Post-16 there has been heavy investment in 'neutral' careers guidance, to help young people improve such decision making.

Market theories derive from Adam Smith, and are rejuvenated in the New Right thinking of the 1980s (Johnson, 1991). Born of a frustration with planning failures, the dead hand of bureaucracy and the expensive subsidy of industrial 'lame ducks', the central ideas that markets are the best (only!) way to allocate scarce resources in a complex capitalist society and that competition in a market is the best (only!) way to improve performance have recently acquired the status of universal truths, except amongst marginalised and beleaguered groups of left-wing academics and politicians. However, within education, as in other public services, it is necessary to set up such markets artificially (Davies, 1992) and there are doubts about how effectively this has been done thus far, or about the extent to which such 'quasi-markets' are working (Le Grand and Bartlett, 1993; Bennett *et al.*, 1994).

The origins of the new managerialism lie in the spread of Japanese approaches in industry, as part of what some call 'flexible specialisation' and others 'post-Fordism' (Atkinson and Meager, 1991; Finegold, 1991; Murray, 1991; Brown and Lauder, 1992). A key part of this approach is the constant search to improve quality and increase efficiency against measurable performance indicators. Such measurement is vital, so that managers can differentiate between essential spending, which affects quality, and inessential spending, which does not. It is assumed that quality can be raised and costs cut simultaneously. Other parts of a TQM approach include the direct involvement of the whole workforce in the constant search for improvement, thus replacing Taylorist bureaucratic hierarchies with fewer layers of management and flexible teams. In British VET, as presently managed, these other parts of a TQM approach are conspicuous by their absence.

It is not our purpose here to challenge these theories individually, though none of them is unproblematic (Capper and Jamison, 1993; Hodkinson and Sparkes, 1993, 1994; Hodkinson, 1995), Rather, we are concerned with the impact of the new management paradigm that derives from them on the quality of VET that young people receive. It is necessary, first, to unpack a little further what is meant by quality in such contexts.

The nature of VET quality

Within the new paradigm quality is seldom defined. Rather, its nature is taken for granted and is assumed to be measurable and largely uncontested. Gleeson and Hodkinson argue that what is understood by educational quality varies according to the beliefs of the individual. One example would be the perennial dispute between those who argue that educational standards follow the Gaussian curve, so that any improvement in pass rates must indicate a fall in assessment requirements, and others who believe that many British young people underachieve, and that quality of achievement can be dramatically expanded, a view exemplified in the NETTS policy. Even within the narrow confines of the new paradigm, it is unclear whether 'quality' is that which customers will buy, that which employers and the economy need, that which leads to a recognised qualification, or some supposedly unproblematic combination of the three.

With the current emphasis on measured achievement, educational or training quality is increasingly being defined by outcomes, by far the most important of which is the achievement of a recognised qualification. Thus, under the drive to increase performance against NETTS, the qualification becomes the sole determinant of quality, rather than one of several possible indicators of it. Especially under NVQs, it is argued that *any* programme that leads to the successful achievement of the qualification must, *ipso facto,* be quality provision and worthwhile experience. We challenge that assumption and argue that the nature of the learning experience itself is an important part of quality and that the achievement of a qualification, even within a market system, cannot guarantee a quality experience.

The training credits in action project

YCs exemplify the best/worst case of this new management paradigm. Young people are issued with vouchers to spend, following provision of professional careers guidance, focused on drawing up an individual action plan. All training is organised by Approved Trainers who have met TEC criteria. All training must lead to an NVQ, at level 2 or higher. Funding for training providers partly depends on the completion of a training programme and the successful award of the qualification. In the scheme under investigation, 30 per cent of the funding was held back for this. Working with Andrew Sparkes, of Exeter University, we conducted a case study investigation of one scheme. It was located in a predominantly rural area with a labour market dominated by small firms, with geographical variations in unemployment and an almost exclusively white population.

We focused on the second cohort of YC trainees, following 10 young people from their final term in school until they were 15 months or more into their training. Sampling was in two stages: we began by interviewing 115 school pupils, mainly in small single-gender groups. Of these, 91 were in year 11 and 26 in the sixth form, 59 boys and 56 girls. They were attending six secondary schools, selected to give geographical spread, because of the potential impact of the youth labour market on youth training (Banks *et al.*, 1992). Pupils were selected, by their careers teachers, as being likely to at least consider using YCs. We also interviewed careers officers and careers teachers from those schools.

From the 115 pupils, we selected 14 to follow through, though this was eventually reduced to 10. They were selected as interesting cases who would be using YCs – with a gender mix, from different geographical locations and working in different occupational areas. For each trainee we also interviewed parents, employer(s), training providers and those finding placements. All were interviewed periodically throughout the 18 months of the study.

As we analysed the stories of these young people, we were struck by the wide variation in their training experiences and that, despite the supposed funding and market controls, some had what can only be described as inadequate experiences. We now turn to one of these stories where things appeared to be less than satisfactory, in order to examine what went wrong and how the new controls influenced the situation. Alison's experiences were better than some of our sample, whilst being worse than others. She did achieve the NVQ level 2 in one year and progressed to level 3 after that.

Alison's story

Alison had embarked on a career in equestrianism. She had approached a local college, where an off-the-job training package was provided, funded through YC. Partly through the college and partly through personal contacts, she had organised a training placement in a local stable, where the bulk of the work centred around riding lessons and trekking. Because the college served a very large area, many trainees, including Alison, lived too far away to travel in for day release provision. The college offered a series of residential weeks to meet this need.

> I've taken the NVQ syllabus level 2, and divided it . . . into approximately 10 weeks . . . and I will teach that subject for a complete week. . . . During that week they will have lectures on the subject, they will have practical lessons on the subject, they will also have riding tuition to their level, they will have lunging lessons, they will possibly go out on a visit relating to that subject, and/or an outside speaker. . . . I'll run all the modules twice over the year because you get the hunting yards that are busy over the winter and quiet through the summer and vice-versa the riding stables. So the work provider then can choose. . . . Whereas perhaps a student will be regularly clipping horses and therefore will have no need really to come in to college to clip horses, they might need to come in for perhaps for the loading of horses and the transportation of horses.
>
> (Tutor)

In order to integrate the on- and off-the-job training, the college employed liaison officers, who were responsible for the day-to-day progress of trainees. They visited trainees in their places of work and liaised with employers. The decision about which training weeks to attend should have been made collaboratively by the trainee, the liaison officer and the employer.

> They sit down with my liaison officer, the student and the work provider and the work provider will say, 'can cover this, I can cover that, I don't think I can cover this subject in as much detail, I think she ought to

attend the week here.' And they also look at their own dates, knowing
. . . how busy they're going to be, and they decide.

(Tutor)

As with all new systems, there were problems. Before this cycle of weekly
courses commenced, the college had run an optional 10 week foundation
programme.

Starting last summer we ran an 8 to a 10 week foundation course
through the summer. So those modules that I've just been talking about
will be covered in those ten weeks. The student will then go away with
all the theory and some of the practice that they will need to reach to
NVQ level 2. . . . Alison came in for the first health and safety week
[only] and then she went back to [the workplace] . . .
    I made a boo-boo. I ran the 10 week foundation course. I then let
a couple of weeks lapse and then I started my module weeks. What I
didn't appreciate, it was obvious that they wouldn't come back in . . .
so soon . . . I thought the third that didn't do the foundation course
would come in. But of course you only get one or two coming in for
each module, then it's very hard to run a module week, using up a lot
of lecturer time and facilities for only one or two people. We had to
cancel a couple.

(Tutor)

Alison could not do the foundation course, as the stables were busiest during
the summer. When we first spoke to her, she was looking forward to doing
six of the separate weeks.

I was going up there [college] for the summer holidays for an 8 week
course . . . but as I was working at a riding school it's really busy in
the summer so I had to work that. I'm going up for 6 weeks throughout
the year . . . just doing different things which I can't train up at the
riding school, or if I can train, it'll be more advanced.

(Alison)

In line with the NVQ philosophy that training must not be time-
related, Alison could attend up to six weeks, but no minimum number
was specified.

She doesn't have to come to training, as long as she and her employer
and hopefully her parents feel she is getting quality progression towards
her NVQ. . . . All our youngsters should have had an induction period
and if they understand the structure of what we offer here and they
make social contacts, they'll want to come in for modules even though

their employers can give them some of the support towards that module, and the better employers will encourage them to do that because they see us as partners in training.

(Training manager)

When interviewed early in the year, the college tutor had marked Alison down as having the prior experience and ability to achieve an NVQ level 2 very quickly.

I have students that come to me having been to the Pony Club, riding lots of different horses, doing regular competition work. . . . I would expect them to get to NVQ level 2 within about the 6 months. . . . Alison would fall into that category.

(Tutor)

The choice of college weeks proved problematic. Despite the rhetoric of meeting needs and filling gaps, the employer felt that Alison would not choose some weeks because she did not think they would be enjoyable.

We're sent a list of various weeks that she would like to go to, and I mean obviously there's some weeks that you couldn't get them to go to . . . like health and safety and things . . . I mean she'll say 'well I'd like to go and do lunging and practice, and I like to do such a thing', so she goes up and does that.

(Employer)

Another factor was how busy the stables were during a week in question. We have already seen how this prevented Alison's attendance on the foundation course. In addition, there were several trainees in the stables and only one could go to college for a particular week.

You have a big list of lots of different things. And on my yard I don't do any bandaging or anything like that. So I wanted to do things on that . . . [My employer] helped me pick them. Or I said what I'm not very good on or what I need practice on, but . . . we had to work it amongst us. We all had to go up at different weeks.

(Alison)

Because of small numbers turning up, the programme for a week was sometimes changed or cancelled, so that Alison did not always get the programme she had chosen. Sometimes she was fitted in with existing groups of full-time students.

But then they kept changing the weeks. . . . So then you ended up with weeks that you didn't want and the weeks you wanted had gone already

> . . . quite often I've been either the one person up there or just 2 or 3.
> . . . So they tend to put you in with the [full-time students] and do
> things that you don't want to do.
>
> (Alison)

There were problems in the stables, because training had to fit in with
the commercial activity, rather than being planned, though in general terms
Alison herself, her mother and the college tutor all felt she learned a lot
whilst working there and that it was a generally good placement.

> They were saying, 'Oh we're so busy – well we'll do some so and so
> today, practise your plaiting or something.' Then when we get round
> to it people would turn up for hacks and they'd say, 'Oh, you have to
> take a hack out now.' 1t was always . . . the customers first and then
> you fitted in when and if you could, and that was very rarely.
>
> (Alison)

Another cause of problems was the difficulty of consultation and
co-operation between everyone involved. In Alison's case this included her
mother, who had a personal knowledge of the horse world.

> [The liaison officer] comes down and liaises with you and with Alison
> as to what courses she wants to do, the dates, the facilities, the travelling
> arrangements, the accommodation . . . any worries or problems you can
> go to her, although she doesn't seem always to liaise with the college.
> . . . The problems that we had when Alison went to the college for the
> week were quite confusing, and I phoned the college and spoke to the
> head chappie there. . . . He said, 'Oh, it's the liaison officer's fault.'. . .
> We put her on the train then I had a phone call from the employer
> at the riding school saying, 'Where's your daughter . . . she should be
> here working.' I said, 'Oh but she's on her week health and safety course
> at the college.' . . . I said, 'Well it was all booked and arranged, and I
> phoned [the liaison officer] the previous week . . . and she knows. 'She
> said, 'Well I was at [the liaison officer's] on Friday, and she never told
> me. 'So then I'm phoning the college saying, 'is Alison really meant
> to be there?' . . . Alison did stay there, she did need to go for the health
> and safety thing, although her employer said she didn't really need to,
> but I was happier that she'd been on that.
>
> (Mother)

A more serious problem, given the outcomes-dominated focus of NVQs,
arose over assessment. As Alison demonstrated competence at the various
parts of the qualification, her log book should have been ticked off and
signed and the evidence recorded. This should have been done partly by

her employer, partly by the liaison officer and partly by tutors in college. For much of the year, no-one did it. The employer claimed to be too busy, and felt that the college should do the assessment because they were paid to do it and she was not.

> While she's there [college], she'll be assessed, because I'd rather they assessed her because I haven't the time really, so I mean if she's up there she might as well be assessed. . . . I am actually an assessor for that [NVQ] anyway . . . [but] I'd rather they did it.
>
> (Employer)

At the same time, the college tutor expected most of the assessment to be done in the stables. 'The employer will do most of them [assessments] there . . . we trained her to be an assessor' (Tutor).
The liaison officer did not do much assessing either.

> There were new girls starting and leaving all the time so [liaison officer] would come down when a new one started . . . and she would also do a quarterly review for me then. But she didn't actually come out on the yard. She would just say, 'What have you been doing?' And she would just write down things that we said but she didn't actually come and tick off any of them. . . . I was just being passed around. . . . In the end [my employer] ticked off what she thought.
>
> (Alison)

As a result, very little assessment was done until matters came to a head when Alison was called to the college to have her award verified.

> I went up in January, because they was going to put me in for my verification then . . . on NVQ2, because by then I should have had all my things ticked, because I'd done them all. But every time I went up to college they said, 'Oh, we'll do your assessments at the end of the week' and then they'd forget or they didn't actually get them done. So when I went up in January to do it . . . and they was like rushing trying to tick them all really quickly saying, 'Oh have you done that?' and I'd say, 'Well not really.' And they'd say, 'Oh, well we'll tick it anyway.' . . . They were saying, 'Oh, your employer should be ticking them as well.' But my employer was saying, 'Well it's the college.' So I was in between. And in the end, the day of the exam [verification] I was sat waiting to go in . . . and they said, 'Well, no way we can put you in for it.'

Though not concerned about waiting for her final award, Alison resented the time wasted in repeating things she had done before, simply because they had never been ticked off.

They say, 'Oh have you done so and so?' and I'll say, 'Yes, I was up here for a whole week and did lots of it.' And they'll say 'Oh, well if we've got enough time we'll just check that you can do it.' Then they'll have to watch you do it again, which is like extra time when you've only got 2 days to do 50 assessments.

(Alison)

She also felt that some sections were ticked even though she lacked experience and competence.

It was mainly the stud work which I hadn't done a lot on. . . . I know a little bit through my own knowledge but not in depth at all – which we were meant to know quite a bit about really. We went to, like, a stud a couple of days before to watch a mare being teased and things like that. But that was like my stud section ticked, really.

(Alison)

Alison's employer was angry about what she felt was poor quality training, though she did not accept responsibility for filling any gaps in Alison's experience. She also felt that competences had been ticked which Alison did not possess.

The actual assessments themselves were a shambles, I was jumping when she came back because a lot of the stuff they'd signed she not only didn't know much on, she knew nothing about. . . . They weren't even given a lecture on breeding . . . they were taken to a stud for half a day, shown around the stud, now what can you learn on that and then everything ticked that they knew it all. . . . When she came back, [my daughter] said, 'Well, how do you tell when a mare's in season?' 'Well I don't know.' Now that's basic. . . . There were feeding and things that they'd ticked and signed. I wouldn't have signed them. They sent a whole pile back for me to sign, and I sent them back saying I wasn't signing them. One was preparing linseed and feeding a horse linseed. Now they ticked that and signed that as if she knew how to do it. Now that is a dangerous thing because that could poison a horse . . . and she didn't know anything about it at all.

(Employer)

The liaison officer confirmed that there had been problems, but felt that everything came right in the end. The root cause had been Alison's failure to attend the foundation course.

I think what happened was, she didn't do the foundation course and then, when she was coming into college, it was unfortunate that . . . we put on the module weeks from September to Christmas and of course we didn't have anything like the number of students, so we had to either cancel weeks or block people together for different subjects, and Alison got muddled around basically over that. So then the list went out for module weeks for the new year and that unfortunately had to be changed, so poor Alison felt that she'd tried twice. And then the third time she managed to get to college to do what she was supposed to. But again I understand there was a mix up when she came in to do what she thought was one subject and somehow she was doing something different. But she had her assessments and she got her NVQ2. . . . Someone should have done it [assessed her], but . . . 16 year olds being 16 year olds, she didn't stand up and shout and say, 'Hey I'm here. I need my assessments done.'

(Liaison officer)

The tutor also agreed that things had gone wrong.

[The employer's] a good work provider but she became very short of time . . . it's very difficult to . . . be work provider and make an assessment. . . . It wasn't all [the employer's] fault, but there was things like the mucking out hadn't been [ticked off] but . . . she does it every day. . . . And it just looked wrong if we kept signing them. But in fact we knew she mucked out. . . . The other thing is that [the liaison officer] is also very busy. [She] went out a couple of times and did some assessments as well. . . . It's very difficult to make the time, especially the odd assessments where you have to make a simulated situation. . . . When they come in on module weeks they actually come in for the training on the module week therefore I don't identify for them to have the assessments. What it really needs is for them to say, I need to come in to complete some assessments.' . . . We should have identified it earlier. It was a problem. We did overcome it and she had a very good report written from the verifier.

(Tutor)

Despite the tutor's earlier prediction, Alison was one of the last in her group to get an NVQ2.

The nature and control of quality

In any VET programme there will be successes and failures. We do not claim that Alison's experiences were 'typical', nor are we passing judgement on the employer or college concerned. Another of our sample attended the same college and had a much more satisfactory experience. Rather, we wish to examine what Alison's story can tell us about the nature of quality in VET and the ways in which the new controls failed to address it.

The central point is obvious. Despite possessing the credit and achieving her NVQ level 2 in a system where the trainer was paid by results, where the NVQ assessment was externally verified and the training organisation was vetted by the TEC, no-one involved felt that Alison had received 'quality training'. She had wasted time, had not received enough help with some areas where she felt weak or inexperienced and had not been regularly or properly assessed. It follows that quality education or training involves much more than the successful achievement of the qualification. It is possible to draw out from Alison's story some key aspects of such quality.

Just because there are numerous different ways of acquiring the competence to achieve an NVQ, it does not follow that all are equally good. Alison felt that she needed to work at the stud unit and her employer regarded some theoretical instruction as important. Time-wasting, unnecessary repetition, boredom and the interruption of training by unrelated work activity (hacking, in this case) are indicators of a low quality experience. Payment by results and the removal of a time-serving requirement did not reduce time wasting. If anything, it was those areas where more intensive training was necessary that were cut.

Alison's story also demonstrates that coherence is not guaranteed by a combination of choice and negotiation. This was because all three parties to the negotiation, the employer, Alison and the college tutor, had different priorities and constraints. In a tourism-focused stables, the long foundation course during the summer was impossible for the employer to accept. For the college, groups which did turn up had to be large enough to be viable, so that the nature of some weeks could not remain as advertised and Alison had to be patched in to other courses. For both the employer and the tutor, these contextual imperatives were more important than providing Alison with a coherent programme. Yet, in the specification for NVQs and in the market driven YC funding regulations, there is no requirement for a planned or co-ordinated experience, nor any mechanism that is likely to encourage such an approach if it runs counter to the other interests of key participants.

A perennial problem for part-time training has always been the relationship between on- and off the job components. Under YTS, the problem was seen to be unstructured work experience which did not contribute to an effective learning programme (Lee *et al.*, 1990). In the new paradigm this concern is reversed, for NVQs give a clear priority to on-the-job learning, which can be in any order and occur at any time, whilst off-the-job work should be directed towards work-based competence. Yet for Alison, just as under the worst YTS schemes, there was little integration between the two parts. Not only were the new controls unable to ensure a positive relationship, but there are clear indications that the current obsessive view that 'employer knows best' is misguided. Like many other small employers we spoke to, the stable owner was primarily concerned with running a business. She had neither time nor inclination to take training provision seriously, beyond the needs of her own commercial activity.

The final lesson to be drawn from Alison's story is that quality VET depends crucially on effective personal and social relationships, which in turn derive from the skills, attitudes, beliefs and professionalism of the personnel involved. With hindsight, changes in the attitude and/or behaviour of the employer, the tutor and the liaison officer might all have improved the quality of Alison's experience. Yet the new paradigm of outcomes, markets and financial pressures never addresses the central issues of professionalism, staff development and staff morale directly. We return to this point below.

Ensuring a quality process

No system for providing VET quality can be foolproof. We are not claiming that the combination of policies that make up the current policy paradigm in British VET caused Alison's problems, although they did contribute to them. Nor are we claiming that previous regimes, such as YTS, would necessarily have been any better. What we do claim is that the assumption that the new policy paradigm will lead to improvements in training quality is fallacious. At the level of choice and 'customer spending', it is based on a fundamental misunderstanding of the ways in which young people make decisions about training (Hodkinson and Sparkes, 1993, 1995). Choices most often arise out of local contacts and experiences, and young people have neither the power nor knowledge to challenge either employers or professional trainers about what they should be doing, who with, where or when.

A careful analysis of our interview data suggests that, though Alison 'chose' the college concerned, she never considered alternatives. Furthermore, although she had previously worked in the stables where she was eventually placed, it was the college who decided to place her there, despite Alison's reservations about the scope for training. Once the programme was under way, the power to purchase had been used. Neither Alison, her mother nor her employer could do anything through the market about the problems that developed. The supposed option to take their custom elsewhere did not occur until after the NVQ2 had been achieved. At this point, Alison and her mother did decide to go to a different stable and a different college for her NVQ3 training, a change that was facilitated by the YC, but crucially depended on the mother's knowledge of the equestrian scene. Likewise, the employer claimed she would use a different training organisation. However, this happened too late to influence the problems of quality already experienced.

Theory suggests that market forces would compel both college and employer to change their provision in subsequent years, in order to remain competitive in the training marketplace. In this case, there was no sign that the employer felt any need to alter her training provision. The college did recognise the need to change, but there is no indication that it was reacting purely, or even mainly, to market pressures. As we have seen, the mistake over the combination of foundation programme and optional weeks had been recognised by the tutor very early in the year. She had already decided to change things for the future because, as a professional educator, she was unhappy with the unforeseen consequences of her initial planning.

Equally spurious is the central principle of NVQs, NETTS and payment by results, that educational or training quality can be measured and controlled by the outcomes. As Alison's training manager said,

> The TEC are concerned at the moment with what they call an Audit Trail but not so concerned with the quality of training inputs. . . . They're looking at quality in measuring it by outcomes, and the outcomes . . . are of doubtful quality.

If we are serious about raising the quality of the British workforce, then urgent attention must be directed to the specification and management of a quality learning process.

This requires more investigation of what a high quality process is. Experiential learning does take time. Learning particular skills or competences are only part of the development of one's personal identity as a riding school operative or any other job. Brown *et al.* (1989) demonstrate that understanding, activity and context are all closely related during learning. Trainees need time to absorb the culture of the workplace. Alison was flagged as likely to complete her NVQ quickly, because such enculturation was already well advanced, through her earlier work with horses and around stables. Another of our sample trainees, Becky, was training to be a dental surgery assistant. Both her trainer and employer believed that this training process took time, and that funding for YCs pressured them to reduce that time artificially, a view endorsed by Alison's training manager.

> Training Credits are looking at NVQs as outcomes and putting cash values on outcomes which makes it very very difficult for trainers to resist the pressures put upon them by their managers to achieve the outcomes. . . . There's bound to be some pressure to pass them . . . and where there's a marginal case where the people who are assessing and teaching would prefer to see someone have a bit more practice, you could say yes, OK, they 'can do'.

We need to know much more about what differentiates quality training time, including enculturation, from time wasting, so we can develop a VET policy which maximises quality time in a young person's training programme. At best, NVQs deflect attention from this important issue. Also, the practice of funding all trainees for a particular qualification at the same level militates against those who need more quality time to achieve high standards. For any trainer working with such a young person, all the current pressures are to push them through quickly, rather than drive for the high quality which the system is supposed to provide. To recruit only those likely to succeed quickly is another obvious commercial response, which risks abandoning those young people most in need of high quality training.

High quality VET crucially depends upon the skills and professionalism of those providing the training. Yet in the scheme we investigated, such training providers were coerced or enticed by funding, rather than being involved in the scheme as valued fellow professionals. Definitions of quality were externally imposed, through funding related targets that had to be met. Many felt threatened and excluded, and morale seemed low. In the wider field of education, there is abundant evidence that quality derives from the commitment, sense of ownership and high morale of teachers, especially where radical change to systems is concerned (Fullan, 1991; Rudduck, 1991; Hargreaves, 1993). Yet the current funding pressures on training organisations and further education colleges are driving their teaching workforces in the opposite direction, towards the use of lower skilled training technicians, with low job security, limited professional development opportunities and, for increasing numbers, part-time employment.

As we have seen with Alison, the role of the employer is fundamental. There is a current policy obsession that employers know best, and that all training should be directed to meeting employers' needs. At a national level Field (1995) argues that NVQs are not actually controlled by employers as the Industry Lead Bodies that draw them up are dominated by a few large employers and a raft of professional consultants. Furthermore, he claims that the NVQ system is being driven by government regulations for programmes such as Youth Training and YC, rather than real employer demand. We found several situations where employer attitudes undermined training quality. Clive, for example, was doing a business and administration NVQ, because his employer insisted he studied business. However, his job was car valeting and car sales, and he was not given enough opportunity to develop on-the-job skills related to the business qualification. In the end, the trainers cut their losses by awarding him an NVQ level 1, after 15 months of training which all felt was of low quality. Helen got a placement training as a car body sprayer. A major problem occurred when her employer made her redundant. As she had no placement, her training had to stop part way through. Payment by results could not facilitate, let alone ensure, the completion she desperately wanted, as the system supposedly designed to reduce drop-outs actually enforced one.

There may be many good features of the new VET paradigm and we are not suggesting that everything should be scrapped to start again. British VET has been plagued by far too many such abrupt policy switches in the immediate past. Rather, we would suggest that a much more careful analysis is conducted of the strengths and weaknesses of current approaches. One partial solution may be to spread the FE inspection system to private training organisations and to employers, but this still begs the fundamental question about what quality training is.

In the meantime, government policy making appears bent on reinforcing the impact of market forces through credits, payment by results, cutting costs and defining quality by qualification gained into the whole of post-compulsory education and training (White Paper, 1994). This dangerous trend, to spread markets and crude outcome measurements wholesale, risks lowering training quality despite increasing qualification levels.

Acknowledgements

This research was funded by the Economic and Social Research Council (ESRC), award no. R00023 3582. Its support is gratefully acknowledged. We would like to thank John Robinson and Martin Bloomer for their helpful advice on an earlier draft of this chapter.

References

Atkinson, J.S. and Meager, N. (1991) Changing working patterns: how companies achieve flexibility to meet new needs, in G. Esland (ed.) *Education, Training and Employment. Volume 1: Educated labour – the changing basis of industrial demand.* Wokingham: Addison-Wesley.

Audit Commission (1993) *Unfinished Business: full-time educational courses for 16–19 year olds.* London: HMSO.

Banks, M., Bates, I., Breakwell, G., Bynner, J., Elmer, N., Jamieson, L. and Roberts, K. (1992) *Careers and Identities: adolescent attitudes to employment, training and education, their home life, leisure and politics.* Milton Keynes: Open University Press.

Bennett, R.J., Wicks, P. and McCoshan, A. (1994) *Local Empowerment and Business Services: Britain's experiment with Training and Enterprise Councils.* London: UCL Press.

Brown, J.S., Collins, A. and Duguid, P. (1989) Situated cognition and the culture of learning, *Educational Researcher,* 18(1), pp. 32–42.

Brown, P. and Lauder, H. (1992) Education, economy and society: an introduction to a new agenda, in P. Brown and H. Lauder (eds) *Education for Economic Survival.* London: Routledge.

Capper, C.A. and Jamison, M.T. (1993) Let the buyer beware: total quality management and educational research and practice, *Educational Researcher, 22(8),* pp. 25–30.

CBI (1989) *Towards a Skills Revolution,* Report of the Vocational Education and Training Task Force. London: CBI.

CBI (1993) *Routes for Success – Careership: a strategy for all 16-19 year old learning.* London: CBI.

Davies, H. (1992) *Fighting Leviathan: building social markets that work.* London: The Social Market Foundation.

ED/DES (1991) *Education and Training for the 21st Century.* London: HMSO.

Elster, J. (1978) *Logic and Society.* Chichester and New York: Wiley.

Elster, J. (1986) *Rational Choice.* Oxford: Blackwell.

Field, J. (1995) Reality testing in the work place. Are NVQs employment led? In P. Hodkinson and M. Issitt (eds) *The Challenge of Competence: professionalism in vocational education and training.* London: Cassell.

Finegold, D. (1991) Institutional incentives and skill creation: preconditions for a high skill equilibrium, In P. Ryan (ed.) *International Comparisons of Vocational Education and Training for Intermediate Skills.* London: Falmer.

Fullan, M. (1991) *The New Meaning of Educational Change.* London: Cassell.

Gleeson, D. and Hodkinson, P. (1995) Ideology and curriculum policy: GNVQ and mass post-compulsory education in England & Wales. *British Journal of Education and Work*, 6(2), pp. 29–40.

Green, A. and Steedman, H. (1993) *Educational Provision, Educational Attainment and the Needs of Industry: a review of the research for Germany, France, Japan, the USA and Britain,* Report No. 5. London: National Institute of Economic and Social Research.

Hargreaves, A. (1993) *Changing Teachers, Changing Times: teachers' work and culture in the postmodern age.* London: Cassell.

Hodkinson, P. (1995) Competence and professionalism, in P. Hodkinson and M. Issitt (eds) *The Challenge of Competence: professionalism through vocational education and training.* London: Cassell.

Hodkinson, P. and Sparkes, A.C. (1993) Young people's choices and careers guidance action planning: a case study of training credits in action, *British Journal of Guidance and Counselling,* 21, pp. 246–61.

Hodkinson, P. and Sparkes, A.C. (1994) The myth of the market: the negotiation of training in a youth credits pilot scheme, *British Journal of Education and Work*, 7(3), pp. 2–20.

Hodkinson, P. and Sparkes, A.C. (1995) Taking credits: a case study of the guidance process into a training credits scheme, *Research Papers in Education*, 10(1), pp. 75–99.

Johnson, R. (1991) My New Right education, in Education Group II *Education Limited: schooling and training and the New Right since 1979.* London: Unwin Hyman.

Lee, D., Marsden, D., Rickman, P. and Duncombe, J. (1990) *Scheming for Youth: a study of YTS in the enterprise culture.* Milton Keynes: Open University Press.

Le Grand, J. and Bartlett, W. (1993) (eds) *Quasi-Markets and Social Policy.* Basingstoke: Macmillan.

Murray, R. (1991) Fordism and post-Fordism, in G. Esland (ed.) *Education, Training and Employment. Volume 1: Educated labour – the changing basis of industrial demand.* Wokingham: Addison-Wesley.

Rudduck, J. (1991) *Innovation and Change.* Buckingham: Open University Press.

White Paper (1994) *Competitiveness: helping business to win.* London: HMSO.

Chapter 13

Policy and accountability

Lee Harvey and Peter Knight

Preface

The worldwide impetus to expand higher education, by increasing participation rates, is driven in great measure by a future vision of the world economy. Competitive advantage in the global economy is seen as dependent upon having a well-educated workforce. The world is changing rapidly and there is a growing perception that there is a need for people who can accommodate to and initiate change. As technology, competition and social upheaval transform the world at an accelerating pace, so higher education is increasingly seen as crucial in producing an adequately educated population.

If higher education is to play an effective role in education for the twenty-first century then it must focus its attention on the transformative process of learning. A prime goal should be to transform learners so that they are able to take initiative, work with independence, to choose appropriate frames of reference, while being able to see the limitations of those frameworks, and to stand outside them when necessary. To be an effective transformative process, higher education must itself be transformed, we argue, so that it produces transformative agents: critical reflective learners able to cope with a rapidly changing world.

Higher education policy in Britain, and in many other countries since the mid-1980s, has increasingly focused on issues of 'quality'. Almost universally, quality has been employed in the service of accountability: an accountability predicated on budgetary constraint within the context of a highly competitive world economy (CEC, 1991; Gungwu, 1992; Green and Harvey, 1993). There are several reasons for this, including:

- a widespread concern about the size of public expenditure and the share of higher education, especially in the face of competing demands such as health and social welfare;
- a concern about the future competitiveness of the economy and hence the labour needs of a post-industrial society;

- the problem of monitoring the input, process and output of higher education in a diverse and rapidly expanding system that is constrained by a shrinking unit of resource;
- the internationalization of higher education and attempts to ensure greater explicitness about the nature and equivalence of academic and professional qualifications, especially as far as employers are concerned;
- an ideological commitment, in some countries, to making public services, including education, more efficient and more responsive to the needs of customers (Moodie, 1988; Cave and Kogan, 1990). 'Quality' provides the vehicle for expressing this ideological commitment in Britain.

'Accountability' has a variety of nuances (Vroeijenstijn, 1995) but a central feature of accountability is:

> that of 'rendering an account' of what one is doing in relation to goals that have been set or legitimate expectations that others may have of one's products, services or processes, in terms that can be understood by those who have a need or right to understand the 'account'. For this reason, accountability is usually, if not always, linked to public information and to judgements about the fitness, soundness, or level of satisfaction achieved.
>
> (Middlehurst and Woodhouse, 1995: 260)

Curiously, the drive for quality at a policy level has been almost independent of a clear assessment of the learning outcomes of higher education and implementation of procedures that are likely to lead to them. This lack of integration occurs despite concurrent innovations in teaching and learning within higher education.

. . . Internal and external stakeholders in higher education have raised questions about the appropriateness of the outcomes of higher education. In policy terms, this concern has been translated into economic issues. At one level, it involves questions about whether the higher education system is producing sufficient graduates to enhance the growth and competitiveness of the economy. Concern in the European Union about the 'skills gap' and efforts in some countries to encourage young people into science and technology are indicative of an economic, utilitarian approach (IRDAC, 1994).

At another level, economic considerations simply reflect pressure on government budgets. With so many competing claims for budgetary consideration, higher education has had to become more accountable for the money it receives. In effect, this means that higher education must not only be explicit about where it spends the money but also must endeavour to provide good value for the money it receives.

This emphasis on accountability is the primary reason why there has been very little linkage between quality policy and the encouragement of innovative approaches to teaching and learning. Accountability focuses attention on quality as value for money, although this may be mediated by other notions of quality.[1]

What this accountability orientation overlooks is the transformative process. If quality is viewed as a process in which key stakeholders are participants, rather than as a product made available to customers or clients, then it is necessary to explore the nature, development and evolving outcomes of that transformative process. It is not very meaningful to assess a continually evolving participatory process by inspecting it at a single point in time. A transformative notion of quality requires a focus on *change*.

In essence, the failure to unite quality policy and learning development in common cause is a function of the tension between accountability and improvement that besets the quality debate. A review of the quality policy in Britain shows the nature of the accountability–improvement tension and demonstrates the failure to link quality with innovations in teaching and learning.

The tension between accountability and improvement is also indicative of an organizational tension between managerialism and collegialism. Before reviewing the policy agenda and exploring the way in which it prioritizes accountability, it is appropriate to explore the relationship between collegialism and managerialism.

Managerialism

Managerialism in higher education refers to the tendency for professional managers, through their decision-making role, to alter academic processes on the basis of non-academic criteria, amongst which financial criteria have been prominent, or in response to management theories and fashions (Bowtell, 1993; Miller, 1994). Accounting procedures dominate decision-making, finance is raised from the status of a parameter within which to work to the guiding operating principle, and financial arguments are used to manipulate political aims (Wilkins, 1994).

The rise of managerialism involves a shift towards a more formalized management structure and control at the institutional level which is reflected in more direct management of the higher education system by the government (Holmes, 1993; Trow, 1993).

Higher education, it is argued, is faced with the emergence of unelected, oligarchic managerial élites, which wield great power without accountability either externally or internally (Wilkins, 1994). In Britain, this managerialist tendency first appeared in the former polytechnic sector. Following the incorporation of the then polytechnics, there was a centralizing of control and an erosion of the contribution of academics to institutional policy-making and 'a sense of alienation from senior management began to manifest itself' (Yorke, 1993: 5). This has subsequently spread into the traditional university sector. In Europe, the professional higher education manager is still a rarity as most systems require that university rectors and deans are elected and serve relatively short terms of office. However, the system is beginning to change (Acherman, 1995).

There is a view that managerialism does not threaten academic freedom. On the contrary:

> good management of the universities is essential as a defence against further erosion of their autonomy . . . For the good of all the academic departments and for the job security of their staff, the universities need to be managed by people who understand and respect academic values but who have not only the time and expertise but the interest to do it well; who do not just see management as a regrettable distraction from their real work; and who are willing to immerse themselves in the job and to learn about it.
>
> (Rear, 1994a)

This view is possibly sustainable at the level of the university although it arguably relies on the benign paternalism of senior management. The widely publicized events relating to the vice-chancellors at the British universities of Huddersfield and Portsmouth are seen as indicative of a rather more Machiavellian approach.

> Externally, provided they balance their books they are unlikely to be challenged. Internally, in the name of 'effective management', senates and academic boards are being stripped of any worthwhile powers and greatly reduced in their breadth of representation. Governing councils provide little effective check. Appointed members owe too much to the patronage of the élite who put them there, while elected representation is reduced . . . I do not deny the possibility of benign oligarchies and dictators. I would prefer not to be forced to rely on it.
>
> (Wilkins, 1994: 10)

It is not the managerialism operating at the level of the institution that is the major concern. Managerialism also operates at the level of the state. It is manifest in the direct interference in higher education, in the name of accountability, of the government and its agencies, such as the funding council.

Managerialism has been linked to government control of the sector through the emergence of 'hard' as opposed to 'soft' managerialism (Trow, 1993). Soft managerialism, that advocated by John Rear (1994a, 1994b), is based on improving efficiency and sees managerial effectiveness as crucial in producing high quality at lowest cost. The hard conception, which is now central in the reshaping of British higher education, elevates system and institution management to a dominant position and focuses on 'the continual assessment of the outcomes of educational activities, and the consequent reward and punishment of institutions and primary units of education through formulas linking these assessments to funding' (Trow, 1993: 2).

Hard managerialism, in Britain, is characterized by:

- a desire to treat education as a product that can be continually improved whilst lowering the unit cost;
- withdrawal of trust by government in the academic community and academia's capacity to critically assess and improve its own activities (Annan, 1993; Mulgan, 1995).

This has led to the creation of bureaucratic machinery and formulae that are imposed on the universities from outside the higher education system. These agencies create criteria of performance and rules for accountability and apply formulae that link funding to quality to ensure the automatic improvement of efficiency and effectiveness of higher education. In effect, 'external assessment linked to funding is thus a substitute not only for trust but also for the effective competitive market which is the chief control both of quality and cost in commercial enterprises' (Trow, 1993: 4). Under the guise of competition, the British Government has used managerialism to impose a 'command economy' on higher education. It is not, therefore, surprising that academics are growing increasingly suspicious of quality and of the burgeoning quality industry.

Collegialism

Higher education institutions are often assumed to embody a collegiate ethos (Moore and Langknecht, 1986; Cannon, 1994; Dearlove, 1995). A college, in one sense, is nothing more than a community of scholars. However, there is underlying 'philosophy' implicit in the notion of collegiality, which will be referred to as 'collegialism' (Harvey, 1995c).

Collegialism is characterized by three core elements:

- a process of shared decision-making by a collegial group in relation to academic matters;
- mutual support in upholding the academic integrity of members of the group;
- conservation of a realm of special knowledge and practice.

There has been a revival of interest in collegialism in the wake of managerialism of the late 1980s. Collegialism can be seen to span a continuum from, 'cloisterism' to 'new collegialism' (Harvey, 1995a).

Cloisterism embodies a conservative reassertion of academic autonomy and freedom. It emphasizes the absolute right of the collegial group to make decisions relating to academic matters, regards the integrity of members as inviolable (except where exceptionally challenged from within), and considers the role of the group as that of developing and defending its specialist realm, which is usually discipline-based. Cloisterism tends to be staff-directed, producer-oriented and research-dominated. It relates to the internal concerns of the group and sees students as novices to be initiated into the mysteries of the discipline. It is effectively inward-looking. The knowledge it possesses is revealed incrementally and according to the dictates of the self-appointed 'owners'. The skills and abilities it expects students to develop are often implicit and obscure. Sometimes what is expected of students is deliberately opaque and shrouded in mystifying discourse.

New collegialism sees the collegial group as the forum for academic decision-making but is prepared to enlarge that group to allow discourse and negotiation with significant others, not least students. It emphasizes accountable professional expertise rather than inviolable academic integrity. New collegialism is outward-looking and responsive to changing circumstances and requirements. It is learning-oriented. It focuses on facilitating student learning rather than teaching, and explicitly encourages the development of a range of skills and abilities. It prefers explicitness to obfuscation. It values team work. It sees its role as one of widely disseminating knowledge and understanding through whatever learning-facilitation and knowledge-production processes are most effective. New collegialism disavows the inwardness of the cloisterist approach while retaining its scepticism of management-dominated quality assurance processes. New collegialism embodies an approach to teaching and learning that is responsible, responsive and transparent and sees quality in terms of transformation of a participant rather than attempting to fit the purpose of a customer.

Table 13.1   Comparison of cloisterism and new collegialism

Cloisterism	New collegialism
Secretive	Open
Isolationist	Networking
Individual	Teamwork
Defensive	Responsive
Traditional approach	Innovative
Producer-oriented	Participant-oriented
Clings to power	Empowering
Wary of change	Welcomes change
Élitist	Open access
Implicit quality criteria	Explicit quality criteria
Information provider	Facilitates active learning

Source: Harvey (1995b).

The core of a new-collegiate approach is the development of a quality culture of continuous improvement. Table 13.1 summarizes these distinctions.

The new collegialism is self-critical and concerned continually to improve its processes and practices rather than rest content with traditional modes of functioning. Academic autonomy in the new collegialism is manifested through ownership and control of an overt, transparent process of continuous quality improvement rather than in the retention of a non-accountable, mystifying, opaque cloisterism. In short, the new collegialism is about the development of an explicit professionalism (Elton, 1992).

Quality in mass higher education

Quality crept on to the British political agenda for higher education in the middle of the 1980s (Burrows, Harvey and Green, 1992). It was hardly noticed at first, and was considered to be a marginal concern. After all, by definition, universities were quality institutions (Kogan, 1986).

The mid-1980s saw the establishment of an agenda that would drive the development of higher education policy in Britain for the next decade. At root was the shift from an élite to a mass higher education system. Four interrelated themes dominated the mass higher education agenda: accountability and value for money, maintaining standards, measuring outputs, and external quality monitoring (EQM). We consider the first three in this chapter. . . .

Accountability and value for money

Accountability takes two forms, one pitched at the level of economic planning and the other at the level of institutional efficiency. In Britain, for example, both elements have been highlighted by government policy statements.

The Jarratt Report (CVCP, 1985) on efficiency recommended that universities and the system as a whole should work to clear objectives and achieve value for money. It was suggested that the University Grants Committee (UGC) and the Committee of Vice-Chancellors and Principals of the Universities of the United Kingdom (CVCP) should jointly develop performance indicators designed for use both within individual universities and for making comparisons between universities. The recommendations for universities included: the development of rolling academic and institutional plans and the introduction of arrangements for staff development, appraisal and accountability. This requirement reflected a general requirement for the public sector to be efficient and effective (Joseph, 1986; DES, 1987; Secretary of State for Education, 1988; Pollitt, 1990; PCFC, 1990c). It also parallels the situation in the United States where the initial impetus for a serious re-evaluation of higher education originated from demands for more accountability (NGATF, 1986; Jennings, 1989; Cross, 1990; Hutchings and Marchese, 1990; Millard, 1991).

Accountability on the level of economic planning was evident in the United Kingdom Green Paper, *The Development of Higher Education into the 1990s* (DES, 1985) and in the ensuing White Paper *Higher Education: Meeting the Challenge* (DES, 1987). The British Government stressed the need for higher education to serve the economy more effectively and to have closer links with industry and to promote enterprise. It noted that other countries produced more qualified scientists, engineers, technologists and technicians than the United Kingdom and, therefore, wanted British higher education to develop the flexibility to be able to respond to future change. An increase in the 'age participation rate' (that is, the percentage of those in the 18–21 age group) to 18 per cent was proposed. In the United States, similar concerns were being expressed about the needs of the economy (AAC, 1985; NGA, 1986), a theme that was coming to preoccupy the European Union (IRDAC, 1990, 1994; CEC, 1991).

The White Paper also indicated that efficiency was to be increased by improvements in institutional management, changes in the management of the system and the development and use of performance indicators. Accountability was firmly established at centre-stage in higher education policy debates in Britain, prefacing similar concerns around the world. Quality improvement, *per se,* was not on the agenda. At this stage, accountability was not wrapped up in a 'quality' cloak but was simply couched in terms of efficiency gains and of clarifying responsibility for maintaining standards. This changed somewhat the following year when institutions covered by the Polytechnics and Colleges Funding Council (PCFC) were expected to provide, in return for public funds, a method for monitoring institutional performance and assuring quality. The Secretary of State recommended that the PCFC should develop indicators of both the quality and quantity of institutions' teaching in relation to funding (Secretary of State for Education, 1988). This recommendation came to partial fruition in 1989 with the establishment of a funding 'premium' for courses of 'outstanding quality' in the PCFC sector (PCFC, 1989).

The shift from 'raw' value-for-money accountability to a more subtle quality-linked accountability, went one step further in a later UK White Paper, *Higher Education: A New Framework* (DES, 1991a), which enjoined further efficient expansion in student numbers while stressing the need to maintain and enhance quality in higher education. The Further and Higher Education Act (HM Government, 1992) firmly linked efficiency and effectiveness to quality. It was axiomatic in the plan for an annual 5 per cent increase in student numbers with no comparable increase in resources. In addition, efficiency concerns underpinned the link between quality assessment and funding, which rewarded good provision rather than using resources to improve inadequate provision. It was proposed that, whatever the method of quality assessment, the funding methodology should give more resources either through increased student numbers or through a funding premium to those institutions assessed as providing high quality teaching and learning in particular academic subject categories and that institutions with areas assessed as being of unacceptable quality would be warned of a possible withdrawal of funds if improvements were not put in place (PCFC/UFC, 1992a, 1992b).

Quality assessment was, at least in theory, to be based not on any absolute measure of excellence but upon the ability of an institution to deliver what it promised through its mission statement and programme aims and objectives, a recurring theme in other countries.

Maintaining and controlling standards

Throughout the last decade, standards have been a continuing concern of all stakeholders in higher education, although at times this has been camouflaged by the preoccupation with quality.

The sub-text of the Lindop Report (Lindop, 1985) was a concern with standards. Among other things it suggested that the best safeguard of academic standards is not external validation or any other form of external control, but the growth of the teaching institution as a self-critical academic community. It suggested a code of practice (published two years later (CVCP, 1987)) noting, in particular, that 'the external examining system is an important and currently under-exploited safeguard of academic standards'. A prolonged debate about the rôle and effectiveness of the external examiner system in Britain has ensued, culminating in the predominant view that it should be retained but needs modifying (CNAA, 1992; Silver, 1993; Harvey and Mason, 1995; HEQC, 1995a; Silver, Skennett and Williams, 1995; Warren Piper, 1995).

> The external examining system is not to be dismissed as an expensive cosmetic . . . It is a vigorous system involving a high proportion of the country's leading academics and the work is undertaken with great seriousness and care. It is a necessary function if there is to be a policy of parity between awards and it confers a number of incidental benefits . . . One thing, however, seems certain – the external examiner system cannot go on as it is. It has either to be scrapped or revamped . . . External examiners can no longer fulfil their traditional function. The gap between examiner and candidate widens; fewer external examiners actually see any students and are inexorably pushed towards judging the teaching and examining system and away from judging the candidates. This is an unplanned shift to a meta-level of quality assurance – an incidental effect of adopting modular degree structures and the progressive move to mass higher education. Indeed, the very nature of

a degree program is changed to one in which an academic discipline is no longer the central organizing force giving shape and coherence to undergraduate study . . . There is a shift from the subject-based view to the academy-based view of the examiner.

(Warren Piper, 1994: 237–9)

Policy advisers and researchers in other countries, including Australia, Sweden and the United States have also explored the possibility of establishing or extending the external examiner systems to assist in the maintenance of standards (for example, Fong, 1988).

The Lindop Report noted that, if academic standards were to be effectively maintained, it would be necessary to develop safeguards, other than validation, to ensure the quality of certain key factors including recruitment of staff, quality of students admitted, and professional and vocational relevance of degree courses. The traditional concern with inputs also implicitly reaffirmed an exceptional notion of quality. Indeed, it has been 'excellence' that has mediated the value-for-money requirements of subsequent legislation, rather than any concern with the effectiveness of enhancement or empowerment process in higher education. The British Government has also clearly linked improved standards in higher education to the quality of teaching, while doing nothing directly to enable or motivate changes in this area.

Managers in higher education have been of the view, prompted by government requirements for efficiency gains, that there is slack in the system and that an increase in staff:student ratios and more pressure on capital and equipment will have minimal impact on the student experience. However, even here there is seen to be a practical limit:

Government and Industry are entitled to expect universities to be innovative and efficient, but repeated annual squeezes of unit cost will not deliver the desired expansion of HE at a quality necessary to face international competition . . . The UK deserves a better policy for expansion than one based on marginal costs.

(Harrison, 1991: 1)

Even the British Government has changed its position. Initially it used output statistics to legitimate its position that more does not mean worse by referring to the increased proportion of first- and upper-second-class degrees to justify underfunded expansion (HM Government, 1991; PCFC/UFC, 1992a, para 251; Secretary of State for Education, 1988). According to Kenneth Clarke, then Secretary of State for Education and Science,

The statistics speak for themselves, with the proportion of graduates in PCFC sector institutions gaining first and upper seconds having risen alongside the surge in student numbers. There are plenty of examples from HMI to show how increasing numbers need not adversely affect quality – quite the reverse.

(DES, 1991b: 1)

However, the British Government, spurred, amongst others, by employers, professional bodies, and higher education organizations, has required a closer look at standards and asked the HEQC to develop a methodology as part of academic audit to ensure comparability of standards (HEQC, 1995b). Given that audit has a fitness-for-purpose approach to quality assurance mechanisms, it is difficult to see how an absolutist comparability will be accommodated. Furthermore, universal standards are also undermined by the further extension of competition between institutions, encouraging them to find their niche in the 'education market' (Richards, 1992; Rothblatt, 1992).

Measuring outputs

The Green Paper, *The Development of Higher Education into the 1990s* (DES, 1985) gave notice of a shift towards output indicators. It suggested that external judgements about quality can be attempted by comparing the success of students in obtaining jobs, their relative salaries, and their reported performance in employment, and by reference to the international standing of our academic qualifications in addition to comparative judgements by external agencies.

The concern with outputs in Britain has been focused on the search for institutional and system performance indicators rather than a specific concern with the outcomes of the learning process: that is, on what students know and can do. A considerable amount of innovation in teaching and learning in higher education, backed up by research, had been developed up to the mid-1980s (Entwistle and Ramsden, 1983; Kolb, 1984; Marton, Hounsell and Entwistle, 1984; Biggs, 1987; Ramsden, 1988). However, this was somehow dissociated from the accountability-based political imperatives despite the White Paper of 1987.

Higher Education: Meeting the Challenge (DES, 1987) indicated that academic standards and the quality of teaching in higher education should be judged primarily on the basis of students' achievements. It encouraged development of broader courses in some circumstances and further emphasis on transferable skills and positive attitude to enterprise. To that end, in December 1987, the Enterprise in Higher Education (EHE) initiative was launched by the Secretary of State for Employment with the support of the Secretaries of State for Education and Science, Trade and Industry, Scotland, and Wales. It was originally designed to encourage the 'development of qualities of enterprise' amongst those undertaking higher education courses but there has been a focus on the development of personal skills related to future employment (HMI, 1993), curriculum change and staff development (ED TEED, 1990, 1991; TIHR, 1990), all of which suggest that EHE has a wider rôle as an agent of institutional change (Elton, 1993).

Despite this emphasis on student achievement, output preoccupations have been mainly directed at the search for performance indicators, such as staff:student ratios, ratio of private fees to public funds, the number and mix of enrolled students by level of study and mode of attendance, wastage and completion rates, rather than any meaningful evaluation of student abilities (CVCP/UGC, 1986, 1987a, 1987b, 1988, 1989, 1990; PCFC, 1990; PCFC/UFC, 1992c). Such indicators are used as crude measures of institutional (and programme) *efficiency* (HMI, 1990). Output indicators have, therefore, been used for accountability purposes and directed at a value-for-money notion of quality rather than seriously attempting to address transformation (Yorke, 1995).

There have been some attempts to construct performance indicators that are pertinent to *learning* outcomes. However, most of these are very crude and tend to be surrogates for measuring teaching quality rather than learning. In the last resort they are based on those things that are already measured or which are easily measurable, such as graduate destinations, wastage rates and degree classifications, but which, at best, provide tenuous indicators of learning and, at worst, are completely misleading (Bourner and Hamed, 1987; Johnes and Taylor, 1990). For example, the balance of subjects in an institution will have a strong bearing on the degree classification profile. Science subjects tend to award a greater percentage of first- and upper-second-class degrees (Table 13.2). Similarly, there are significant differences in the employment pattern between different occupations and different employment rates occur in different subject areas at any given time (Porrer, 1984; Brennan and McGeevor, 1988). Measures of value added and student evaluations are the only serious attempts to obtain indicators of learning.

Value added

Approaches have been developed that attempt to measure the 'value added' to a student. These take into account the abilities of the student when entering higher education and offset some of the criticisms relating to the use of degree classifications as performance indicators.

The most significant research in the United Kingdom in this area was the jointly funded PCFC/CNAA project that evaluated a range of different approaches to calculating value added (CNAA, 1990). The report advocates a comparative value-added approach. This approach has two stages: the calculation, on the basis of empirical evidence, of the degree classification that a student with a given set of entry qualifications could be expected to achieve, followed by a comparison with the degree classification that they actually achieve. A single score is produced, which is negative if the student achieves less than expected and positive if they achieve more. The size of the positive or negative score is relative to the size of the difference between the actual and anticipated degree classification achieved. Thus a student whose anticipated degree class is a 'third' and whose actual class is a 'first' will achieve a higher score than a student whose anticipated class was a 'third' and whose actual score was a 'lower second'.

The report also notes that the positive and negative scores achieved by students can be aggregated to produce a single score for an institution, course or department, thus providing a basis for comparison with other similar units.

The approach has been criticized because, although avoiding arbitrary weighting of the inputs, it assumes an interval scale for outcomes – the difference in value between a first and upper second is the same as the difference in value between an unclassified degree and a fail (Gallagher, 1991). This does not preclude the possibility of a suitable weighting of outcomes or, alternatively, that aggregates could not be defined in terms of the ratio of 'better than expected' to 'worse than expected' results.

A second criticism is that it assumes that degree classifications between sectors and between institutions are comparable and there has been some question concerning the validity of that assumption (CVCP, 1986; CNAA/ DES, 1989; Cave et al., 1991; Alexander and Morgan, 1992) (see also Table 13.2).

A more fundamental criticism of the value-added approach developed in the United Kingdom concerns the narrow interpretation of what counts as value. What is the value that the degree classification represents? What does degree classification measure? An approach developed in the USA attempts to address these issues. McClain, Krueger and Taylor (1986) describe the Northeast-Missouri State University Value-Added Assessment Program. In this system, the value added to the student is evaluated along three different dimensions: performance in the liberal arts and science component of the programme (usually first two years); performance in affective learning which considers cultural awareness, interpersonal skills, self-esteem, problem-solving and functioning in the larger society; and evaluation of students' performance in the major field of study. Using this system, therefore, the breadth of the learning, transferable skills and specialist subject knowledge are all separately assessed using a range of tests. Similar approaches have been used in other institutions and as part of other research programmes designed to explore value added in the United States (Jacobi, Astin and Ayala, 1987; Pike et al., 1991).

This concurrent approach to value added (Cave et al., 1991), where each student's achievements are assessed at different points in their university careers, has been criticized on the grounds that, first, the tests are not of

Table 13.2   Honours graduates awarded first-class or 'good' degrees in
universities and polytechnics in the United Kingdom (1971–86)

Subject	First-class degrees (%)	'Good' degrees (%)
Physics	17	45
Computing and maths, physics	17	43
Engineering (general)	16	47
Chemistry	16	45
Chemical engineering	13	46
Aeronautical engineering	13	40
Mechanical engineering	12	42
Electrical engineering	12	41
Mining engineering	11	46
Metallurgy	11	44
Technology (general)	11	44
Industrial engineering	10	47
Art and design	10	47
Civil engineering	10	39
Biology	8	48
Philosophy	7	50
Health studies	7	46
Pharmacy	7	46
English	7	46
Theology	7	43
Combined science	7	37
History	6	50
Modern languages	6	44
Environmental sciences	6	41
Architecture and planning	6	34
Drama	5	47
Music	5	41
Education	5	38
Psychology	4	44
Hotel management, food sciences	4	42
Geography	4	41
Surveying	4	41
Economics	4	35
Law	4	34
Social studies	3	37
Business studies	3	36
Combined arts	3	36
Government and public administration	2	38
Accountancy	2	30

Source: CNAA Transbinary Database. Based on a reorganization of two tables in
Warren Piper (1994: 190).

benefit to the students and that they have no incentive to do well. Second, it is questionable whether the tests accurately and validly assess the concepts that they are intended to measure. Third, the system is extremely time-consuming and costly. Fourth, it might encourage 'teaching to the test'. The use of the approach to make inter-institutional comparisons is also questioned as it might lead to a reduction in diversity. Value-added systems of this nature need to take account of the individual missions of institutions (Bauer, 1986; Cave *et al.*, 1991).

Despite the reservations and criticism of various methodologies for value added, the approach provides one of the few attempts to measure the enhancement side of transformative quality. It is one of the few areas where quality policy comes close to the evaluation of student attributes. However, at the policy level, value added has not seriously been adopted as a system, or as a comparative performance indicator.

Student evaluations

A significant amount of research into student evaluations of teaching has taken place in the USA where student-feedback questionnaires are widespread and have been in use since the 1930s. Academic staff often raise questions about the validity and reliability of student evaluations of teaching quality. Concerns are expressed that the views of students are influenced by variables unrelated to the quality of teaching, such as class size, workload, degree of difficulty of the subject and prior student interest in the subject. The development of an instrument for Students' Evaluation of Educational Quality (SEEQ) casts doubt on these concerns, as it has demonstrated that nine evaluation factors (learning; enthusiasm; organization; group interaction; individual rapport; breadth of coverage; examination grading; assessment of students; and workload) are to be found across different academic disciplines and different academic years (Marsh, 1982).

Arguments concerning validity focus on issues such as whether or not there is a correlation between effective student learning and high student evaluations of teaching quality. It has been suggested that students may not be best placed to evaluate teaching quality at the time of study and that they may be able to take a more objective view after they have had the opportunity to apply what they have learned in later study or after graduation. However, research has demonstrated that student evaluations are quite reliable when based on responses of ten students or more and suspected sources of bias in student ratings have little impact. Retrospective ratings by former students agree remarkably well with the evaluations that they made at the end of a course. Similarly, student evaluations correlate moderately well with student learning, as measured by standardized examination, and with affective course consequences, such as application of the subject matter and plans to pursue the subject further. In addition, staff self-evaluations of their own teaching show agreement with student ratings (Murray, 1984). Student evaluations are frequently used as a feedback mechanism to staff in the United States to help them improve their teaching and there is some evidence that they are effective in this (Marsh, 1982).

Although student evaluations can be valuable within institutions, it is more debatable whether they can be used to make comparisons between institutions (Cave *et al.*, 1991). Student characteristics are an important potential moderator of the comparative validity of student feedback (Dowell and Neal, 1982). Even where an instrument is developed and provides a useful tool for local policy decisions, the particulars of the student characteristics may render it unsuitable for inter-institutional comparative purposes.

A major problem with typical student evaluations of taught units or even whole programmes is that they tend to be limited to fairly narrow concerns with teaching rather than a wider consideration of the student learning experience.

Research on the use of student evaluations as a performance indicator for comparison between institutions and subject areas has been prompted by the AVCC/ACDP working party on performance indicators in Australia, which advocated that student evaluations of teaching quality should be used as a performance indicator. Paul Ramsden (1991) has attempted to develop a technique for using a student-evaluation questionnaire to provide valid data at the departmental and institutional level. On the basis of his previous research on teaching quality and effective learning, Ramsden argues that there are four characteristics of teaching quality at the departmental level which correlate highly with effective learning by students. The key characteristics are good teaching (clarity of explanation, level at which material is pitched, enthusiasm and help with study problems), freedom in learning, clear goals and standards, and appropriate workload. The Course Experience Questionnaire (CEQ) was designed to measure differences between educational units (departments and faculties) on these factors. Ramsden recognizes that there might be other factors which contribute to teaching quality, such as course design and relevance of content.

Following a national trial, a short form of the CEQ (25 items) is being used as part of a national annual survey of all graduates organized by the Graduate Careers Council of Australia (GCCA). The results of the trial suggest that the instrument is capable of showing the existence of medium to very large differences in perceived teaching quality within the fields of study represented in the trial. However, significant differences were found in average ratings between fields of study on a national basis, which 'argues for making any comparisons among institutions within fields and disciplines, rather than across them'. Recurring differences were also found between disciplines within a field of study and the author suggests that caution should be exercised in interpreting differences among institutions across broad fields of study.

From 1995, results of the annual survey were aggregated by field of study and made publicly available. This will enable prospective students to find out how the courses they are thinking of applying for are rated by graduates. There is a commercial *Good Universities Guide* that gives the ratings alongside other information like entry requirements, as well as a universities-sponsored code of practice for interpreting the results.

Despite some initial reluctance, universities are beginning to see the value of the results as evidence of their strengths and for purposes of internal quality assurance and improvement. There is as yet no other satisfactory indicator of university teaching performance available in Australia. 'The evidence from our own studies is that satisfaction with the university experience as a whole is much more strongly related to the CEQ results than to perceptions of facilities and resources' (Ramsden, 1995: 1).

Ramsden indicates some difficulties in using CEQ as a performance indicator for reporting to funding bodies. He points out that performance on different scales could be combined to produce a single average score, thus making inter-institutional comparisons easier, but questions the validity of so doing when the interrelations among the scales are small. He also questions the appropriateness of using CEQ mean scores to rank units as the data would be norm-referenced and therefore say nothing about whether a unit is good or bad but only whether or not it is better or worse than another unit. He therefore recommends the use of absolute data as well as norm-referenced data.

The student evaluations so far reported concentrate mainly on the quality of teaching in terms of the lecturer's interaction with the students. The Student Satisfaction Approach at the University of Central England (UCE) in Birmingham . . . takes a broader view, linking satisfaction to the student learning experience and basing the research instrument on the expressed views of students during focus-group discussions. All areas that impact on student learning are included, ranging from teaching, through the provision of learning resources, to accommodation, cafeterias and financial circumstances.

The aim of the research is to produce indicators that will help the institution measure, and thereby improve, the quality of the student experience. Indeed, the survey is embedded in a top-down accountability process that identifies responsibility for action to address student concerns. Nonetheless, despite its very important role in quality assurance within the institution, it is doubtful whether it could be the basis of inter-institutional comparisons. The very nature of the process inhibits such comparability (Green, 1990; Harvey and Mason, 1995). Each year students identify the key elements of their learning experience and the research instrument changes and evolves over time. The main concerns in one institution are not necessarily the same as in another. There are, it is true, a core of items that change little over time and between institutions, but simply to adopt these as the basis for inter-institutional comparisons would probably result in the omission of major areas of impact on the student learning experience at the local level.

Crucially, the issue is not one of identifying statistical indicators that measure performance, but of providing insights into student perceptions that are used to set up specific institutional, faculty or programme-level initiatives to improve on provision. Student Satisfaction at UCE is a process that is locked into attempting to enhance the transformative learning experience.

The benefit of using student evaluations as a performance indicator is that they are a direct measure of teaching quality, and, in some cases, of student learning. The validity and reliability of student evaluations have been shown to be quite high. There are difficulties, however, in adopting them as performance indicators for inter-institutional comparisons because they are rarely universal, that is to say that they vary depending on the character of the subject being studied, the character of the institution and so on. Although some countries, such as Australia, are pressing ahead with identifying performance indicators that can be linked to funding, quantitative indicators do not figure prominently in Britain. In 1990, a comparison of Britain and Netherlands suggested that, after 1985, Dutch higher education emphasized peer judgements while performance indicators appeared to dominate British quality assurance (Goedegebuure, Maassen and Westerheijden, 1990). The situation no longer applies, although the image seems hard to shake off on the international stage (Murphy, 1994). The critical determinant of British funding allocations is performance against contract. In England, money is allocated on the basis of type of student, mode of study and subject area, modified by historical circumstances, efficiency gains, and so on. Higher education institutions contract to deliver student numbers in various categories and failure results in a clawback of funds by HEFCE. Performance indicators are not used in this process, although they are used by the National Audit Office to monitor the financial health of each institution.

Indeed, in the development of quality monitoring in Britain, there has been a tendency to shift away from *performance indicators* and instead place far more emphasis on a process of audit and assessment in which a variety of statistical indicators is taken into account in more or less rigorous ways by peer review groups assessing research quality, teaching quality or the effectiveness of quality assurance mechanisms . . .

Conclusion

Higher education policy since the mid-1980s has increasingly been concerned with accountability and value-for-money as the sector has expanded. The notion of 'quality' has been employed as a vehicle to legitimate a policy of steadily reducing the unit of resource and increasing centralized control. Quality, as value-for-money or as fitness-for-purpose, is rooted in a 'philosophy' that asserts that the economy cannot support the full cost of expansion in higher education, while at the same time arguing that higher education is a central element in the future competitiveness of the economy in the world market.

Although 'quality' crept on to the British political agenda for higher education in the middle of the 1980s, initial concerns about universities were dominated by issues of efficiency, effectiveness and the maintenance of standards. Slowly, a focus on outputs rather than inputs came to dominate policy. With the rapid increase in higher education the emphasis was placed firmly on accountability and value for money. A concern with outputs became ever more prominent with the search for sector and institutional performance indicators. However, little attempt was made to develop performance indicators of student learning, and those that might appear to relate to learning are tenuous. It was left to institutions to develop a transformative, improvement orientation to institutional, learning-related performance indicators, such as the Student Satisfaction approach at UCE.

In essence, in Britain, as in many other countries, the primary concern has been with accountability rather than improvement. At root, quality policy has not addressed transformative learning. It has been preoccupied with other notions of quality, such as value for money and fitness for purpose, which . . . are insubstantial operationalizations of transformative quality.

We have concentrated in this chapter mainly on the impact of quality-policy on the development of an educated workforce. However, references to the impact of policy on research show a corresponding process. The Research Assessment Exercise and the growing centralized control of the research councils are indicative of the short-term, value-for-money, pragmatic approach to research funding dressed up as rewards for excellence. There is a dearth of evidence for any long-term support for research that could really underpin Britain's economic recovery.

There is little to suggest that current policy on research in higher education has much to do with developing a transformative research culture. While the Research Assessment Exercise has required clearer accountability, there is little to suggest that it has palpably improved research output. Results of research into the impact of the Research Assessment Exercise are not yet published. Initial impressions and anecdotal evidence suggest that, rather than a transformative research culture, government policy has encouraged a compliance culture that has produced an over-reporting of underdeveloped research, with little transformative potential. Furthermore, there is a suggestion that it has a negative impact on teaching and learning (Jenkins, 1995). Similar concerns occupy UNESCO:

Emphasis on short-term gains and the pressure of budgetary constraints can lead to serious long-term consequences for higher education institutions as the proper seats for the advancement of knowledge and the training of future scientists and industrial researchers. Research departments in higher education institutions, although costly, are a crucial source of skills and ideas in the context of the global economy based on knowledge and constant technological change. The best way to make the general public, government bodies and economic organization aware of the role of research in higher education is to demonstrate, through convincing results, the scholarly quality, economic value, humanistic perspective and cultural relevance of research and the related study programmes and teaching.

(UNESCO, 1995: 29, para 81)

Note

1   For example, value for money for research funding is often based on peer assessment of the 'worth' of the research. This is the case in Britain, where expert panels assess the research output of all the universities receiving government research funding. Panels rate the research on a scale of excellence, which directly informs funding allocations. In this case, value for money is mediated by an exceptional notion of quality. In the case of teaching and learning, 'excellence' often serves as the basis of accountability assessments as it does, for example, in Australia. In other countries, such as Britain, value-for-money accountability is mediated by mission-related fitness-for-purpose.

References

Acherman, H. (1995) 'Meeting quality requirements', abstract of paper, with additional comments, presented at the Organisation for Economic Co-operation and Development (OECD), Programme on Institutional Management in Higher Education (IMHE) Seminar, at OECD, Paris, 4–6 December 1995.

Alexander, D. and Morgan, J. (1992) 'Quality assurance in a European context', paper presented to the AETT conference on 'Quality in Education', University of York, 6–8 April, 1992.

Annan, Lord (1993) Opening address on 'Universities' in Hansard, 6 December 1993, 5.33 p.m., p. 788.

Bauer, M. (1986) 'A commentary on the Northeast Missouri and Tennessee Evaluation Model' in Kagen, M. (ed.) Evaluating Higher Education, pp. 53–5, London, Jessica Kingsley.

Biggs, J. B. (1987) Student Approaches to Learning and Studying, Hawthorne, Victoria, Australian Council for Educational Research.

Bourner, T. and Hamed, M. (1987) Entry Qualifications and Degree Performance, Publication 10, London, CNAA Development Services.

Bowtell, C. (1993) Bulletin: Stop Work, Academics' Federation of Victoria.

Brennan, J. and McGeevor, P. (1988) Graduates at Work: Degree Courses and the Labour Market, London, Jessica Kingsley.

Burrows, A., Harvey, L. and Green, D. (1992) *The Policy Background to the Quality Debate in Higher Education 1985–1992: A Summary of Key Documents*, Birmingham, QHE.

Cannon, R. A. (1994) 'Quality and traditional university values: policy development through consultation', *The Australian Universities' Review*, 37(1), pp. 26–30.

Cave, M. and Kogan, M. (1990) 'Some concluding observations' in Cave, M., Kogan, M. and Smith, R. (eds) *Output and Performance Measurement in Government: The State of the Art*, pp. 179–87, London, Jessica Kingsley.

Cave, M., Hanney, S., Kogan, M. and Trevett, G. (1991) *The Use of Performance Indicators in Higher Education: A Critical Analysis of Developing Practice*, London, Jessica Kingsley.

Commission of the European Communities (CEC) (1991) *Memorandum on Higher Education in the European Community*, Brussels, European Commission.

Committee of Vice Chancellors and Principals of the Universities of the United Kingdom (CVCP) (1985) *Report of the Steering Committee for Efficiency Studies in Universities* (The Jarratt Report), London, CVCP.

Committee of Vice Chancellors and Principals of the Universities of the United Kingdom (CVCP) (1986) *Academic Standards in Universities* (with an introduction by Prof. P. A. Reynolds), London, CVCP.

Committee of Vice Chancellors and Principals of the Universities of the United Kingdom (CVCP) (1987) *Academic Staff Training – Code of Practice* (The Jarratt Report), Circular, April, London, CVCP.

Committee of Vice Chancellors and Principals of the Universities of the United Kingdom and Universities Grants Committee (CVCP/UGC) (1987a) *Performance Indicators in Universities: A Second Statement*, London, CVCP/UGC.

Committee of Vice Chancellors and Principals of the Universities of the United Kingdom and Universities Grants Committee (CVCP/UGC) (1987b) *University Management Statistics and Performance Indicators*, London, CVCP/UGC.

Committee of Vice Chancellors and Principals of the Universities of the United Kingdom and Universities Grants Committee (CVCP/UGC) (1988) *University Management Statistics and Performance Indicators in the UK*, second edition, London, CVCP/UGC.

Committee of Vice Chancellors and Principals of the Universities of the United Kingdom and Universities Grants Committee (CVCP/UGC) (1989) *University Management Statistics and Performance Indicators in the UK*, third edition, London, CVCP/UGC.

Committee of Vice Chancellors and Principals of the Universities of the United Kingdom and Universities Grants Committee (CVCP/UGC) (1990) *University Management Statistics and Performance Indicators in the UK*, fourth edition, London, CVCP/UGC.

Council for National Academic Awards (CNAA) (1990) *The Measurement of Value Added in Higher Education*, London, CNAA.

Council for National Academic Awards (CNAA) (1992) *The External Examiner and Curriculum Change*, Discussion Paper 7, London, CNAA.

Council for National Academic Awards and Department of Education and Science (CNAA/DES) (1989) *The Role of External Examiner: A Summary of the Principal Findings of a Project on the Role of the External Examiners in Undergraduate Courses in the United Kingdom during 1986*, Swindon, ESRC.

Cross, K. P. (1990) 'Streams of thought about assessment' in AAHE Assessment Forum (1990) *Assessment 1990: Understanding the Implications* (Assessment Forum Resource), pp. 1–14, Washington, DC, American Association for Higher Education.

Dearlove, J. (1995) 'Collegiality, managerialism and leadership in English universities', *Tertiary Education and Management*, 1(2), pp. 161–9

Department of Education and Science (DES) (1985) *The Development of Higher Education into the 1990s*, Green Paper, Cmnd. 9524, London, HMSO.

Department of Education and Science (DES) (1987) *Higher Education: Meeting the Challenge*, White Paper, Cm. 114, London, HMSO.

Department of Education and Science (DES) (1991a) *Higher Education: A New Framework*, White Paper, Cm. 1541, London, HMSO.

Department of Education and Science (DES) (1991b) 'Clarke tells polytechnics to plan for changes next year', *The Department of Education and Science News*, White Paper, 294/91, September 1991.

Dowell, D. and Neal, J. (1982) 'A selective review of the validity of student ratings of teaching', *Journal of Higher Education*, 53(1), pp. 51–62.

Elton, L. (1992) 'University teaching: a professional model for quality and excellence', paper to the 'Quality by Degrees' Conference at Aston University, 8 June 1992.

Elton, L. (1993) 'Enterprise in Higher Education: an agent for change', in Knight, P. T. (ed.) *University-Wide Change, Staff and Curriculum Development*, Staff and Educational Development Association, SEDA Paper, 83, May 1994, pp. 7–14, Birmingham, SEDA.

Employment Department Group, Training, Enterprise and Education Directorate (ED TEED) (1990) *Higher Education Developments – The Skills Link*, Sheffield, Employment Department Group.

Employment Department Group, Training, Enterprise and Education Directorate (ED TEED) (1991) *Enterprise in Higher Education. Key Features of Enterprise in Higher Education, 1990–91*, Sheffield, Employment Department Group.

Entwistle, N. and Ramsden, P. (1983) *Understanding Student Learning*, London, Croom Helm.

Fong, B. (1988) 'Old wineskins: the AAC external examiner project', *Liberal Education*, 74, pp. 12–16.

Gallagher, A. (1991) 'Comparative value added as a performance indicator', *Higher Education Review*, 23(3), pp. 19–29.

Goedegebuure, L. C. J., Maassen, P. A. M. and Westerheijden, D. F. (eds) (1990) *Peer Review and Performance Indicators: Quality Assessment in British and Dutch Higher Education*, Culemborg, Lemma.

Green, D. (1990) 'Student Satisfaction: assessing quality in HE from the customer's view' in *Proceedings of the Second International Conference on Assessing Quality in HE*, Tennessee, University of Tennessee.

Green, D. and Harvey, L. (1993) 'Quality assurance in Western Europe, trends, practices and issues', paper presented at the Fifth International Conference on 'Assessing Quality in Higher Education', Bonn, 21 July 1993.

Gungwu, W. (1992) 'Universities in transition in Asia', *Oxford Review of Education*, 18(1), pp. 17–27.

HM Government (1991) *Further and Higher Education Bill*, HL Bill, 4 50/5, London, HMSO.

HM Government (1992) *Further and Higher Education Act*, London, HMSO.

HM Inspectorate (HMI) (1990) *Performance Indicators in Higher Education. A Report by HMI*, Reference 14/91NS, January–April 1990, London, DES.

HM Inspectorate (HMI) (1993) *A Survey of the Enterprise in Higher Education Initiative in Fifteen Polytechnic and Colleges on Higher Education. September 1989–March 1991*, London, DFE.

Harrison, D. (1991) 'Challenges and opportunities for institutions', paper to the CBI Conference on 'Higher Education in the 1990s', 21 November 1991.

Harvey, L. (1995a) *Quality Assurance Systems, TQM and the New Collegialism*, Birmingham, QHE.

Harvey, L. (1995b) 'The new collegialism: improvement with accountability', *Tertiary Education and Management*, 2(2), pp. 153–60.

Harvey, L. and Mason, S. (1995) *The Role of Professional Bodies in Higher Education Quality Monitoring*, Birmingham, QHE.

Harvey, L., Burrows, A. and Green, D. (1992) *Total Student Experience: A First Report of the QHE National Survey of Staff and Students' Views of the Important Criteria for Assessing the Quality of Higher Education*, Birmingham, QHE.

Higher Education Funding Council for England (HEFCE) (1992) 'New Funding Council to review library provision in higher education: and to decide in July on a funding method for teaching', press release, HEFCE 1/92, 17 June 1992, Bristol, HEFCE.

Higher Education Quality Council (HEQC) (1995a) *The Future Development of the External Examiner System*, HEQC Consultative Document, June, London, HEQC.

Higher Education Quality Council (HEQC) (1995b) *Graduate Standards Programme: Progress Report*, HEQC Consultative Document, June, London, HEQC.

Holmes, G. (1993) 'Quality assurance in further and higher education: a sacrificial lamb on the altar of managerialism', *Quality Assurance in Education*, 1(1), p. 4.

Hutchings, P. and Marchese, T. (1990) 'Watching assessment: questions, stories, prospects', *Change*, September/October, pp. 12–38.

Industrial Research and Development Advisory Committee of the Commission of the European Communities (IRDAC) (1990) *Skills Shortages in Europe: IRDAC Opinion*, November, Brussels, EC.

Industrial Research and Development Advisory Committee of the Commission of the European Communities (IRDAC) (1994) *Quality and Relevance: Unlocking Europe's Human Potential*, March, Brussels, EC.

Jacobi, M., Astin, A. and Ayala, F. (1987) *College Student Outcomes Assessment: A Talent Development Perspective*, Washington, DC, Association for the Study of Higher Education.

Jenkins, A. (1995) 'The Research Assessment Exercise: funding and teaching quality', *Quality Assurance in Education* 3(2), pp. 4–12.

Jennings, E. T. Jr. (1989) 'Accountability, program quality, outcome assessment, and graduate education for public affairs and administration', *Public Administration Review*, 49(5)

Johnes, J. and Taylor, J. (1990) *Performance Indicators in Higher Education*, Buckingham, Society for Research into Higher Education/Open University Press.

Joseph, K. (1986) *Degree Courses in the Public Sector: Quality and Validation*, Circular, London, DES.

Kogan, M. (ed.) (1986) *Evaluating Higher Education: Papers from the Journal of Institutional Management in Higher Education*, London, Jessica Kingsley.

Kolb, D. A. (1984) *Experiential Learning: Experience as the Source of Learning and Development*, Englewood Cliffs, NJ, Prentice-Hall.

Lindop, N. (ed.) (1985) *Academic Validation in Public Sector Higher Education*, London, HMSO.

McClain, C. J., Krueger, D. W. and Taylor, T. (1986) 'Northeast Missouri State University value-added assessment program: a model for educational accountability' in Kogan, M. (ed.) *Evaluating Higher Education*, pp. 33–42, London, Jessica Kingsley.

Marsh, H. W. (1982) 'SEEQ: a reliable, valid, and useful instrument for collecting student evaluations of university teaching', *British Journal of Educational Psychology*, 52, pp. 77–95.

Marton, F., Hounsell, D. J. and Entwistle, N. J. (eds) (1984) *The Experience of Learning*, Edinburgh, Scottish Academic Press.

Middlehurst, R. and Woodhouse, D. (1995) 'Coherent systems for external quality assurance', *Quality in Higher Education*, 1(3), pp. 257–68.

Millard, R. M. (1991) 'Governance, quality and equity in the United States' in Berdahl, R. O., Moodie, G. C. and Spitzberg, I. J. (eds) *Quality and Access in Higher Education: Comparing Britain and the United States*, pp. 42–57, Buckingham, Society for Research into Higher Education/Open University Press.

Miller, H. D. R. (1994) *The Management of Change in Universities: Universities, State and Economy in Australia, Canada and the United Kingdom*, Buckingham, Society for Research into Higher Education/Open University Press.

Moodie, G. C. (1988) 'The debates about higher education quality in Britain and the USA' in Berdahl, R. O., Moodie, G. C. and Spitzberg, I. J. (eds) *Studies in Higher Education*, 13, pp. 5–13.

Moore, J. W. and Langknecht, L. F. (1986) 'Academic Planning in a political system', *Planning for Higher Education*, 14(1).

Mulgan, G. (1995) 'Trust me they owe it to us', *Times Higher Education Supplement*, 17 November 1995, p. 14.

Murphy, P. (1994) 'Research quality, peer review and performance indicators', *The Australian Universities' Review*, 37(1), pp. 14–18.

Murray, H. (1984) 'The impact of formative and summative evaluation of teaching in North American universities', *Assessment and Evaluation in Higher Education*, 9(2), pp. 117–32.

National Governors' Association (NGA) (1986) *Time for Results: The Governors' 1991 Report on Education*, Washington, DC, NGA.

National Governors' Association Task Force (NGATF) (1986) 'Task Force on college quality' in *Time for Results: The Governors' 1991 Report on Education*, pp. 153–71, Washington, DC, NGA.

Pike, G. R., Phillippi, R. H., Banta, T. W., Bensey, M. W., Milbourne, C. C. and Columbus, P. J. (1991) *Freshman to Senior Gains at the University of Tennessee, Knoxville*, Knoxville, The University of Tennessee, Center for Assessment Research and Development.

Pollitt, C. (1990) 'Measuring university performance: never mind the quality, never mind the width', *Higher Education Quarterly*, 44(1), pp. 60–81.

Polytechnics and Colleges Funding Council (PCFC) (1989) *Recurrent Funding Methodology 1990–91: Guidance for Institutions*, Circular, London, PCFC.

Polytechnics and Colleges Funding Council (PCFC) (1990) *Recurrent Funding and Equipment Allocations 1990–91*, London, PCFC.

Polytechnics and Colleges Funding Council and Universities Funding Council (PCFC/UFC) (1992a) *The Funding of Teaching in Higher Education*, Bristol, PCFC.

Polytechnics and Colleges Funding Council and Universities Funding Council (PCFC/UFC) (1992b) *A Funding Methodology for Teaching in Higher Education*, Bristol, PCFC.

Polytechnics and Colleges Funding Council and Universities Funding Council (PCFC/UFC) (1992c) *Macro Performance Indicators*, May, Bristol, PCFC.

Porrer, R. (1984) *Higher Education and Employment*, London, Association of Graduate Careers Advisory Services.

Ramsden, P. (ed.) (1988) *Improving Learning: New Perspectives*, London, Kogan Page.

Ramsden, P. (1991) 'A performance indicator of teaching quality in higher education: the Course Experience Questionnaire', *Studies in Higher Education*, 16(2), pp. 129–50.

Ramsden, P. (1995) Personal correspondence, November 1995.

Rear, J. (1994a) 'Defenders of academic faith', *Times Higher Education Supplement*, 21 October 1994, p. 15.

Rear, J. (1994b) 'Freedom with responsibility', *Times Higher Education Supplement*, 2 December 1994, p. 12.

Richards, H. (1992) 'University op-out call', *Times Higher Education Supplement*, No. 1020, 22 May 1986.

Rothblatt, S. (1992) 'National standards or local interests?' *Times Higher Education Supplement*, No. 1020, 7 February 1992, p. 14.

Secretary of State for Education (1988) Letter to the Chairman of the PCFC, Circular, 1 November 1988, London, DES.

Silver, H. (1993) *External Examiners: Changing Roles?*, London, CNAA.

Silver H., Skennett, A. and Williams, R. (1995) *External Examiner System: Possible Futures*, report of a project commissioned by HEQC, May, London, QSC.

Tavistock Institute of Human Relations (TIHR) (1990) *The First Year of Enterprise in Higher Education. Final Report of the Case Study Evaluation of EHE*, Sheffield, Employment Department Group.

Trow, M. (1993) 'Managerialism and the academic profession: the case of England', paper presented to the 'Quality Debate Conference', Milton Keynes, 24 September 1993.

United Nations Educational, Scientific and Cultural Organization (UNESCO) (1995) *Policy Paper for Change and Development in Higher Education*, Paris, UNESCO.

Vroeijenstijn, T. I. (1995) 'Improvement and accountability', in *Proceedings of the Third Meeting of the International Network for Quality Assurance Agencies in Higher Education*, 21–22 May 1995, pp. 25–35, Utrecht, Holland, VSNU/Inspectorate of Education.

Warren Piper, D. J. (1994) *Are Professors Professional? The Organisation of University Examinations*, London, Jessica Kingsley.

Warren Piper, D. J. (1995) 'Assuring the quality of awards', *Quality in Higher Education*, 1(3), pp. 197–210.

Wilkins, J. (1994) 'Letter to the editor', *Times Higher Education Supplement*, 28 October 1994, p. 10.

Yorke, M. (1993a) 'Total quality higher education?', paper at the 15th EAIR Forum, University of Turku, 15 August 1993.

Yorke, M. (1993b) 'Shouldn't quality be enhanced rather than assessed?', paper at the 17th Annual EAIR Forum, 'Dynamics in Higher Education: Traditions Challenged by New Paradigms', Zurich, Switzerland, 27–30 August 1995.

Yorke, M. (1995) 'Siamese twins? Performance indicators in the service of account-ability and enhancement', *Quality in Higher Education*, 1(1), pp. 13–30.

Index